Android Programm
and
Open Source Tools

Fore June

Android Programming and Open Source Tools

CreateSpace, a DBA of On-Demand Publishing, LLC.

ISBN-13: 978-1502336712

ISBN-10: 1502336715

First Edition: September, 2014

Contents

About the Author

Fore June is an independent Internet Service Provider (ISP) who provides various kinds of Internet services to the public and information technology consulting to a couple of small companies. Fore has written a few books and holds an M.S.E.E. degree in Electrical Engineering and Computer Science.

Preface

I described in my book *Windows Fan, Linux Fan* that I worked for a toy company in the Far East for a couple of years more than ten years ago. After I returned to the US, I resumed my job as an independent Internet Service Provider (ISP). I enjoy every bit of the freedom and the peaceful life such a job can provide, and I am grateful for all the abundance around us. One day, when I sat down and reviewed my work, I suddenly found that ten years had past and I was shocked by the rapid advance of the computing technologies in this period. Mobile devices have become ubiquitous and their computing capacities are amazingly huge. Ten years ago, ARM processor was a popular but small player in the microprocessor market. Then suddenly people are talking about the rivalry between ARM and Intel, the world's largest microprocessor designer and manufacturer. Open source movement is no longer a quixotic thought but has become a reality and has made profound impact in this world. The open source mobile OS Android came from nowhere a few years ago to become the major mobile system. If we measure the wealth of someone in terms of the computing power they can purchase, almost everyone in this nation has become a multimillionaire overnight.

This book is about basic Android programming as well as developing applications in the platform with use of some popular open source tools. This area is very broad. If I include all related topics, or include all materials in a topic, then I could never finish this book. So only a small scope of basic materials have been covered but they will provide interested readers a foundation to further explore this exciting technolgy.

The main reason of writing this book is that I hope I can make some contributions to the open source community as I have benefited so much from it in the past twenty years. This will be my last technology book as I am approaching retirement age and have difficulties reading a computer screen. However, I still hope I could contemplate the advancement in technology in the future and will have the capacity to revise my books, correcting mistakes, in particular typos, and incorporating more new materials.

Since Android is a new computing platform, I obtain most of the information about it from its official developers Web site, *http://developer.android.com/*.

Some of the images used in the book, such as those presented in the *Grid View Demo* example of Chapter 2 were downloaded from the Internet over some years, and I have lost track the exact URLs of the sources. I would like to thank the authors of the images.

The source code of this book can be obtained from the web site

http://www.forejune.com/android/

by entering the password **democracy**.

Fore June
September 2014

x

Chapter 1   Introduction

1.1   The Value of Knowledge

Most of us might have heard about the value of knowledge but many of us may overlook the underlying significance of acquiring knowledge in the modern world, not recognizing fully its real value. Even when our nation is in recession like the situation in 2011, when the jobless rate hovered around 9%, there is a serious shortage of good engineers and scientists. Many large newspapers such as New York Times and Wall Street Journal reported in 2011 that Silicon Valley saw strong hiring demand in the year. In July, 2011, more than 6,500 new jobs were advertised online for IT related openings in the Silicon Valley, up 9% from the same period a year ago. Some claimed that recruiting in Silicon Valley was more competitive and intense and furious than college football recruiting of high school athletes.

In March 2011, New York Times reported: "As the rest of the country fights stubbornly high unemployment, the shortage of qualified engineers has grown acute in the last six months, tech executives and recruiters say, as the flow of personal or venture capital investing has picked up. In Silicon Valley, along the southern portion of the San Francisco Bay in California, and other tech hubs such as New York, Seattle and Austin, start-ups are sprouting by the dozen, competing with well-established companies for the best engineers, programmers and designers. At the same time, all the companies are seeking ever more specialized skills. Tech recruiters have also expanded their searches. They still scout college campuses, particularly Stanfords computer science department, where this year it was common for seniors to receive half a dozen offers by the end of first quarter. But since college degrees are not mandatory, recruiters are also going to computer coding competitions and parties, in search of talent that is reminiscent of the dot-com mania."

This book is written in the spirit of helping readers acquire a knowledge that will be valuable to their own development. Even though the book presents the materials at an introductory level, some readers may still find some of the materials difficult, depending on their background and willingness of paying efforts in learning. But our knowledge is valuable only if we need to pay effort to gain it. The more effort we pay to acquire knowledge, the wealthier and happier we will be. Topics that are easy to us are also easy to our competitors. In the coming decades, the competition between nations will be a competition of acquiring knowledge. The economic regions that censor information and block the flow of knowledge would eventually fall behind.

Renowned management specialist Peter Drucker (1909 - 2005) had long advocated the emergence of knowledge society and the importance of knowledge workers. The social transformations from an industrial society to a knowledge society would be the most significant event of the century and its lasting legacy. Science and technology have been advancing so rapidly that manufacturing becomes irrelevant in the modern society. A DVD containing certain data that we pay twenty dollars to purchase may just cost a few cents to manufacture. Though it is very rare for the productivity between two labour workers differs by a factor more than two, the productivity of a good knowledge worker can be easily a factor of 100 or higher than that of an average knowledge worker. Nathan Myhrvoid, former Chief Technology Officer at Microsoft Corporation, and a co-founder of Intellectual Ventures, once said the following:

> *The top software developers are more productive than*
> *average software developers not by a factor of 10X or*
> *100X or even 1000X but by 10,000X.*

Putting this in another perspective, we see that under an ideal situation (discarding exploition by 'leaders'), if an average engineer earns \$100K a year, a top engineer could earn $10000 \times \$100K = \$1$ billion a year.

To become proficient in a certain field, one must learn with his or her heart, overcoming difficulties, barriers and frustrations. After enduring the hard work, one would enjoy the pleasure of understanding difficult materials and acquiring valuable knowledge. Fauja Singh, the 100-year-old marathoner runner who became the world's oldest person to complete a full-length marathon in October 2011 after crossing the line at the Scotiabank Toronto Waterfront event in eight hours and 25 minutes, said: "Anything worth doing is going to be difficult."

While the position of a labour worker can be easily substituted by another one with little training, it is very difficult to replace a specialist of a field in the knowledge economy, for the new worker must also go through the same learning barriers and hard work to acquire the knowledge.

1.2   The Open Source Movement

In the past few decades, the open source movement may be the most important development in the software industry and in knowledge acquirement. Open source software is made available to anybody to use as its source code can be read by everyone. Open source software promotes learning and understanding, and expedite software development, making software more robust.

Nowadays, open source applications are abundant and they have been propelling the technolgy world moving forward rapidly. Most of the world's top super computers are built using the open system, Linux. This book along with its programs and utilities are 100% written using open source software.

An example open source contribution to the society is the exceptional success of the stereoscopic 3D movie *Avatar* of 2009, which had set off a phenomenal trend in making 3D films. The movie has also become the top grossing movie of all time, eclipsing James Cameron's former top grossing movie, *Titanic*. One of the main reasons of its huge success is the use of open source technologies to create the fantastic stereoscopic 3D effects. It is interesting to note that Cameron wrote the script for the film more than 15 years ago, but the open source technology was not mature enough to portray his vision of the film, which might be the major cause of the long delay of its production.

While the audience are moved and amazed by the realistic 3D effects, few realise that open source software is the driving force behind the creation of those 3D graphics and animation rendering. Linux has played a silent but an important role in the creation of the movie. Weta Digital, co-founded by Peter Jackson, is a digital visual effects company that gave life to the flora and fauna of Pandora in the movie. It uses Linux and other Linux-based software to achieve all those cutting edge graphics.

In 2011, open source movement scored a couple of stunning triumphs. In February of the year, the whole world was watching with great interest and excitement the human-versus-machine competition on the quiz show *Jeopardy*. On the human side were Brad Butter, the biggest all-time money winner on *Jeopardy*, and Ken Jennings, the record holder for the longest championship streak. On the machine side was an artificial intelligence computer system named *Watson*, which was capable of answering questions posed in natural language, and was developed in IBM's DeepQA project by a research team led by principal investigator David Ferrucci. Watson was named after IBM's first president, Thomas J. Watson. In a two-game, combined-point match, broadcast in three *Jeopardy* episodes, Watson beat both Brad Rutter and Ken Jennings without any connection to the Internet during the game. The audience was much amazed by the intelligence of Watson. However, much of the audience might not know that Watson was actually powered by open source software. IBM did not build Watson from scratch but had leveraged existing open source projects to provide many of the building blocks for the Watson project. Watson's software was written in both Java and C++ and uses Apache Hadoop framework for distributed computing, Apache UIMA (Unstructured Information Management Architecture) framework, IBMs DeepQA software and SUSE Linux Enterprise Server 11 operating system. Watson can run on a few operating systems but to compete on *Jeopardy*, Watson was running SUSE Linux Enterprise Server OS. Just like the human players, Watson had no access to Google or any other outside sources of information during the competition. It played with its own "knowledge".

Another big triumph of open source software in 2011 is that Android has become the most popular mobile phone operating system, capturing nearly 50% of smart phone market. Google first unveiled Android as a Linux-based open-source mobile operating system in late 2007 and it was embraced immediately by many big carriers such as Sprint, T-Mobile, Verizon and AT&T. Since its debut, Android has been gaining market rapidly. Android is an open-source software stack for mobile devices, and the Android project is led by Google. The Android Open Source Project (AOSP) includes individuals working in a variety of roles. Google is responsible for Android product management and the engineering process for the core framework and platform; however, the project considers contributions from any source, not just Google. The Android team created Android in response to their own experiences of launching mobile apps. They wanted to make sure that there was no central point of failure, so that no industry player can restrict or control the innovations of any other. That's why Android was created, and its source code was made open. For more information, one can refer to the Android official web site at *http://www.android.com*.

1.3   This Book

The work of this book, *Android Programming and Open Source Tools*, is an extension of the author's experience of developing programs in embedded devices. It is an introduction to develop applications in the Android platform with use of open source tools and knowledge. Most of the information can be found on the Internet, in particular the official Android web site (*www.android.com/*). The materials are discussed at an introductory level and the main code is mainly presented in Java. Quite a lot of the code is adopted from the code published in the Android developers web site. The programs presented are mainly for illustrating the basic techniques of developing Android programs; very often error checking and handling are not included, and many of the parameters are hard-coded. Nevertheless, the programs can be used as a starting point for further development.

We have to admit that the programs presented in this book were written over a period of time and thus the notations may not be very consistent. Also, we have not optimized the code for memory usage or computing time. All the code presented in this book can be found at the site,

http://www.forejune.com/android/

and you can download the programs using the password "democracy". The programs have been written using the Eclipse IDE running in a 64-bit Linux CentOS environment. The programs of this book reside in subdirectories with numbering reflecting the related chapters. For example, the programs discussed in Chapter 8 will be in directory *8/*.

In our descriptions, we usually use text in *italics* to refer to classes, variables, files and directories, and **bold** to refer to methods and terminals such as **int**, and **float**. We sometimes refer to a method of a class as a function, and we do not add an 'm' at the beginning of a data member to distinguish it from a local variable as we feel that it is not necessary.

We hope you enjoy reading this book.

Chapter 2   An Introduction to Android

2.1   Introduction

If you were not shut off from the world in the past couple of years, you must have heard about Android. Development in communication has been shrinking the world and thanks to the advancement of Wi Fi technologies, some developing countries are able to leapfrog into the twenty-first century without the burden of dismantling the infrastructure and equipment of wired communication. Mobile devices have become ubiquitous and some are even more sophisticated than PCs. Transitioning from working with PCs to mobile devices such as smart phones and tablet computers has become a trend. Android is developed in response to this trend. It is an open source operating system based on the Linux kernel with applications developed using the Java programming language. The Android operating system was first developed by Android, Inc. Google acquired Android, Inc. in July 2005, and became the leading developer of the Android OS. In November 2007, the Open Handset Alliance, which initially was a consortium of 34 companies formed to develop Android. The consortium was later expanded to absorb many more companies in a joint effort to further develop the platform, which is the real innovation in the mobile technology. Because of its openness, in less than two years, Android has come from nowhere to become the dominant smart phone operating system in the US, eclipsing all other major players in the field. News, details and relevant links of Android can be found from its official web site,

http://www.android.com/

Wikipedia has a good article about the history and miscellaneous information of Android at

http://en.wikipedia.org/wiki/Android_(operating_system)

Technical information can be obtained from Android's official developer web site at:

http://developer.android.com/guide/index.html

This site provides a lot of information and how-to for developing Android applications and publishing them. The site defines Android as follows:

> *Android is a software stack for mobile devices that includes an operating system, middleware and key applications. The Android SDK provides the tools and APIs necessary to begin developing applications on the Android platform using the Java programming language.*

The developer site also lists various features of Android, including

1. **Application framework** enabling reuse and replacement of components
2. **Dalvik virtual machine** optimized for mobile devices
3. **Integrated browser** based on the open source WebKit engine
4. **Optimized graphics** powered by a custom 2D graphics library
5. **3D graphics** based on the OpenGL ES 1.0 and ES 2.0 specifications
6. **SQLite** for structured data storage
7. **Media support** for common audio, video, and still image formats (MPEG4, H.264, MP3, AAC, AMR, JPG, PNG, GIF)
8. **GSM Telephony** (hardware dependent)
9. **Bluetooth, EDGE, 3G**, and **WiFi** (hardware dependent)

10. **Camera, GPS, compass**, and **accelerometer** (hardware dependent)
11. **Rich development environment** including a device emulator, tools for debugging, memory and performance profiling, and a plugin for the Eclipse IDE

The following figure shows the architecture of Android.

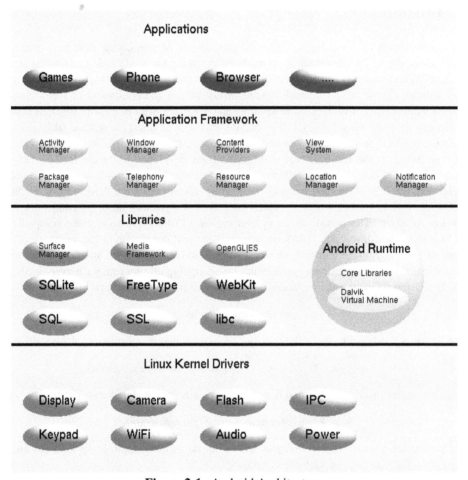

Figure 2-1 Android Architecture

In summary, Android is a software stack for mobile devices that includes an operating system, middleware and key applications. The Android SDK provides the tools and APIs necessary to develop applications on the Android platform using the Java programming language. Moreover, Android includes a set of C/C++ libraries that can be used by various components of the Android system. These capabilities are exposed to developers through the Android application framework as shown in Figure 2-1.

Figure 2-1 also shows that an Android application runs in its own process, with its own instance of the Dalvik virtual machine (VM). The Dalvik Executable (.dex) format is used to execute files in the Dalvik VM; the format is optimized for minimal memory footprint. After a Java program has been compiled, the classes will be transformed into the *.dex* format by the **dx** tool so that it can be run in the Dalvik VM. The Linux kernel provides underlying functionality such as threading and low-level memory management for the Dalvik VM.

Like the rest of Android, Dalvik is open source software and is published under the terms of the Apache License 2.0. Dalvik is known to be a clean-room implementation rather than a development on top of a standard Java runtime. This could mean that it does not inherit copyright-based license restrictions from either the standard-edition or open source-edition Java runtimes.

Android has undergone several versions of revision. Each new version is named after a dessert in increasing alphabetic order:

1. Android 1.6 (Donut)
2. Android 2.02.1 (Eclair)
3. Android 2.2 (Froyo)
4. Android 2.3 (Gingerbread)
5. Android 3.0 (Honeycomb)
6. Android 4.0 (Icecream Sandwich)
7. Android 4.1 (Jelly Bean)
8. Android 4.4 (KitKat)

Version 4.0 (Android Icecream Sandwich) was released in November, 2011. This version merges Android 2.3 (Gingerbread) and Android 3.0 (Honeycomb) into one operating system for use on all Android devices. This will allow us to incorporate Honeycomb's features such as the holographic user interface, new launcher and more (previously available only on tablets) into our smart phone apps, and easily scale our apps to work on different devices. Ice Cream Sandwich will also add new functionality.

Most of the Android programs presented in this book are developed and tested with Android version 4.X API level 16 or above with an emulator running in a 64-bit Linux machine, which runs CentOS 6.4, a 64-bit Linux OS. We mainly use the Eclipse IDE to do the development but command line tools are also used occasionally and discussed in this book.

Though Android apps are written in Java, 3D graphics programs are written with OpenGL ES. The graphics functions, OpenGL commands that we use in 3D graphics examples are open standards in the industry. They have the same form and syntax, whether they are presented in C/C++ or Android Java. Both of the OpenGL ES versions 1.0 and 2.0 will be discussed.

2.2   Development Tools

The Android official site provides the information and tools to develop Android applications. One can refer to the site

> *http://developer.android.com/index.html*

to learn the details and download the development tools. The following link shows how to install Android and set up the development environment for the first time:

> *http://developer.android.com/sdk/installing.html*

Since Android applications are written in java, in most situations developing an Android application is simply writing some java programs utilizing the Android libraries. The programs can be compiled and built with use of *Apache Ant*, a software tool for automating software build processes. Ant is similar to *Make* but it is implemented in java, and is best suited to building java projects. In many cases it may be more convenient to do the development using **Eclipse**, a multi-language open *software development environment* consisting of an *integrated development environment* (IDE) along with an extensible plug-in system. Eclipse is mostly written in java, and is an ideal IDE for developing java applications; it can be also used to develop applications of other programming languages such as C/C++ and PHP by means of various plug-ins. However, running **Eclipse** consumes a lot of resources.   We always have the option of developing Android programs using a simple traditional editor such as **vi**, and compiling and running it using the *Android* command.

2.2.1 Eclipse IDE

One can obtain information of Eclipse and download it from its official web site at

http://www.eclipse.org/

Eclipse can be easily installed and run in any supported platform. Using Linux as an example, the following steps show how to install Eclipse along with the Android Development Tools (ADT):

1. Go to *http://www.eclipse.org/*; click **Download Eclipse**; choose **Eclipse for RCP and RAP Developers**, and download the package into a local directory, say, */apps/downloads*.
2. Unpack the downloaded package into the directory */apps* by:

   ```
   $ cd /apps
   $ gunzip -c /apps/download/eclipse-rcp-helios-SR2-linux-gtk.tar.gz | tar xvf -
   ```
3. Then start Eclipse by:

   ```
   $ cd eclipse
   $ ./eclipse
   ```
4. From the eclipse IDE, install the **Android Development Tools** (ADT):

   - Click **Help** > **Install New Software**
   - In the "Work with" box, type *http://dl-ssl.google.com/android/eclipse/*; hit "Enter"; select all the "Development Tools"; click **Next**; click **Next**; accept the license "agreement to", and click **Finish** to install ADT.
5. After the ADT installation, restart Eclipse.
6. Click **Window** and you should see the entry **Android SDK and AVD Manager**.
7. Add the Android SDK directory by clicking **Preference**; select **Android** and enter the location of your Android SDK. Now click on **Android SDK and AVD Manager** to proceed.
8. If you are new to eclipse, click on **Tutorials** and follow the instructions to create a **Hello World** application.

Hello World Example

As an example of writing Android applications in the Eclipse IDE, we present the steps of writing a **Hello World** application. In this example, we will run the application in the Android Emulator. You can also find this example at the Android tutorial web site at

http://developer.android.com/resources/tutorials/hello-world.html

In the description, we use the specified Android version 4.2.2.

1. Start Eclipse.
2. In the Eclipse IDE, choose **Preferences** > **Android**.
3. Install a platform in Eclipse:

   (a) Choose **Window** > **Android SDK Manager**, which displays a panel showing the Android platform packages in your system like the screen shot shown in Figure 2-2.
   (b) As an example, choose **Android 4.2.2(API 17)** and its subcomponents "SDK Platform" and "SDK Samples"; then click **Install 2 packages**; check **Accept All**; click **Install**. Eclipse will download the package from the Internet and install it.
   (c) When it is finished you can press the key 'ESC' to clear the panel.

Name	API	Rev.	Status
▽ ☐ 🗀 Tools			
☐ ✗ Android SDK Tools		21.1	Installed
☐ ✗ Android SDK Platform-tools		16.0.2	Installed
▽ ☐ Android 4.2.2 (API 17)			
☐ Documentation for Android SDK	17	2	Installed
☐ SDK Platform	17	2	Installed
☐ Samples for SDK	17	1	Installed
☐ ARM EABI v7a System Image	17	2	Installed
☐ Intel x86 Atom System Image	17	1	Installed
☐ MIPS System Image	17	1	Installed
☐ Google APIs	17	2	Installed
☐ Sources for Android SDK	17	1	Installed
▽ ☐ Android 4.1.2 (API 16)			
☐ SDK Platform	16	4	Installed
☐ Samples for SDK	16	1	Installed
☐ ARM EABI v7a System Image	16	3	Installed
☐ Intel x86 Atom System Image	16	1	Installed
☐ *MIPS System Image*	16	4	*Not installed*
☐ Google APIs	16	3	Installed

Show: ☑ Updates/New ☑ Installed   ☐ Obsolete Select New or Updates

Sort by: ⦿ API level   ○ Repository   Deselect All

Figure 2-2   Sample Packages

4. Create an Android Virtual Device (AVD), which defines the system image and device settings of the emulator:

   (a) In Eclipse, choose **Window** > **AVD Manager**, which displays the *Android Virtual Device Manager* panel.
   (b) Click **New..**, which displays the *Create new Android Virtual Device (AVD)* dialog.
   (c) Enter a name for the AVD, say, "avd422".
   (d) Select the target to be *Android 4.2.2 – API Level 17*.
   (e) Click **Create AVD**.
   (f) Press 'ESC' to exit the AVD panel.

5. Create a new Android project:

   (a) In Eclipse, select **File** > **New** > **Project**, which displays the *New Project* dialog as shown in Figure 2-3 below.
   (b) Select **Android Project** and click **Next**, which displays the *New Android Project* dialog.
   (c) Enter "HelloWorldProject" for *Project Name* and click **Next**.
   (d) Choose *Build Target* to be *Android 4.2.2* and click **Next**.
   (e) Enter "HelloWorld" for *Application Name*, "android.hello" for *Package Name*, "HelloWorld" for *Create Activity*, select **API 17 (Android 4.22)** for Minimum and target SDK, click **Next** > **Next** > **Next** > **Finish**.

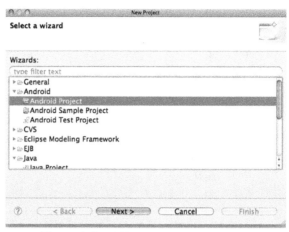

Figure 2-3 Eclipse New Project Dialog

The *HelloWorldProject* Android project is now ready. It should be visible in the *Package Explorer* on the left of the Eclipse IDE. (You may need to click **Plug-in Device.** on the left to display **Package Explorer**.)

6. From the **Package Explorer**, choose **HelloWorldProject > src > android.hello > Main-Activity.java**. Double-click on **MainActivity.java** to open it, which should look like the following:

```
package android.hello;

import android.app.Activity;
import android.os.Bundle;

public class HelloWorld extends Activity {
  /** Called when the activity is first created. */
  @Override
  public void onCreate(Bundle savedInstanceState) {
    super.onCreate(savedInstanceState);
    setContentView(R.layout.activity_main);
  }
}
```

7. Revise "MainActivity.java" to the following that constructs a user interface (UI):

```
package android.hello;
import android.app.Activity;
import android.os.Bundle;
import android.widget.TextView;
public class MainActivity extends Activity {
  @Override
  public void onCreate(Bundle savedInstanceState) {
    super.onCreate(savedInstanceState);
      TextView tv = new TextView(this);
      tv.setText("Hello, Android!");
      setContentView(tv);
  }
}
```

8. Run the application by choosing from Eclipse, **Run > Run**. Then select **Android Application** and click **OK**. The Android emulator will start and run the application. You should see on your screen something like Figure 2-3 below. (You may need to use the mouse to drag the lock to the right side of the screen to unlock the device.)

Figure 2-3   HelloWorld Android Application

If you do not see the message "Hello, Android!", click the **menu** button of the Android emulator which will run the application.

2.3   Android Basics

2.3.1 Manifest File

One of the most important part of an Android application is the manifest file, which is an xml file named *AndroidManifest.xml*. It is a resource file containing all the details needed by the android system to run and test the application. Every application must have an *AndroidManifest.xml* file in its root directory. We can edit it in the Eclipse IDE by clicking on a project in the **Package Explorer** and the menus:

Res > AndroidManifest.xml > Manifest General Attributes

The file *AndroidManifest.xml* outlines the crucial features for an application, including the following information:

1. It presents to the Android system the properties of the application.
2. It describes the application's components, such as activities, services, broadcast receivers, and content providers.
3. It specifies the application's Java package name, which serves as a unique identifier for the application.
4. It determines the processes that will host the application components.
5. It specifies permissions required to run the applications, such as Internet access, and user data access.
6. It declares the minimum Android API level that the application needs. The API levels determine whether the application can run on an Android platform. For example, setting the minimum API level to 11 would require honeycomb or later Android versions to run the application.
7. It lists the libraries that the application has to link with.
8. It lists the Instrumentation classes that provide profiling and other information to run the application. These declarations are for testing and they will be removed when the application is published.

Manifest File Structure

We can edit the manifest file using the Eclipse IDE. Figure 2-3 below shows a screen shot of a panel for editing the manifest file.

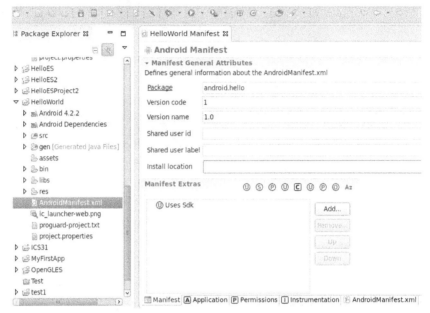

Figure 2-3   Manifest File of Hello World Example

Alternatively, we can edit the xml source file directly. (In Eclipse IDE, click the tab **Android-Manifest.xml** shown at the bottom of Figure 2-2.) The listing below shows the source code of the **HelloWorld** *AndroidManifext.xml* file.

Program Listing 2-1   Source Code of **HelloWorld** *AndroidManifext.xml*

```
<?xml version="1.0" encoding="utf-8"?>
<manifest xmlns:android="http://schemas.android.com/apk/res/android"
    package="android.hello"
    android:versionCode="1"
    android:versionName="1.0" >
    <uses-sdk
        android:minSdkVersion="17"
        android:targetSdkVersion="17" />
    <application
        android:allowBackup="true"
        android:icon="@drawable/ic_launcher"
        android:label="@string/app_name"
        android:theme="@style/AppTheme" >
        <activity
            android:name="android.hello.MainActivity"
            android:label="@string/app_name" >
            <intent-filter>
                <action android:name="android.intent.action.MAIN" />
                <category android:name="android.intent.category.LAUNCHER" />
            </intent-filter>
        </activity>
    </application>
</manifest>
```

The Android developer web site shows a more complete general structure of the manifest file and every element that it can contain. Each element is documented in a separate file along with all of its attributes. We can view detailed information about any element by clicking on the element name.

The following list shows in alphabetical order all the elements that can appear in the manifest file. They are the only legitimate elements allowed. We are not allowed to add our own elements or attributes.

```
<action>              <activity>            <activity-alias>
<application>         <category>            <data>
<grant-uri-permission>                      <instrumentation>
<intent-filter>       <manifest>            <meta-data>
<permission>          <permission-group>    <permission-tree>
<provider>            <receiver>            <service>
<supports-screens>    <uses-configuration>  <uses-feature>
<uses-library>        <uses-permission>     <uses-sdk>
```

2.4 Command Line Development

We always have the option of developing Android applications using command-line terminals without using any IDE. Using command-line tools could be simpler and lets the developer have a clearer picture of the working environment. We use a particular working directory to illustrate this method. In the examples, the symbol '$' denotes the command prompt. In a command, *italics* denote variable names, which should be substituted by actual names. This convention only applies to a command, not a description. Also note that in a command, the symbol – is composed of two dashes.

Suppose we have created the directory '/workspace', where we will develop our Android programs. We first go to the directory by the command

$ cd /workspace

The Android SDK comes with a tool called **android** that is usually integrated into the ADT of Eclipse. But we can always use this command as a stand alone development tool which lets us to

1. create, view, and delete Android Virtual Devices (AVDs),
2. create and update Android projects,
3. update our Android SDK with new platforms, add-ons, and documentation,
4. and to perform many other project management tasks.

We can find out its usage by issuing the command,

$ android –help

which displays a menu similar to the following:

```
    Usage:
     android [global options] action [action options]
     Global options:
 -h --help       : Help on a specific command.
 -v --verbose    : Verbose mode, shows errors, warnings and all messages.
    --clear-cache: Clear the SDK Manager repository manifest cache.
 -s --silent     : Silent mode, shows errors only.

 Valid actions are composed of a verb and an optional direct object:

 -    sdk            : Displays the SDK Manager window.
 -    avd            : Displays the AVD Manager window.
 -    list           : Lists existing targets or virtual devices.
```

```
  -   list avd            : Lists existing Android Virtual Devices.
  -   list target         : Lists existing targets.
  -   list sdk            : Lists remote SDK repository.
  - create avd            : Creates a new Android Virtual Device.
  -   move avd            : Moves or renames an Android Virtual Device.
  - delete avd            : Deletes an Android Virtual Device.
  - update avd            : Updates an Android Virtual Device to match the
                            folders of a new SDK.
  - create project        : Creates a new Android project.
  - update project        : Updates an Android project (must already have
                            an AndroidManifest.xml).
  - create test-project   : Creates a new Android project for a test package.
  - update test-project   : Updates the Android project for a test package
                            (must already have an AndroidManifest.xml).
  - create lib-project    : Creates a new Android library project.
  - update lib-project    : Updates an Android library project (must already have
                            an AndroidManifest.xml).
  - create uitest-project : Creates a new UI test project.
  - update adb            : Updates adb to support the USB devices declared in the
                            SDK add-ons.
  - update sdk            : Updates the SDK by suggesting new platforms to install
                            if available.
```

2.4.1 Listing Targets

We can list all the image targets in the system using the command,

> $ android list targets

which generates a target list similar to the following:

```
----------
id: 1 or "android-4"
    Name: Android 1.6
    Type: Platform
    API level: 4
    Revision: 3
    Skins: WVGA854, WVGA800 (default), QVGA, HVGA
    ABIs : armeabi
----------
..............
----------
id: 23 or "Google Inc.:Google APIs:17"
    Name: Google APIs
    Type: Add-On
    Vendor: Google Inc.
    Revision: 3
    Description: Android + Google APIs
    Based on Android 4.2.2 (API level 17)
    Libraries:
     * com.google.android.media.effects (effects.jar)
         Collection of video effects
     * com.android.future.usb.accessory (usb.jar)
         API for USB Accessories
     * com.google.android.maps (maps.jar)
         API for Google Maps
    Skins: WQVGA400, WVGA854, WSVGA, WXGA800-7in, WXGA720, HVGA,
           WQVGA432, QVGA, WVGA800 (default), WXGA800
    ABIs : armeabi-v7a
----------
id: 24 or "android-18"
    Name: Android 4.3
    Type: Platform
```

```
API level: 18
Revision: 1
Skins: WXGA800, WXGA720, WXGA800-7in, WVGA854, WVGA800 (default),
       WSVGA, WQVGA432, QVGA, WQVGA400, HVGA
ABIs : armeabi-v7a
```

Such a list is generated by the **android** command, which scans, in our example, the directories, **/android-sdk-linux/platforms/**, and **/android-sdk-linux/add-ons/** for valid system images.

2.4.2 Creating AVDs

We can list all the available Android Virtual Devices (AVDs) by the command

$ android list avd

To create an avd, we can issue the command

$ android create avd –name *name* –target *targetID* [*–option value*] ...

where *name* specifies the new AVD and *targetID* specifies the image we want to run on the emulator when the AVD is invoked. We can specify other options such as the emulated SD card size, the emulator skin, or a custom location for the user data files. The following is an example of such a command,

$ android create avd –name comAvd –target 24

which displays a message similar the following:

```
Auto-selecting single ABI armeabi-v7a
Android 4.3 is a basic Android platform.
Do you wish to create a custom hardware profile [no]
Created AVD 'comAvd' based on Android 4.3, ARM (armeabi-v7a) processor,
with the following hardware config:
hw.lcd.density=240
vm.heapSize=48
hw.ramSize=512
```

We can use the tool to delete an AVD. For example,

$ android delete avd –name comAvd

removes **comAvd** we just created.

We can also specify the path to hold the AVD files. For example,

$ android create avd –name comAvd –target 24 –path /workspace/avds/

generates the files "config.ini" and "userdata.img" for **comAvd** in the directory */workspace/avds*. We can check this using the UNIX **ls** command:

$ ls avds

which displays the file names,

config.ini   userdata.img

We can examine the configure file "config.ini" using a text editor such as **vi**, which would display some text similar to the following:

```
avd.ini.encoding=ISO-8859-1
hw.lcd.density=240
skin.name=WVGA800
skin.path=platforms/android-18/skins/WVGA800
hw.cpu.arch=arm
abi.type=armeabi-v7a
hw.cpu.model=cortex-a8
vm.heapSize=48
hw.ramSize=512
image.sysdir.1=system-images/android-18/armeabi-v7a/
```

For more details and the use of other options, one can refer to the Android official developer web site at

```
developer.android.com/tools/devices/managing-avds-cmdline.html#AVDCmdLine
```

2.4.3 Creating Project

We can use the **android** tool to create a project using a command like the following:

$ android create project –target *targetID* –name *appsName* \
    –path *path-to-workspace/appsName* –activity *mainActivity* \
    –package *packageName*

(Remember that the symbol – is composed of two dashes.)

For instance, consider an example of creating a simple *HelloWorld* application called **helloCom**. We first make the directory *helloCom* by

$ mkdir helloCom

(Remember that we are working in the directory */workspace*.)

Then we issue the command

$ android create project –target 24 –name helloCom \
    –path ./helloCom –activity SayHello –package example.helloCom

to create the project. The command generates the following message:

```
Created directory /workspace/helloCom/src/example/helloCom
Added file ./helloCom/src/example/helloCom/SayHello.java
Created directory /workspace/helloCom/res
Created directory /workspace/helloCom/bin
Created directory /workspace/helloCom/libs
Created directory /workspace/helloCom/res/values
Added file ./helloCom/res/values/strings.xml
Created directory /workspace/helloCom/res/layout
Added file ./helloCom/res/layout/main.xml
Created directory /workspace/helloCom/res/drawable-xhdpi
Created directory /workspace/helloCom/res/drawable-hdpi
Created directory /workspace/helloCom/res/drawable-mdpi
Created directory /workspace/helloCom/res/drawable-ldpi
Added file ./helloCom/AndroidManifest.xml
Added file ./helloCom/build.xml
Added file ./helloCom/proguard-project.txt
```

We can check the file structure created using the command **du**:

$ du -a helloCom

which displays all the directories and files created for the project:

```
4          helloCom/src/example/helloCom/SayHello.java
8          helloCom/src/example/helloCom
12         helloCom/src/example
16         helloCom/src
4          helloCom/AndroidManifest.xml
4          helloCom/local.properties
4          helloCom/bin
4          helloCom/libs
4          helloCom/ant.properties
4          helloCom/project.properties
4          helloCom/proguard-project.txt
4          helloCom/res/drawable-ldpi/ic_launcher.png
8          helloCom/res/drawable-ldpi
16         helloCom/res/drawable-xhdpi/ic_launcher.png
20         helloCom/res/drawable-xhdpi
4          helloCom/res/layout/main.xml
8          helloCom/res/layout
4          helloCom/res/values/strings.xml
8          helloCom/res/values
12         helloCom/res/drawable-hdpi/ic_launcher.png
16         helloCom/res/drawable-hdpi
8          helloCom/res/drawable-mdpi/ic_launcher.png
12         helloCom/res/drawable-mdpi
76         helloCom/res
4          helloCom/build.xml
128        helloCom
```

In particular, the *build.xml* file will be used by the **ant** utility to continue to build the project. To execute the commands specified in *build.xml*, we go into the *helloCom* directory by

$ cd helloCom

and execute

$ ant debug

which builds a sample package. If the build is successful, the message "BUILD SUCCESSFUL" will be displayed at the end of the process.

We can now install the package by issuing the command,

$ adb install bin/helloCom-debug.apk

Most likely, you will see an error message like the following:

```
* daemon not running. starting it now on port 5037 *
* daemon started successfully *
error: device not found
- waiting for device -
```

This is because we have not started the android device emulator yet. At this point, you can terminate the command by typing *Crtl-C*.

We first start the emulator by the command

$ emulator -avd comAvd

Then we execute the command

    $ adb install bin/helloCom-debug.apk

This time you will see a success message like the following:

```
* daemon not running. starting it now on port 5037 *
* daemon started successfully *
2544 KB/s (37063 bytes in 0.014s)
pkg: /data/local/tmp/helloCom-debug.apk
Success
```

The emulator should have an icon showing our application *SayHello*. (If you cannot find the application, restart your emulator.) We can run it by clicking on the icon, which displays the "Hello World, SayHello" message.

The source code of the app, *SayHello.java* is in the directory *src/example/helloCom*. We can view its content using the *vi* editor:

    $ vi src/example/helloCom/SayHello.java

which displays the source code *SayHello.java*:

```
package example.helloCom;

import android.app.Activity;
import android.os.Bundle;

public class SayHello extends Activity
{
    /** Called when the activity is first created. */
    @Override
    public void onCreate(Bundle savedInstanceState)
    {
        super.onCreate(savedInstanceState);
        setContentView(R.layout.main);
    }
}
```

The file *main.xml* defines the app output. We can view or edit its content using the *vi* editor:

    $ vi res/layout/main.xml

which displays the content of *main.xml*:

```
<?xml version="1.0" encoding="utf-8"?>
<LinearLayout xmlns:android="http://schemas.android.com/apk/res/android"
    android:orientation="vertical"
    android:layout_width="fill_parent"
    android:layout_height="fill_parent"
    >
<TextView
    android:layout_width="fill_parent"
    android:layout_height="wrap_content"
    android:text="Hello World, SayHello"
    />
</LinearLayout>
```

To verify that this file defines the output, we can change the "Hello World" text to something else, say, "Hello World the Beautiful!". For the modification to take effect, we have to recompile and reintall the app with the "-r" option:

```
$ ant debug
$ adb install -r bin/helloCom-debug.apk
```

When we run the *SayHello* application in the emulator, we should see the message "Hello World the Beautiful!" displayed.

2.5   Simple Examples

We present some simple examples here to give you a quick start and get familiar with the process of compiling and running an Android application using an emulator. Discussions of the items, widgets and attributes are given in the next chapter.

2.5.1 Button and ImageButton

We discuss in this section how to create buttons and in particular how to create an image button, which is represented by an image. When we click on the button, a text message is displayed. Through the development of this application, one can learn the layout basics and some fundamental techniques of writing an Android application. We will use the Eclipse IDE to create this application. Suppose we call both the project name and application name *ImageButton* and the package name *example.imagebutton*. The following presents the detailed steps of the process.

1. **Create Project** *ImageButton*:

   (a) Click **File > New > Project > Android > Android Application Project**
   (b) Specify the names of the project, the application and the package as *ImageButton*, *ImageButton*, and *example.imagebutton* respectively. Then click **Next > Next > Next > Next** to use the defaults of Eclipse. So the names of **Activity** and **Layout** are *MainActivity* and *activity_main* respectively. The **Navigation Type** is *None*. Then click **Finish** to create the project *ImageButton*.

2. **Prepare an Image for the Button**:
   Copy an image, say, *icon.png*, which is used to represent a button to a *drawable* directory inside resource directory *res*. If you are not sure about the resolution of your screen, simply copy it to all the listed drawables such as *drawable-hdpi* and *drawable-mdpi*. Now your Eclipse **Package Explorer** will show a menu similar to the one shown on Figure 2-4(a).

3. **Define Buttons in Layout**:
   Modify the file *res/layout/activity_main.xml* to the following, which defines an ordinary *Button* named as *resetButton* and an *ImageButton* named *imageButton1* represented by the image *icon.png*. The file also specifies a *TextView* object, which is identified as *message*. The main program *MainActivity.java* will correspondingly define variable to refer to *resetButton*, *imageButton1*, and *message* objects. A variable name in the Java program is associated with the corresponding object name defined in the layout XML file through the method **findViewById**:

   variable_name = **findViewById** (**R.id.***xml_object_name*)

```
<?xml version="1.0" encoding="utf-8"?>
```

```
<LinearLayout xmlns:android=
    "http://schemas.android.com/apk/res/android"
    android:layout_width="fill_parent"
    android:layout_height="fill_parent"
    android:orientation="vertical" >

    <ImageButton
        android:id="@+id/imageButton1"
        android:layout_width="wrap_content"
        android:layout_height="wrap_content"
        android:src="@drawable/icon" />
    <Button
        android:id="@+id/resetButton"
        android:layout_height="wrap_content"
        android:layout_width="match_parent"
        android:text="Reset"
        android:textSize="10pt" >
    </Button>
    <TextView
        android:layout_height="wrap_content"
        android:layout_width="match_parent"
        android:layout_marginLeft="6pt"
        android:layout_marginRight="6pt"
        android:textSize="12pt"
        android:layout_marginTop="4pt"
        android:id="@+id/message"
        android:gravity="center_horizontal">
    </TextView>
</LinearLayout>
```
----

4. **Modify Main Java Program**:
   Modify the Java program *src/example/imagebutton/MainActivity.java* to the following. The code is simple and self-explained. The method **addListenerOnButton** specifies how the two buttons will respond when they are clicked.

```
package example.imagebutton;

import android.view.View.OnClickListener;
import android.widget.ImageButton;
import android.widget.TextView;
import android.widget.Button;
import example.imagebutton.R;
import android.app.Activity;
import android.os.Bundle;
import android.view.View;

public class MainActivity extends Activity {
    ImageButton imageButton;
    Button resetButton;
    TextView message;

    @Override
```

```java
public void onCreate(Bundle savedInstanceState) {
  super.onCreate(savedInstanceState);
  setContentView(R.layout.activity_main);
  addListenerOnButton();
}

//define Listeners
public void addListenerOnButton() {
  imageButton = (ImageButton) findViewById(R.id.imageButton1);
  resetButton = (Button) findViewById(R.id.resetButton);

  imageButton.setOnClickListener(new OnClickListener() {
    @Override
    public void onClick(View view) {
      message = (TextView) findViewById(R.id.message);
      message.setText("Image Button Clicked!");
    }
  });

  resetButton.setOnClickListener(new OnClickListener() {
    @Override
    public void onClick(View view) {
      message = (TextView) findViewById(R.id.message);
      message.setText(" ");
    }
  });
}
}
```

The **onCreate** method is auto-generated by the Eclipse when we create the app's project. It is called by the system when an *Activity* is started. This method typically initializes the Activity's instance variables and layout. It should be kept simple so that the app loads quickly. Actually the system will display an ANR (Application Not Responding) if the app takes too long to load. We should use a background thread to do time consuming initializations rather than using **onCreate**.

While the app is running, the user could change its device configuration by rotating the device or sliding out a hard keyboard. To ensure smooth operations during configuration changes, the system passes a *Bundle* parameter, *savedInstanceState*, which contains the activity's saved state, to **onCreate**. Typically, the state information is saved by the *Activity*'s **onSaveInstanceState** method.

The button variables have been defined in the layout file *activity_main.xml*. You may refer to the explanations of the next example on how the variables defined in the Java program relate to those defined in the layout file.

5. We can now compile and run the program from the Eclipse IDE by choosing the **Run** menu. We can also set the run configuration by choosing **Run** > **Run Configurations....** The emulator will show an ImageButton represented by the icon image and a regular button labeled *Reset*. Clicking on the icon image, which represents the *ImageButton* will display the message *Image Button Clicked!* as shown in Figure 2-4(b). Clicking the *Reset Button* clears the message.

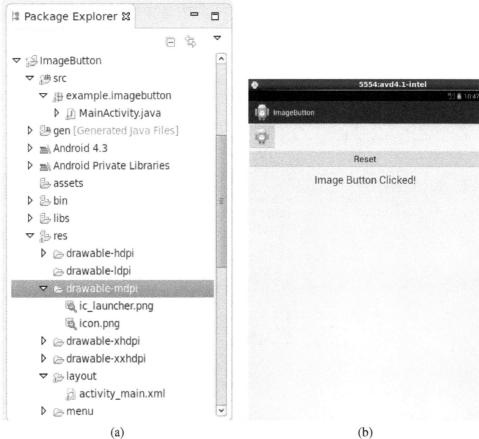

(a)   (b)

Figure 2-4 ImageButton Example: (a) Eclipse IDE Project Explorer Menu (b) Sample Screen
Shot of Application Output

2.5.2 Interest Calculator

In this section, we discuss creating an interactive practical application – the *Interest Calculator*. This Android app simply calculates the interest of an amount of money entered by the user at a certain rate. It also calculates and displays the total amount, which is the sum of the principal and the interest. It is a very simple Android app but through this example, we will explain many basic Android programming features, such as defining strings and text attributes, some of which we have explained in previous sections without concrete examples.

We define the app's GUI in the file *res/layout/activity_main.xml*, where we use a *TableLayout* to organize GUI components into cells specified by rows and columns. Each cell in a *TableLayout* can be empty or can have one component, which in turn can be a layout containing other components. A component can span multiple columns. We use*TableRow* to create the rows.

The number of columns in a *TableLayout* is defined by the *TableRow* that contains the most components. The height of each row is determined by the highest component and the width of each column is determined by the widest element in the column. However, we can specify the table columns to stretch to fill the width of the screen, which may result in wider columns. Components are added to a row from left to right by default. One can refer to the Android developer site for more details about the class *TableLayout* at:

   http://developer.android.com/reference/android/widget/TableLayout.html
and the class *TableRow* at

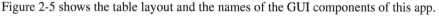

http://developer.android.com/reference/android/widget/TableRow.html
Figure 2-5 shows the table layout and the names of the GUI components of this app.

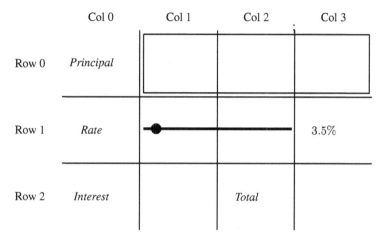

Figure 2-5 . *TableLayout* of App's GUI Labeled by Rows and Columns

The following steps guide you through the development of the app along with explanations of various Android programming features and some classes used. Suppose we use Eclipse IDE, calling both the project name and application name *InterestCalc* and the package name *example.interestcalc*.

1. **Create Project** *InterestCalc*:

    (a) Click **File** > **New** > **Project** > **Android** > **Android Application Project**
    (b) Specify the names of the project, the application and the package as *InterestCalc*, *InterestCalc*, and *example.interestcalc* respectively. Then click **Next** > **Next** > **Next** > **Next** to use the defaults of Eclipse. So the names of **Activity** and **Layout** are *MainActivity* and *activity_main* respectively. The **Navigation Type** is *None*. Then click **Finish** to create the project *InterestCalc*.

2. **Define the GUI Layout**:
    We define the GUI layout of the app in the XML file *res/layout/activity_main.xml*. Modify this file to the following.

```
-----------------------------------------------------------------------
<?xml version="1.0" encoding="utf-8"?>
<!-- Interest Calculator's XML Layout -->
<TableLayout xmlns:android="http://schemas.android.com/apk/res/android"
    android:id="@+id/tableLayout" android:background="#eeeeee"
    android:layout_width="match_parent"
    android:layout_height="match_parent"
    android:stretchColumns="1,2,3" android:padding="5dp">

    <!-- row0 -->
    <TableRow android:id="@+id/row0"
      android:layout_height="wrap_content"
      android:layout_width="match_parent">
      <TextView android:id="@+id/principalStr"
        android:layout_width="wrap_content"
        android:layout_height="wrap_content"
```

```
        android:text="@string/principal" android:textColor="#000"
        android:textSize="14pt" android:gravity="right"
        android:paddingRight="5dp">
    </TextView>
    <EditText android:id="@+id/principalEditText"
        android:layout_width="wrap_content" android:textSize="12pt"
        android:text="@string/principalValue"
        android:layout_height="wrap_content" android:layout_span="3"
        android:inputType="numberDecimal" android:layout_weight="1">
    </EditText>
</TableRow>

  <!-- row1 -->
  <TableRow  android:id="@+id/row1"
    android:layout_height="wrap_content"
    android:layout_width="match_parent">
    <TextView android:id="@+id/rateStr"
      android:layout_width="wrap_content"
      android:text="@string/rate"  android:textSize="14pt"
      android:textColor="#000"     android:paddingRight="5dp"
      android:gravity="right|center_vertical"
      android:layout_height="match_parent"
      android:paddingBottom="5dp"
      android:focusable="false">
    </TextView>
    <SeekBar android:id="@+id/seekBar"
      android:layout_height="wrap_content"
      android:layout_width="match_parent"
      android:layout_span="2"
      android:max="1000" android:progress="35"
      android:paddingLeft="8dp" android:paddingRight="8dp"
      android:paddingBottom="5dp"
      android:layout_weight="1">
    </SeekBar>
    <TextView android:id="@+id/rateTextView"
      android:layout_width="wrap_content" android:text="3.5%"
      android:textColor="#000" android:gravity="center_vertical"
      android:textSize="12pt" android:layout_height="match_parent"
      android:paddingLeft="5dp" android:paddingBottom="5dp"
      android:focusable="false" android:layout_weight="1">
    </TextView>
  </TableRow>

  <!-- row2 -->
  <TableRow android:id="@+id/row2"
    android:layout_height="wrap_content"
    android:layout_width="match_parent">
    <TextView android:id="@+id/interestStr"
      android:layout_width="wrap_content"
      android:layout_height="wrap_content"
      android:text="@string/interest" android:textSize="14pt"
      android:textColor="#00ff00" android:gravity="right"
      android:paddingRight="5dp">
    </TextView>
    <TextView android:id="@+id/interestTextView"
```

```
            android:layout_width="wrap_content"
            android:layout_height="wrap_content"
            android:text="3.5" android:gravity="center"
            android:focusable="false" android:layout_weight="1"
            android:textSize="12pt" android:cursorVisible="false"
            android:longClickable="false">
        </TextView>
        <TextView android:id="@+id/totalStr"
            android:layout_width="wrap_content"
            android:layout_height="wrap_content"
            android:text="@string/total" android:textColor="#ff1111"
            android:gravity="right" android:textSize="14pt"
            android:paddingRight="5dp" android:layout_weight="1">
        </TextView>
        <TextView android:id="@+id/totalTextView"
            android:layout_height="wrap_content"
            android:layout_width="wrap_content"
            android:text="@string/totalValue"
            android:gravity="center" android:focusable="false"
            android:layout_weight="1" android:textSize="12pt"
            android:cursorVisible="false" android:longClickable="false">
        </TextView>
    </TableRow>
</TableLayout>
```

This file is mostly self-explained. we have purposely used different ways to specify some attributes to introduce the techniques. By default, the layout width and height attributes are set to **match_parent** so that the layout fills the entire screen. Each padding attribute is set to 5dp to ensure that there will be 5 density-independent pixels around the border of the entire layout. The *stretchColumns* attribute is set to "1, 2, 3", indicating that columns 1, 2 and 3 should be stretched horizontally to fill the layout's width. The stretch does not include column 0, so the width of this column is equal to that of the widest element plus any padding space specified for the element.

The background color of the *TableLayout* is specified near the top of the file by the attribute and parameter

    android:background="#eeeeee"

where the parameter "#eeeeee" defines a grey color.

Attribute *textSize* specifies the font size of the displayed text and attribute *gravity* specifies the text alignment. For example, in the *TextView* element of row 0, the statements

    android:textSize="14pt" android:gravity="right"

specify a font size of 14 points and a right-aligned text.

The statement

    android:text="@string/principal"

defines the string of the *TextView* to be displayed. The @ sign in the paremeter indicates that the actual string is defined in the file *res/values/strings.xml* and in this example, it is referenced by the variable *principal*. (See the next step.) If there is no @ sign in the param-eter, the value for the parameter is simply the text enclosed inside the double quotes. For example, in column 3 of row 1, the statement android:text="3.5%"

specifies that the string to be displayed is simply **3.5%**.

In the <*SeekBar*> element of row 1, the statement

android:layout_span="2"

means that the *SeekBar* will occupy two columns as shown in Figure 2-5. The statements

android:max="1000" android:progress="35"

specify that the maximum value of the bar is 1000 and the initial value is 35, which corresponds to $35/1000 = 3.5\%$. The values of attribute **Focusable** in **TextView** are set to false so that when the SeekBar's value is changed by the user, the **TextView** still maintains the focus. This helps keep the keyboard on the screen on a device that displays the soft keyboard.

3. **Specify Text Strings**:
The strings denoted with an @ sign in the layout can be defined in the the file *res/values/strings.xml*. So modify this file to the following.

```
<?xml version="1.0" encoding="utf-8"?>
<resources>
    <string name="app_name">Interest Calculator</string>
    <string name="principal">Principal</string>
    <string name="principalValue">100.00</string>
    <string name="interest">Interest</string>
    <string name="total">Total</string>
    <string name="rate">Rate</string>
    <string name="totalValue">103.5</string>
    <string name="zero">0.00</string>
    <string name="action_settings">Settings</string>
</resources>
```

In the notation here, the text inside a pair of double quotes is a variable name and the text between the *string* tags is the actual value of the variable. For example, in

<string name="principal">Principal</string>

principal is the variable name and **Principal** is the actual string represented by the variable, which is defined in row 0 of the *TableLayout* discussed above:

android:text="@string/principal"

4. **Modify Main Java Program**:
Modify the Java program *src/example/interestcalc/MainActivity.java* to the following.

```
//Interest Calculator
package example.interestcalc;

import android.os.Bundle;
import android.app.Activity;
import android.text.Editable;
import android.widget.TextView;
import android.widget.EditText;
import android.text.TextWatcher;
```

```java
import android.widget.SeekBar;
import android.widget.SeekBar.OnSeekBarChangeListener;

//main Activity class for Interest Calculator
public class MainActivity extends Activity
{
  private double principal;    //amount entered by the user
  private double ratePercent;  //inter rate in % set with SeekBar
  private EditText principalEditText; //user input for principal
  private TextView rateTextView;      //displays rate percentage
  private TextView totalTextView;
  private TextView interestTextView;  //displays interest amount

  //constants used in saving/restoring state
  private static final String PRINCIPAL = "PRINCIPAL";
  private static final String INTEREST_RATE = "INTEREST_RATE";

  // Called when the activity is first created.
  @Override
  public void onCreate(Bundle savedInstanceState)
  {
    super.onCreate(savedInstanceState); //call superclass's version
    setContentView(R.layout.activity_main); //inflate the GUI

    //check whether app just started or is being restored from memory
    if ( savedInstanceState == null ) // the app just started running
    {
      principal = 100.0;    //initialize the principal to 100
        ratePercent = 3.5; //initialize the interest rate to 3.5%
      } else { // restore app from memory, not executed from scratch
        // restore saved values
        principal = savedInstanceState.getDouble(PRINCIPAL);
        ratePercent = savedInstanceState.getDouble(INTEREST_RATE);
    }

    // get the TextView displaying the rate percentage
    rateTextView = (TextView) findViewById(R.id.rateTextView);

    // get the interest  and total TextView
    interestTextView=(TextView) findViewById(R.id.interestTextView);
    totalTextView = (TextView) findViewById(R.id.totalTextView);

    // get the principal editText
    principalEditText=(EditText)findViewById(R.id.principalEditText);

    // editTextWatcher handles editText's onTextChanged event
    principalEditText.addTextChangedListener(editTextWatcher);

    // get the SeekBar used to set interest rate
    SeekBar seekBar = (SeekBar) findViewById(R.id.seekBar);
    seekBar.setOnSeekBarChangeListener(seekBarListener);
  } // end method onCreate

  // updates the interest and total EditTexts
  private void updates()
```

```java
   {
     rateTextView.setText(String.format("%.02f %s",ratePercent,"%"));
     // calculate interest
     double interest = principal * ratePercent * .01;

     // calculate the total, including principal and interest
     double total = principal + interest;

     // display interest and total  amounts
     interestTextView.setText( String.format("%.02f", interest));
     totalTextView.setText( String.format("%.02f", total));
   }

   // save values of editText and SeekBar
   @Override
   protected void onSaveInstanceState(Bundle outState)
   {
     super.onSaveInstanceState(outState);

     outState.putDouble(PRINCIPAL, principal);
     outState.putDouble(INTEREST_RATE, ratePercent);
   }

   // called when the user changes the position of SeekBar
   private OnSeekBarChangeListener seekBarListener =
      new OnSeekBarChangeListener()
   {
      // update ratePercent, then call updates
      @Override
      public void onProgressChanged(SeekBar seekBar, int progress,
                                                    boolean fromUser)
      {
         // sets ratePercent to position of the SeekBar's thumb
         ratePercent = seekBar.getProgress() /10.0;
         updates(); // update interest and total
      }

      @Override
      public void onStartTrackingTouch(SeekBar seekBar)
      {
      }

      @Override
      public void onStopTrackingTouch(SeekBar seekBar)
      {
      }
   }; // end OnSeekBarChangeListener

   // event-handling object that responds to editText's events
   private TextWatcher editTextWatcher = new TextWatcher()
   {
     // called when the user enters a number
     @Override
     public void onTextChanged(CharSequence s, int start,
        int before, int count)
```

```
    {
        // convert editText's text to a double
        try
        {
            principal = Double.parseDouble(s.toString());
        }
        catch (NumberFormatException e)
        {
            principal = 0.0; // default if an exception occurs
        }
        updates(); // update the values
    }

    @Override
    public void afterTextChanged(Editable s)
    {
    }

    @Override
    public void beforeTextChanged(CharSequence s, int start,
            int count, int after)
    {
    }
  }; // end editTextWatcher
} // end class MainActivity
```

When the system runs the application, the ADT Plugin tools build and generate a resource class called *R* from the resource XML files such as *strings.xml* and *activity_main.xml*. This class contains nested static classes representing the resources specified in the project's *res* directory. This class can be found in the project's *gen* directory, which contains source-code files generated by the system. In our case, the file generated is *gen/example/interestcalc/R.java*. The class is compiled to binary files in *bin/classes/example/interestcalc*, which contains the binary codes of all the classes of the package *example.interestcalc*. Within the nested classes of class *R*, the tools have created static final **int** constants that let us refer to these resources programmatically from our app's Java code, *src/example/interestcalc/MainActivity.java*. Examples of the nested classes of *R* include

(a) class *drawable*, which contains constants for any drawable items, such as images and button images, that we put in various drawable directories inside *res*,
(b) class *id*, which contains constants for the GUI components defined in your xml layout files,
(c) class *layout*, which contains constants that represent each layout file in the project such as, *activity_main.xml*,
(d) class *string*, which contains constants for each string defined in *strings.xml*.

The following is a portion of the generated file *gen/example/interestcalc/R.java* in this example:

```
  package example.interestcalc;
  public final class R {
    .....
    public static final class drawable {
```

```
        public static final int ic_launcher=0x7f020000;
    }
    public static final class id {
        public static final int action_settings=0x7f08000d;
        public static final int interestStr=0x7f080009;
        public static final int interestTextView=0x7f08000a;
        public static final int principalEditText=0x7f080003;
        public static final int principalStr=0x7f080002;
        public static final int rateStr=0x7f080005;
        public static final int rateTextView=0x7f080007;
        public static final int row0=0x7f080001;
        public static final int row1=0x7f080004;
        public static final int row2=0x7f080008;
        public static final int seekBar=0x7f080006;
        public static final int tableLayout=0x7f080000;
        public static final int totalStr=0x7f08000b;
        public static final int totalTextView=0x7f08000c;
    }
    public static final class layout {
        public static final int activity_main=0x7f030000;
    }
    public static final class string {
        public static final int action_settings=0x7f050008;
        public static final int app_name=0x7f050000;
        public static final int interest=0x7f050003;
        public static final int principal=0x7f050001;
        public static final int principalValue=0x7f050002;
        public static final int rate=0x7f050005;
        public static final int total=0x7f050004;
        public static final int totalValue=0x7f050006;
        public static final int zero=0x7f050007;
    }
    . . . . .
}
```

In **OnCreate**() of class *MainActivity*, the call

> setContentView (R.layout.activity_main);

takes the constant *R.layout.activity_main* as parameter, which in this example is 0x7f030000 as shown in *R.java* above, and it represents the *activity_main.xml* file. In general, **setContentView** uses the constant argument to load the corresponding xml document, which is then parsed and converted to the app's GUI components and the process is known as inflating the GUI.

Once the layout is inflated, we can get references to the individual widgets using the **findViewById** method as shwon in the *MainActivity* code above.

In the code of *MainActivity.java* listed above, we also define an anonymous inner class that implements interface *OnSeekBarChangeListener*. which creates the anonymous inner-class object *seekBarListener* that responds to seekBar's events. Java requires us to override a few methods that include: **onProgressChanged**, **onStartTrackingTouch**, and **onStopTrackingTouch**. In our app, we only implement **onProgressChanged**, which we need, and simply provide an empty shell for each of the other two, that we do not actually use. In our code, we use the *getProgress* method of the class *SeekBar* to obtain the SeekBar's indicator position. The **getProgress** returns an integer in the range $0 - 1000$, which is defined by us with the statement

>   android:max="1000"

in the file *activity_main.xml* discussed above. We divide the returned value by 10 to obtain the percentage interest rate, which can have a value ranging from 0.0 to 100.9. The method then calls **updates**() to calculate the interest and the total amount.

5. **Run the Application**:
   When we run the application, we will see a screen similar to one shown in Figure 2-6. We can enter a value for *principal* by clicking the mouse at the text area of *principal*. If you want to erase the original value (100.00), you have to point the mouse cursor to the right side of the number and press the key *Backspace* to erase the digits.

   We can change the interest rate by sliding the seekBar indicator using the mouse.

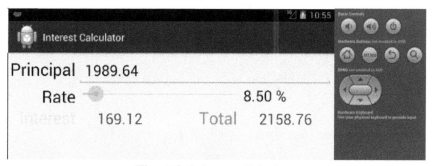

Figure 2-6   Interest Calculator

2.5.3 Grid View Demo

In this example, we demonstrate the use of *GridView* to display an array of images. This example is adopted from the example *HelloGridView* presented in the official Android developer web site.

  GridView is a *ViewGroup*, which displays items in a two-dimensional and scrollable grid. A *ListAdapter* is used to automatically insert grid items to the layout. In this example, we will construct an image gallery using *GridView*. Each grid displays an image thumbnail. When an item is clicked, a toast message will show the position of the grid selected.

  We use Eclipse IDE to develop this application and we call the project and application *Grid-ViewDemo*, and the package, *example.gridviewdemo*:

1. Like what we did in previous examples, we create a project named *GridViewDemo* using Eclipse IDE.

2. We create the directory *res/drawable*, find some images from the Internet or other sources. and save them in the directory, naming the images as *sample0.jpg, sample1.jpg*, and *sample2.jpg* etc.

3. We modify the layout file *res/layout/activity_main.xml* to the following:

```
<?xml version="1.0" encoding="utf-8"?>
<GridView xmlns:android="http://schemas.android.com/apk/res/android"
    android:id="@+id/gridview"
    android:layout_width="match_parent"
    android:layout_height="match_parent"
```

```
      android:columnWidth="100dp"
      android:numColumns="auto_fit"
      android:verticalSpacing="10dp"
      android:horizontalSpacing="10dp"
      android:stretchMode="columnWidth"
      android:gravity="center"
  />
```

This *GridView* will fill the entire screen. The **numColumns** attribute, representing number of columns, is set to *auto_fit*, which sets the number of columns to fit the screen. One may set it to a number such as 3 and 4.

4. We modify the main java program, *MainActivity.java* to the following:

```
package example.gridviewdemo;

import android.widget.AdapterView.OnItemClickListener;
import android.content.Context;
import android.app.Activity;
import android.os.Bundle;
import android.widget.*;
import android.view.*;

public class MainActivity extends Activity
{
  public void onCreate(Bundle savedInstanceState) {
    super.onCreate(savedInstanceState);
    setContentView(R.layout.activity_main);

    GridView gridview = (GridView) findViewById(R.id.gridview);
    gridview.setAdapter(new ImageAdapter(this));

    gridview.setOnItemClickListener(new OnItemClickListener() {
      public void onItemClick(AdapterView<?> parent, View v,
                                       int position, long id) {
        Toast.makeText(MainActivity.this, "" + position,
                                     Toast.LENGTH_LONG).show();
      }
    });
  }
}

class ImageAdapter extends BaseAdapter {
  private Context context;
  // reference the  images
  private Integer[] imageIds = {
    R.drawable.sample2, R.drawable.sample3,
    R.drawable.sample4, R.drawable.sample5,
    R.drawable.sample6, R.drawable.sample7,
    R.drawable.sample0, R.drawable.sample1,
    R.drawable.sample2, R.drawable.sample3,
    R.drawable.sample4, R.drawable.sample7,
  };
  public ImageAdapter(Context context0) {
```

```
      context = context0;
  }
  public int getCount() {
    return imageIds.length;
  }
  public Object getItem(int position) {
    return null;
  }
  public long getItemId(int position) {
      return 0;
  }
  // create a new ImageView for each item referenced by the Adapter
  public View getView(int position,View convertView,ViewGroup parent){
    ImageView imageView;
    if (convertView == null) {//Initialize attributes for first time
      imageView = new ImageView(context);
      imageView.setLayoutParams(new GridView.LayoutParams(220, 220));
      imageView.setScaleType(ImageView.ScaleType.CENTER_CROP);
      imageView.setPadding(6, 6, 6, 6);
    } else {
      imageView = (ImageView) convertView;
    }
    imageView.setImageResource(imageIds[position]);
        return imageView;
    }
}
```

We have defined the content view in the layout file *activity_main.xml*. The class *MainActivity* captures the *GridView* from the layout with **findViewById(int)**. The **setAdapter()** method then sets a custom adapter, *ImageAdapter*, as the source for all items to be displayed in the grid. The *ImageAdapter* is a class defined in the same file. We pass a new **AdapterView.OnItemClickListener** to the **setOnItemClickListener()** so that a task will be peformed when an element in the grid is clicked. This anonymous instance defines the **onItemClick()** callback method, which displays a *Toast* message indicating the position of the element in the grid.

The custom adapter class *ImageAdapter* extends the class *BaseAdapter*, and is thus required to implement some methods inherited from *BaseAdapter*. The constructor and the method **getCount()** are self-explained. In general, **getItem(int)** returns the actual object at the specified position in the adapter, but it is not used in this example. Also, **getItemId(int)** returns the row id of the item, but again they are not needed here.

The first useful method is **getView()**, which creates a new *View* for each image added to the *ImageAdapter*. When it is called, a *View* is passed in, which normally is a recycled object, and thus we need to check whether the object is **null**. If it is **null**, an *ImageView* object is created and configured with desired properties for the image presentation including:

q) **setLayoutParams** (*ViewGroup.LayoutParams*) that sets the height and width for the *View*. This ensures that, regardless of the image sizes, each image is resized and cropped to fit in the dimensions.

b) **setScaleType**(*ImageView.ScaleType*), which declares that images should be cropped toward the center if necessary.

c) **setPadding(int, int, int, int)** that defines the padding for all sides. Normally, images with different aspect-ratios, will have more cropping with less padding if its dimensions do not match those of the *ImageView*. At the end of the **getView()** method, an image from the image array, specified by the paramter *position*, is set as the image resource for the *ImageView*.

5. When we run the application, we should see an image gallery. Figure 2-7 shows a sample of the display. If we click on an image, its position in the image array is displayed for a short while as a *Toast* message.

Figure 2-7 Image Gallary Using GridView

2.6   Running On a Real Android Device

When we build a mobile application, it is important that we test the application on a real device before releasing it to users. To do the test, we need to have an Android phone or device that can be used for testing but not all Android phones have this function. So when you purchase an Android phone, make sure that it can be used for development. One can refer to the Android developers web site for detailed information about using hardware devices:

```
http://developer.android.com/tools/device.html
```

The phone that we have used for testing is *Samsung*'s *Galaxy III*, and we will use this as an example to explain how to upload and run an app on the mobile phone.

First, we connect our Samsung mobile phone to our PC (a 64-bit Linux machine) via a USB port and turn on the phone. We can check whether the phone has been attached to the PC using the *adb* command in a terminal, which will list all the attached Android devices:

```
$ adb devices
List of devices attached
479004ad3e8ecfbc device
```

Second, we configure our Eclipse IDE to run the app in the phone by clicking **Run > Run Configurations.. > Target**. Then check **Always prompt to pick device** and click **Apply**. Now when we click **run**, we will see the **Android Device Chooser** dialog as shown in Figure 2-8.

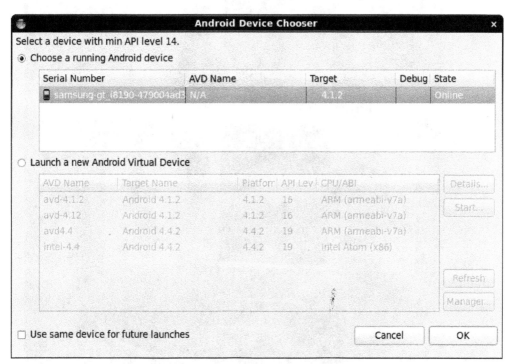

Figure 2-8   Android Device Chooser

We simply select the Samsung device and click **OK**. The app will be uploaded to the Galaxy phone and we can swipe across its screen to unlock to run it. Figure 2-9 shows the *GridViewDemo* app discussed above running on a Samsung Galaxy III phone.

Figure 2-9 Running App on Real Mobile Phone

2.7   Notes on Using Eclipse IDE

Most readers may use Eclipse IDE to learn or develop Android applications as it is a convenient IDE that helps us import the necessary libraries and pinpoints the errors. However, Eclipse is not a very user-friendly IDE and many navigation paths are non-intuitive, requiring a lot of trials to get familiar with its usage. There are also some situations that the IDE may lead us to a wrong direction in the development process, and in this case, you may want to use the command line tools to assist you to find the right ways. For example, occasionally Eclipse may suggest a wrong library to import, which is not the one your application needs, leading to subtle errors, which are hard to debug.

If your machine runs a newly installed operating system such as 64-bit Linux, some generic libraries such as the C++ glib required by the system to run the Android plugins may be missing. The Eclipse IDE could run normally but when it builds the Android environment, it may need a dynamic library that depends on another library, which is missing. The IDE may not generate the correct error messages informing you the missing library, or worse, it may generate an error message that points you to a wrong direction. This can be avoided if you build and compile your Android project using the command-line tools. They will tell you exactly what libraries are missing.

Sometimes, it may import the wrong library for a statement when you click on the error indicator caused by a missing library. For example, you may need the OpenGL *Matrix* class, which requires the import statement,

```
import android.opengl.Matrix;
```

However, if not careful, you may have imported the wrong one:

```
import android.graphics.Matrix;
```

and you are not aware of it; you may then wonder why errors still occur after you have included the *Matrix* import statement.

If sometimes when you start Eclipse and see red dot error indicators in a project that you did not see last time, you may fix them by simply doing a cleaning of the project (Click **Project** > **Clean..** > **Clean all projects** > **OK**) or restarting Eclipse again.

While working on a project using Eclipse, if you have changed a file of the project using another editor, you have to click your project name in *Package Explorer*, and then click **File** > **Refresh** for the changes to take effect in Eclipse.

To change the editor font size, you have to click **Window** > **Preferences** > **General** > **Appearance** > **Colors and Fonts** > **Java** > **Java Text Editor Fonts** > **Edit** ....

Chapter 3   Android Components and Simple Examples

In this chapter, we present some simple examples, which are mostly adopted from the official Android tutorial web site where it explains in each example the meanings of statements and variables in the program but often misses the description of some steps that might be crucial for beginners to compile and run the program. Here we fill in those missing steps but may only describe the program context briefly.

3.1   GUI Example with Eclipse IDE

The first example is about **building a simple user interface** which can be found at

http://developer.android.com/training/basics/firstapp/building-ui.html.

We explain how to develop this user interface application using Eclipse IDE, which offers a lot of assistants to the user in the process. When an error occurs in the code, the IDE shows a small red circle at the left side of the problematic statement and underlines with red the fields that cause the error. The user can click on the red circle or the underlined field and Eclipse will present suggestions to fix the problem. Very often, an error may be caused by missing the import of a class; the user can fix it by clicking on the suggested import statement by Eclipse, which will then add the import statement to the program automatically.

   We can build an Android graphical user interface (GUI) using a hierarchy of *View* and *ViewGroup* objects as shown in Figure 3-1 below. *View* objects in general consist of graphical widgets such as buttons and text fields while *ViewGroup* objects are *View* containers that are invisible, defining how the child views are laid out, such as in horizontal row or in a grid.

   We can use XML to define a user interface (UI) with a hierarchy of UI elements.

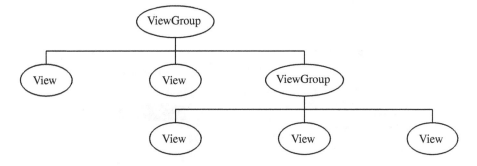

Figure 3-1. A Hierarchy of View and ViewGroup Objects

   Suppose we call our application *SimpleGui* and we shall use the Android Linear Layout to present the interface. To start, we create the project using Eclipse IDE with:

   File > New > Android Application Project

We can enter **SimpleGui**, **SimpleGui**, and **gui.simplegui** for *Application Name*, *Project Name* and *Package Name* respectively as shown in Figure 3-2 below.

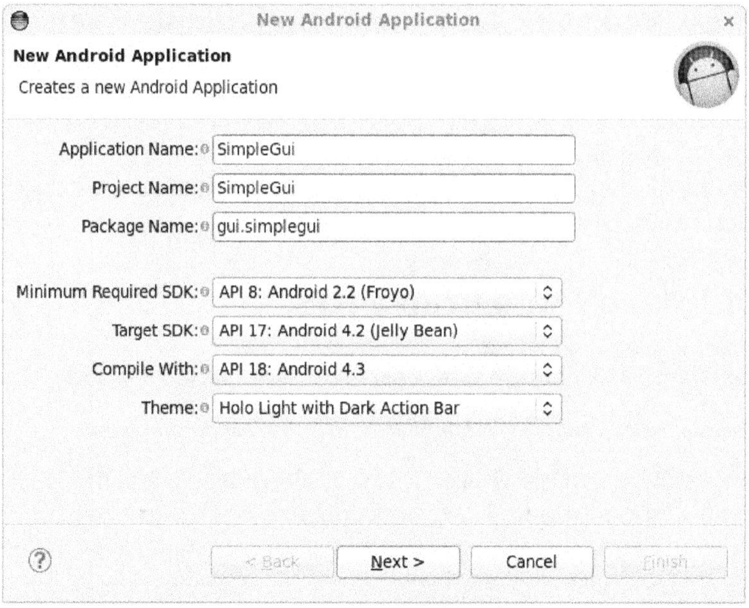

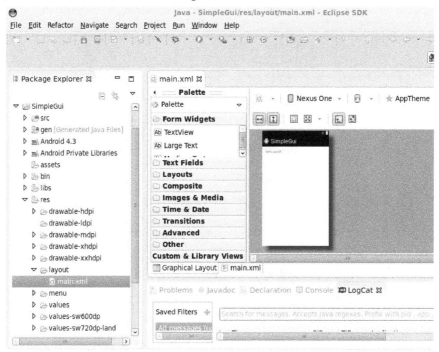

Figure 3-2   Creating SimpleGui Project

Then click **Next** > **Next** > **Next** > **Next**, where we have chosen to create a *Blank Activity*. In the *Blank Activity* panel, rather than using the default values, we enter **GuiMain** for *Activity Name* and *main* for *Layout Name*, and click **Finish** to create the **SimpleGui** project. The Eclipse IDe will show us the content of the layout file *main.xml* in the relative directory *res/layout* in graphical format, which is the default, as shown in Figure 3-3.

Figure 3-3   After Creating SimpleGui Project

To examine the file in text format, we have to click on the tab of *main.xml* shown at the bottom of the Eclipse editor.

3.1.1 Using a Linear Layout

The layout file *main.xml*, which is created by the *Blank Activity* template, defines a *RelativeLayout* and *TextView* child view. We want to change the layout to *LinearLayout*, which is a subclass of *ViewGroup*, laying out child views in either a vertical or horizontal orientation. So we modify the default *main.xml* file to the following:

```
<?xml version="1.0" encoding="utf-8"?>
<LinearLayout xmlns:android="http://schemas.android.com/apk/res/android"
  xmlns:tools="http://schemas.android.com/tools"
  android:layout_width="match_parent"
  android:layout_height="match_parent"
  android:orientation="horizontal">
  <EditText android:id="@+id/message_box"
      android:layout_weight="1"
      android:layout_width="0dp"
      android:layout_height="wrap_content"
      android:hint="@string/message_box" />
  <Button
      android:layout_width="wrap_content"
      android:layout_height="wrap_content"
      android:text="@string/send_button" />
</LinearLayout>
```

Two red error indicators will show up in the IDE editor at the two statements:

> android:hint="@string/message_box"
> android:text="@string/send_button"

This is because we have not defined the strings *message_box* and *send_button* in *string.xml*. To fix the errors we edit the file *strings.xml* in directory *res/values* to

```
<?xml version="1.0" encoding="utf-8"?>
<resources>
  <string name="app_name">SimpleGui</string>
  <string name="action_settings">Settings</string>
   <string name="message_box">Enter a message</string>
  <string name="send_button">Send</string>
</resources>
```

When we run the application, Android will display a GUI looked like Figure 3-4 below.

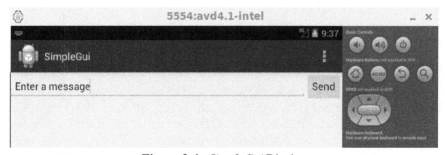

Figure 3-4 *SimpleGui* Display

The details of *layout* properties can be found at:

> http://developer.android.com/guide/topics/ui/declaring-layout.html

What we have defined inside <LinearLayout> in the file *main.xml* above are a user-editable text field, <EditText> called *message_box*, and a <Button> called *send_button*.

The layout has been created in a way that both the **EditText** and **Button** widgets are only as big as necessary to fit their content, as shown in figure 3-4. The attributes and properties of the widgets are explained below.

<Edit Text> Attributes

android:id

> This specifies a unique identifier for the view for further references. The symbol at (@) is required when specifying any resource object using XML. The plus sign (+) is also needed when we define a resource ID for the first time. In our example,

```
<EditText android:id="@+id/message_box"
```

> *message_box* is the resource name and *id* is the resource type.

android:layout_width and **android:layout_height**

> These attributes specify the width and height of the layout. The **wrap_content** value makes layout size to be as big as needed to fit the contents of the view. If the value **match_parent** is used, the *EditText* element will fill the screen, because it will match the size of the parent *LinearLayout*.

android:hint

> This defines a default string for display. In our example, the string is given by *@string/message_box*, which specifies a string defined in the file *res/values/strings.xml*.

android:layout_weight

> This defines the amount of remaining space each view should consume, relative to the amount taken up by other sibling views. The default value for a view is 0, implying that it won't fill any space by default.

<Button> Attributes

The **Button** attributes *layout_width* and *layout_height* of *main.xml* in our example are set to **wrap_content**, which makes the button widget to be as large as necessary to fit its content.

3.1.2 Responding to Clicking

For the button to respond to a user's clicking, we need to add the statement

> android:onClick="transmitMessage"

to the <Button> element of the layout file *main.xml*. The attribute value "transmitMessage" of **android:onClick** is the method in the activity that the system calls when the button is clicked. We have to define this method in the class *GuiMain*. That is, we have to include this method in the file *GuiMain.java* in directory *src/gui/simplegui/* as shown below:

```
...
import android.view.View;
import android.content.Intent;
import android.widget.EditText;
```

```
...

public class GuiMain extends Activity
{
  public final static String EXTRA_MESSAGE = "gui.simplegui.MESSAGE";
  ...

  public void transmitMessage( View view )
  {
    Intent intent = new Intent(this, MessageActivity.class);
    EditText editText = (EditText) findViewById(R.id.message_box);
    String message = editText.getText().toString();
    intent.putExtra(EXTRA_MESSAGE, message);
    startActivity(intent);
  }
}
```

In the code, we have defined an *Intent* object, which provides late runtime binding between separate components such as two activities. In general, an *Intent* class is an abstract description of an operation to be performed, representing an app's "intent to do something". It is mostly used in launching activities, where it establishes a 'bridge' between activities. Detailed descriptions of the class can be found at

> http://developer.android.com/reference/android/content/Intent.html

(Eclipse IDE allows us to look up a class conveniently; it may show a small green triangle on the scrolling bar at the statement of a new class. Clicking on the green triangle loads the information of the class.) In our example, an *Intent* is constructed to start an activity named *MessageActivity* using the constructor,

> Intent intent = new Intent(this, MessageActivity.class);

which takes two parameters:

1. A *Context* object as its first parameter. The parameter *this* refers to the *GuiMain* class. Note that the *Activity* class is a subclass of the *Context* class.
2. The second parameter is an *Activity* that the *Intent* binds with the first.

Besides creating another activity, an *Intent* object can transmit data to the activity as well. In the **transmitMessage**() method, we use **findViewById**() to get the text from the **EditText** element and add it to the *Intent* object *intent*.

In order for the other activity to inquire the extra data, we have to define the key for the intent's extra as a public constant, which is the *String* constant **EXTRA MESSAGE** defined in the *GuiMain* class above.

At this point, the Eclipse editor will indicate an error at the statement referencing *MessageActivity* as we have not defined this class. In the next section we discuss how to create an *Activity* class and define *MessageActivity*.

3.1.3 Creating a New Activity

To create a new *Activity*, click on the Eclipse IDE:

> **File > New > Other..**

A window panel appears. Select the **Android** folder, choose **Android Activity**, and click **Next**. Then select **Blank Activity** and click **Next**, which presents a wizard like the one shown in Figure 3-5 below. Fill in the activity details:

> **Project**: SimpleGui
> **Activity Name**: MessageActivity
> **Layout Name**: activity_message
> **Title**: MessageActivity
> **Hierarchial Parent**: gui.simplegui.GuiMain
> **Navigation Type**: None

and click **Finish**, which creates the new **Activity**.

Figure 3-5   New Activity Wizard in Eclipse

The java file *src/gui/simplegui/MessageActivity.java* is created, consisting of a default template as follow:

```
package gui.simplegui;

import android.os.Bundle;
import android.app.Activity;
import android.view.Menu;
import android.view.MenuItem;
import android.support.v4.app.NavUtils;
import android.annotation.TargetApi;
import android.os.Build;

public class MessageActivity extends Activity
{
  @Override
  protected void onCreate(Bundle savedInstanceState)
  {
    super.onCreate(savedInstanceState);
    setContentView(R.layout.activity_message);
    // Show the Up button in the action bar.
    setupActionBar();
  }

  /*
```

```
   * Set up the {@link android.app.ActionBar},if the API is available.
   */
  @TargetApi(Build.VERSION_CODES.HONEYCOMB)
  private void setupActionBar() {
    if (Build.VERSION.SDK_INT >= Build.VERSION_CODES.HONEYCOMB) {
      getActionBar().setDisplayHomeAsUpEnabled(true);
    }
  }


  @Override
  public boolean onCreateOptionsMenu(Menu menu) {
    //Inflate the menu; this adds items to action bar if it is present.
    getMenuInflater().inflate(R.menu.message, menu);
    return true;
  }


  @Override
  public boolean onOptionsItemSelected(MenuItem item) {
    switch (item.getItemId()) {
    case android.R.id.home:
    //This ID represents the Home or Up button. In the case of this
    //activity, the Up button is shown. Use NavUtils to allow users
    //to navigate up one level in the application structure. For
    //more details, see the Navigation pattern on Android Design:
    /*
  http://developer.android.com/design/patterns/navigation.html#up-vs-back
    */
    NavUtils.navigateUpFromSameTask(this);
    return true;
    }
    return super.onOptionsItemSelected(item);
  }
}
```

We need to modify *MessageActivity* to the following so that it receives the message sent from *GuiMain* and displays it:

```
package gui.simplegui;

import android.os.Bundle;
import android.app.Activity;
import android.view.Menu;
import android.view.MenuItem;
import android.support.v4.app.NavUtils;
import android.annotation.SuppressLint;
import android.annotation.TargetApi;
import android.content.Intent;
import android.os.Build;
import android.view.View;
import android.widget.EditText;
import android.widget.TextView;

public class MessageActivity extends Activity
{
  @SuppressLint("NewApi")
  @Override
```

```
protected void onCreate(Bundle savedInstanceState) {
  super.onCreate(savedInstanceState);
  setContentView(R.layout.activity_message);

  // Need running on Honeycomb or higher to use ActionBar APIs
  if (Build.VERSION.SDK_INT >= Build.VERSION_CODES.HONEYCOMB) {
    // Show the Up button in the action bar.
    getActionBar().setDisplayHomeAsUpEnabled(true);
  }
  // Get the message from the intent
  Intent intent = getIntent();
  String message = intent.getStringExtra(GuiMain.EXTRA_MESSAGE);

  // Create the text view
  TextView textView = new TextView(this);
  textView.setTextSize(40);
  textView.setText(message);

  // Set the text view as the activity layout
  setContentView(textView);
}

@Override
public boolean onOptionsItemSelected(MenuItem item) {
  switch (item.getItemId()) {
  case android.R.id.home:
    NavUtils.navigateUpFromSameTask(this);
    return true;
  }
  return super.onOptionsItemSelected(item);
}
}
```

You may see an error at the statement

   @SuppressLint("NewApi")

To fix the error, you need to make sure that you use an API of 16 or higher and you may need to add to the program the import statement:

   import android.annotation.SuppressLint;

When we run the app, type a message in the text field, and click the *Send* button, the message will show up on the second activity as shown in Figure 3-6 below.

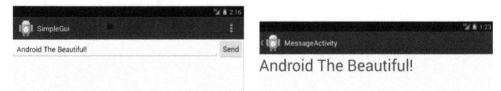

Figure 3-6   Both activities of SimpleGui Running on Android 4.3

3.2   GUI Example using Command Line

In this section we describe how to develop the above simple GUI app using command-line commands. We again assume that our workspace is in */workspace*. We will use the AVD called *SDcard* that we created with Eclipse in the above example:

1. We first go to the workspace directory and create the subdirectory *simpleGui* with commands:

   ```
   $ cd  /workspace/
   $ mkdir  simpleGui
   ```

2. Create the project *simpleGui* by

   > android create project –target 24 –name simpleGui –path ./simpleGui \
   > –activity GuiMain –package gui.simplegui

3. Go into the project directory:

   ```
   $ cd simpleGui
   ```

4. Compile the project by

   ```
   $ ant debug
   ```

   to generate some default files.

5. Modify the activity program *GuiMain.java* using a text editor such as *vi*,

   ```
   $ vi src/gui/simplegui/GuiMain.java
   ```

   to the following:

   ```java
   package gui.simplegui;

   import android.os.Bundle;
   import android.app.Activity;
   import android.content.Intent;
   import android.view.Menu;
   import android.view.View;
   import android.widget.EditText;

   public class GuiMain extends Activity {
     public final static String EXTRA_MESSAGE = "gui.simplegui.MESSAGE";
     @Override
     protected void onCreate(Bundle savedInstanceState) {
       super.onCreate(savedInstanceState);
       setContentView(R.layout.main);
     }
     @Override
     public boolean onCreateOptionsMenu(Menu menu) {
       // Inflate the menu, adding items to the action bar
       getMenuInflater().inflate(R.menu.gui_main, menu);
       return true;
     }
     public void transmitMessage( View view )
     {
       Intent intent = new Intent(this, MessageActivity.class);
       EditText editText = (EditText) findViewById(R.id.message_box);
       String message = editText.getText().toString();
       intent.putExtra(GuiMain.EXTRA_MESSAGE, message);
       startActivity(intent);
     }
   }
   ```

6. Create the other activity file using

$ vi src/gui/simplegui/MessageActivity.java

with the following code:

```
package gui.simplegui;

import android.os.Bundle;
import android.app.Activity;
import android.view.Menu;
import android.view.MenuItem;
import android.support.v4.app.NavUtils;
import android.annotation.SuppressLint;
import android.annotation.TargetApi;
import android.content.Intent;
import android.os.Build;
import android.view.View;
import android.widget.EditText;
import android.widget.TextView;

public class MessageActivity extends Activity {
  @SuppressLint("NewApi")
  @Override
  protected void onCreate(Bundle savedInstanceState) {
     super.onCreate(savedInstanceState);
     setContentView(R.layout.activity_message);

     // Make sure we're running on Honeycomb or higher
     if (Build.VERSION.SDK_INT >= Build.VERSION_CODES.HONEYCOMB) {
        // Show the Up button in the action bar.
        getActionBar().setDisplayHomeAsUpEnabled(true);
     }
     // Get the message from the intent
     Intent intent = getIntent();
     String message = intent.getStringExtra(GuiMain.EXTRA_MESSAGE);

     // Create the text view
     TextView textView = new TextView(this);
     textView.setTextSize(40);
     textView.setText(message);

     // Set the text view as the activity layout
     setContentView(textView);
  }
  @Override
  public boolean onOptionsItemSelected(MenuItem item) {
     switch (item.getItemId()) {
     case android.R.id.home:
       NavUtils.navigateUpFromSameTask(this);
       return true;
     }
     return super.onOptionsItemSelected(item);
  }
}
```

7. Modify *main.xml* with

$ vi res/layout/main.xml

to the following:

```
<?xml version="1.0" encoding="utf-8"?>
<LinearLayout xmlns:android="http://schemas.android.com/apk/res/android"
  xmlns:tools="http://schemas.android.com/tools"
  android:layout_width="match_parent"
  android:layout_height="match_parent"
  android:orientation="horizontal">
  <EditText android:id="@+id/message_box"
      android:layout_weight="1"
      android:layout_width="0dp"
      android:layout_height="wrap_content"
      android:hint="@string/message_box" />
  <Button
      android:layout_width="wrap_content"
      android:layout_height="wrap_content"
      android:text="@string/send_button"
      android:onClick="transmitMessage"/>
</LinearLayout>
```

8. Create **activity_message.xml** using

   $ vi res/layout/activity_message.xml

   with the code:

```
<RelativeLayout xmlns:android="http://schemas.android.com/apk/res/android"
  xmlns:tools="http://schemas.android.com/tools"
  android:layout_width="match_parent"
  android:layout_height="match_parent"
  android:paddingBottom="@dimen/activity_vertical_margin"
  android:paddingLeft="@dimen/activity_horizontal_margin"
  android:paddingRight="@dimen/activity_horizontal_margin"
  android:paddingTop="@dimen/activity_vertical_margin"
  tools:context=".MessageActivity" >

  <TextView
      android:layout_width="wrap_content"
      android:layout_height="wrap_content" />
</RelativeLayout>
```

9. Modify **strings.xml** with

   $ vi res/values/strings.xml

   to the following:

```
<?xml version="1.0" encoding="utf-8"?>
<resources>
  <string name="app_name">SimpleGui</string>
  <string name="action_settings">Settings</string>
  <string name="message_box">Enter a message</string>
  <string name="send_button">Send</string>
  <string name="title_activity_message">MessageActivity</string>
</resources>
```

10. Create **dimens.xml** using

    $ vi res/values/dimens.xml

with the following code:

```
 <resources>
    <!-- Default screen margins, per the Android Design guidelines. -->
    <dimen name="activity_horizontal_margin">16dp</dimen>
    <dimen name="activity_vertical_margin">16dp</dimen>
 </resources>
```

11. Create **styles.xml** using

> $ vi   res/values/styles.xml

with the following code:

```
 <resources>
   <style name="AppBaseTheme" parent="android:Theme.Light">
   </style>
   <!-- Application theme. -->
   <style name="AppTheme" parent="AppBaseTheme">
   </style>
 </resources>
```

12. Modify **AndroidManifest.xml** with

> $ vi   AndroidManifest.xml

to the following code:

```
<?xml version="1.0" encoding="utf-8"?>
<manifest xmlns:android="http://schemas.android.com/apk/res/android"
    package="gui.simplegui"
    android:versionCode="1"
    android:versionName="1.0" >

    <uses-sdk
        android:minSdkVersion="8"
        android:targetSdkVersion="17" />

    <application
        android:allowBackup="true"
        android:icon="@drawable/ic_launcher"
        android:label="@string/app_name"
        android:theme="@style/AppTheme" >
        <activity
          android:name="gui.simplegui.GuiMain"
          android:label="@string/app_name" >
          <intent-filter>
              <action android:name="android.intent.action.MAIN" />
              <category android:name="android.intent.category.LAUNCHER" />
          </intent-filter>
        </activity>
        <activity
          android:name="gui.simplegui.MessageActivity"
          android:label="@string/title_activity_message"
          android:parentActivityName="gui.simplegui.GuiMain" >
          <meta-data
              android:name="android.support.PARENT_ACTIVITY"
              android:value="gui.simplegui.GuiMain" />
        </activity>
```

```
        </application>
    </manifest>
```

13. Create a subdirectory *menu* in *res* by

    $ mkdir res/menu

    and create two files, *gui_main.xml* and *message.xml* inside this directory. Create the first one using command

    $ vi res/menu/gui_main.xml

    with code

```
<menu xmlns:android="http://schemas.android.com/apk/res/android" >
    <item
        android:id="@+id/action_settings"
        android:orderInCategory="100"
        android:showAsAction="never"
        android:title="@string/action_settings"/>
</menu>
```

    and the second one using

    $ vi res/menu/message.xml

    with code

```
<menu xmlns:android="http://schemas.android.com/apk/res/android" >
    <item
        android:id="@+id/action_settings"
        android:orderInCategory="100"
        android:showAsAction="never"
        android:title="@string/action_settings"/>
</menu>
```

14. To compile the programs, we need the android support library *android-support-v4.jar*. We can copy this file to our project library directory using a command similar to the following:

    $ cp ~/Desktop/android-sdk-linux/extras/android/support/v4/android-support-v4.jar libs/   .

    (If the library file is not in the example path, you may locate it using the UNIX **locate** or **find** command.)

15. We start the emulator:

    $ emulator -avd SDcard &

16. We can now install the package:

    $ adb install bin/simpleGui-debug.apk

    When we run the app, we shall see activities similar to those shown in Figure 3-6.
    If you get an error message like *Unfortunately, simpleGui has stopped!* when you enter a message and click the **send** button, you might be using a newer API level for theme customization. In this case, you have to create a directory like "res/values-v*XX*" for the file "styles.xml" that specifies the application theme. For example, for API 14+ devices, the value of *XX* is 14; we first create the directory by

    $ mkdir res/values-v14

    and create the file *styles.xml* inside this directory using command

    $ vi res/values-v14/styles.xml

    with code

```
<resources>
  <style name="AppBaseTheme" parent="android:Theme.Holo.Light.DarkActionBar">
  </style>
</resources>
```

Recompile the app with the command "ant debug" and reintall it using the **adb** command with the "-r" option.

You may refer to the site

http://android-developers.blogspot.com/2012/01/holo-everywhere.html

for a discussion of the Holo theme used in *styles.xml*.

You can exit an activity by pressing the 'ESC' key.

3.3 Activity

3.3.1 Activity and Screen

In Android, an activity represents a screen as we have seen in the example of creating activities discussed above.

An application often consists of multiple activities that are loosely bound to each other. The application may create activities to generate different user-interface screens for various purposes. For example, the application can have a screen sending emails, a second screen for viewing a map and a third one for recording speech. Using activities, one can easily send messages from one screen to another. When we use Eclipse IDE to develop an application, the IDE generates a *main* activity which is a typical step in the development. When we run the application, the *main* activity is presented to us the first time we launch the application. When a new activity is started, the previous activity is stopped and is pushed onto a stack, which is last-in-first-out (LIFO). The stopped activity releases its large resource objects, such as network or database connections and reacquires them when it resumes actions. The state transitions are part of the activity lifecycle.

Android provides a few callback methods that an activity could receive because of a change in its state, regardless the nature of system – whether the system is creating the activity, stopping it, resuming it, or destroying it. Each callback provides the application a way to perform specific work that is appropriate to that state change.

Like a thread, an activity can be in one of several states in its life cycle: **active** (or running), **paused** or **stopped**. It transitions from one state to another in response to an event. In the transition,. it receives a call to a lifecycle method, which is defined in the Activity class

An **active** activity runs in the foreground, and "has the focus". It is visible on the screen, allowing the user to interact with it. A **paused** activity is also visible on the screen but does not have the focus. A **stopped** activity is not visible on the screen.

A paused or stopped activity may be terminated by the system, when the system needs its memory for other tasks such as running another app.; a **stopped** actvitity has a higher priority of getting terminated.

For more details, one can refer to

http://developer.android.com/guide/components/activities.html

which is a link of the Android developers web site.

Readers can refer to the example presented in Section 3.2 and 3.3, where two activities (two screens) are created with one screen accepting an input message from the user and sending it to the other screen which accepts the message and displays it.

The steps of creating two activities called *main1* and *main2* representing two screens can be summarized as follows:

1. **XML Layouts**

   Create two XML layout files, *main1.xml*, and *main2.xml* in the directory *res/layout/* to represent screen 1 and screen 2 respectively:

   (a) File *res/layout/main1.xml*:

```
<?xml version="1.0" encoding="utf-8"?>
<LinearLayout xmlns:android="http://schemas.android.com/apk/res/android"
    android:id="@+id/linearLayout1"
    android:layout_width="fill_parent"
    android:layout_height="fill_parent"
    android:orientation="vertical" >
<TextView
    android:id="@+id/textView1"
    android:layout_width="wrap_content"
    android:layout_height="wrap_content"
    android:text="I&apos;m Screen 1 (main1.xml)"
    android:textAppearance="?android:attr/textAppearanceLarge" />
<Button
    android:id="@+id/button1"
    android:layout_width="fill_parent"
    android:layout_height="wrap_content"
    android:text="Click me to another screen" />
</LinearLayout>
```

   (b) File *res/layout/main2.xml*:

   Same as *main1.xml* except that the text *Screen 1 (main1.xml)* is substituted by *Screen 2 (main2.xml)*

3.3.2 A Simple Calculator

In this section, we present an example of a single activity, which is a calculator performing basic arithmetic operations including addition, subtraction, multiplication, and division. The user enters two numbers and clicks on an operation button. The result will be displayed along with the entered numbers and the operation. The code is simple and mostly self-explained. By studying this example, we can get familiar with the basic Android layout and program development. The following presents the procedures of creating and running this application using the Eclipse IDE.

1. **Create Project** *Calculator*:

   (a) Click **File > New > Project > Android > Android Application Project**
   (b) Specify the names of the project, the application and the package as *Calculator*, *Calculator*, and *example.calculator* respectively. Choose *API 11:Android 3.0(Honeycomb)* or later for the **Minimum Required SDK** entry. Then click **Next > Next > Next > Next** to use the defaults of Eclipse. So the names of **Activity** and **Layout** are *MainActivity* and *activity_main* respectively. The **Navigation Type** is *None*. Then click **Finish** to create the project *Calculator*.

2. **Define Layout of** *MainActivity*:
   In this application, we have four different buttons, which are for the operations $+$, $-$, $*$, and $/$. Clicking on a button will cause the application perform the arithmetic operation on the two numbers entered in the edit-text spaces. So we define four *Button* objects within the main *LinearLayout* and two *EditText* object that allows a user to enter numbers. To accomplish these, we modify the file *res/layout/activity_main.xml* to the following code:

```
------------------------------------------------------------------
<?xml version="1.0" encoding="utf-8"?>
<LinearLayout
```

```
      xmlns:android="http://schemas.android.com/apk/res/android"
      android:orientation="vertical"
      android:layout_width="fill_parent"
      android:layout_height="fill_parent">
  <LinearLayout
      android:layout_width="match_parent"
      android:layout_height="wrap_content"
      android:id="@+id/linearLayout1"
      android:layout_marginLeft="12pt"
      android:layout_marginRight="12pt"
      android:layout_marginTop="4pt">
      <EditText
        android:layout_weight="1"
        android:layout_height="wrap_content"
        android:layout_marginRight="6pt"
        android:id="@+id/t1"
        android:layout_width="match_parent"
        android:inputType="numberDecimal">
      </EditText>
      <EditText
        android:layout_height="wrap_content"
        android:layout_weight="1"
        android:layout_marginLeft="6pt"
        android:id="@+id/t2"
        android:layout_width="match_parent"
        android:inputType="numberDecimal">
      </EditText>
  </LinearLayout>
  <LinearLayout
      android:layout_width="match_parent"
      android:layout_height="wrap_content"
      android:id="@+id/linearLayout2"
      android:layout_marginTop="4pt"
      android:layout_marginLeft="6pt"
      android:layout_marginRight="6pt">
      <Button
        android:layout_height="wrap_content"
        android:layout_width="match_parent"
        android:layout_weight="1"
        android:text="+"
        android:textSize="10pt"
        android:id="@+id/plus">
      </Button>
      <Button
        android:layout_height="wrap_content"
        android:layout_width="match_parent"
        android:layout_weight="1"
        android:text="-"
        android:textSize="8pt"
        android:id="@+id/minus">
      </Button>
  </LinearLayout>

  <LinearLayout
      android:layout_width="match_parent"
```

```
    android:layout_height="wrap_content"
    android:id="@+id/linearLayout3"
    android:layout_marginTop="4pt"
    android:layout_marginLeft="6pt"
    android:layout_marginRight="6pt">

    <Button
      android:layout_height="wrap_content"
      android:layout_width="match_parent"
      android:layout_weight="1"
      android:text="*"
      android:textSize="10pt"
      android:id="@+id/multiply">
    </Button>
    <Button
      android:layout_height="wrap_content"
      android:layout_width="match_parent"
      android:layout_weight="1"
      android:text="/"
      android:textSize="10pt"
      android:id="@+id/divide">
    </Button>
    </LinearLayout>
    <TextView
      android:layout_height="wrap_content"
      android:layout_width="match_parent"
      android:layout_marginLeft="6pt"
      android:layout_marginRight="6pt"
      android:textSize="12pt"
      android:layout_marginTop="4pt"
      android:id="@+id/displayResult"
      android:gravity="center_horizontal">
    </TextView>
</LinearLayout>
```
----

3. Modify the main program *MainActivity.java* to the following code, which is mostly self-explained. One should study it carefully, trying to understand what each statement means.

```
package example.calculator;
import android.os.Bundle;
import android.app.Activity;
import android.content.DialogInterface;
import android.content.DialogInterface.OnClickListener;
import android.text.TextUtils;
import android.view.Menu;
import android.view.View;
import android.widget.Button;
import android.widget.EditText;
import android.widget.TextView;

public class MainActivity extends Activity
                    implements View.OnClickListener{
    EditText t1, t2;
```

```java
Button plus, minus, multiply, divide;
TextView displayResult;
String oper = "";

/** Called when the activity is first created. */
@Override
public void onCreate(Bundle savedInstanceState) {
  super.onCreate(savedInstanceState);
  setContentView(R.layout.activity_main);

  //find the EditText elements (defined in activity_main.xml)
  t1 = (EditText) findViewById(R.id.t1);
  t2 = (EditText) findViewById(R.id.t2);

  plus = (Button) findViewById(R.id.plus);
  minus = (Button) findViewById(R.id.minus);
  multiply = (Button) findViewById(R.id.multiply);
  divide = (Button) findViewById(R.id.divide);

  displayResult = (TextView) findViewById(R.id.displayResult);

  // set  listeners
  plus.setOnClickListener( this );
  minus.setOnClickListener( this);
  multiply.setOnClickListener( this);
  divide.setOnClickListener( this);
}

// @Override
public void onClick( View view ) {
  double num1 = 0;
  double num2 = 0;
  double result = 0;

  // check if the fields are empty
  if (TextUtils.isEmpty(t1.getText().toString())
      || TextUtils.isEmpty(t2.getText().toString())) {
    return;
  }

  // read EditText and fill variables with numbers
  num1 = Double.parseDouble(t1.getText().toString());
  num2 = Double.parseDouble(t2.getText().toString());

  // perform operations
  // save operator in oper for later use
  switch ( view.getId() ) {
  case R.id.plus:
    oper = "+";
    result = num1 + num2;
    break;
  case R.id.minus:
    oper = "-";
    result = num1 - num2;
    break;
```

```
case R.id.multiply:
  oper = "*";
  result = num1 * num2;
  break;
case R.id.divide:
  oper = "/";
  result = num1 / num2;
  break;
default:
  break;
}

// form the output line
displayResult.setText(num1 + " " + oper + " " + num2 +
" = " + result);
  }
}
```
----

4. **Run Application**:
   When we run the application, enter two numbers and click on an operation button, we should see an output screen similar to one shown on Figure 3-7

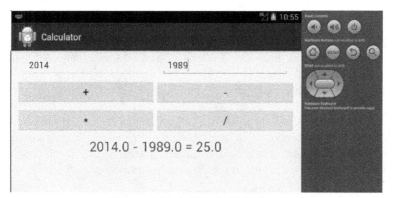

Figure 3-7 A Simple Calculator

3.4 Fragment

A *Fragment* is an independent component representing a behavior or a part of user interface in an Activity, but has its own lifecycle. A fragment may be considered as a modular section of an activity with functionality that can be easily reused within activities and layouts. It receives its own input events that we can easily add or remove while the activity is running. For example, a multi-pane user interface can be built by combining multiple fragments in a single activity and a fragment can be reused in multiple activities.

A fragment is always embedded in an activity; it must 'live' within an activity, running in the context of it. If the activity pauses, it pauses. If the activity terminates, it terminates. However, an activity may have multiple fragments and each fragment can live and operate independently from each other. We can dynamically or statically add fragments to an activity.

A fragment typically has its own user interface but it is also possible to construct a fragment without a user interface which is referred to as a headless fragment.

3.4.1 Why Fragments?

The primary reason for Android to introduce fragments since Android 3.0 (API level 11) is to make the user interface designs on large screens such as tablets, more dynamic and flexible. By dividing the layout of an activity into fragments, we can easily modify the activity's appearance at runtime and preserve the changes in a stack which is managed by the activity.

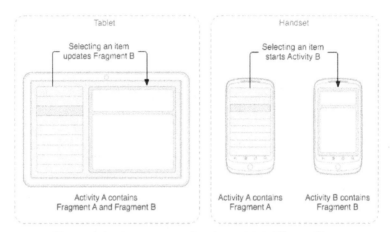

Figure 3-8 Fragments on Devices with Different Sizes
(Downloaded from *http://developer.android.com/guide/components/fragments.html*)

Fragments make an application easy to reuse components in different layouts. Figure 3-8 above, which is downloaded from the Android official site, shows an example of using fragments on devices with very different sizes.

The figure shows a typical example of the flexibility of using fragments, where we build single-pane layouts for a handset (phone) and multi-pane layouts for a tablets, which has a much larger screen size. On the tablet we see a list of details immediately on the same screen on the right hand side if we click on an item. On a smartphone the application presents a new detail screen. In general we should design a fragment as a modular and reusable activity component, which works independently from other fragments; it should be self-contained that defines its own layout.

3.4.2 Fragment Example

As an example of creating and working with fragments, we use the Eclipse IDE to create two fragments, *FragmentA* and *FragmentB* consisting of buttons, *buttonA* and *buttonB* respectively. When we click on *buttonA*, the display shows the *FragmentA* layout, and it shows *FragmentB* when *buttonB* is clicked. We name our project and application *FragmentDemo* with package *fragment.fragmentdemo*. As we need to extend the *Fragment* class, we need to use an Android API of version at least 11. The following are the steps of creating this application with Eclipse:

1. **Create Project** *FragmentDemo*:

   (a) Click **File > New > Project > Android > Android Application Project**
   (b) Specify the names of the project, the application and the package as *FragmentDemo*, *FragmentDemo*, and *fragment.fragmentdemo* respectively. Choose *API 11:Android 3.0(Honeycomb)* or later for the **Minimum Required SDK** entry. Then click **Next > Next > Next > Next** to use the defaults of Eclipse. So the names of **Activity** and **Layout** are *MainActivity* and *activity_main* respectively. The **Navigation Type** is *None*. Then click **Finish** to create the project *FramentDemo*.

2. **Define Layout of** *MainActivity*:
   In this application, we have two different buttons. Clicking on one displays a corresponding fragment interface below them. So we define two *Button* objects within the main *LinearLayout* and a *Fragment* object using the *fragment* tag. To accomplish these, we can modify the file *res/layout/activity_main.xml* to the following code:

```xml
<?xml version="1.0" encoding="utf-8"?>
<LinearLayout xmlns:android=
    "http://schemas.android.com/apk/res/android"
  android:layout_width="match_parent"
  android:layout_height="match_parent"
  android:orientation="vertical" >

  <Button
    android:id="@+id/buttonA"
    android:layout_width="fill_parent"
    android:layout_height="wrap_content"
    android:text="Fragment A"
    android:onClick="chooseFragment" />
  <Button
    android:id="@+id/buttonB"
    android:layout_width="fill_parent"
    android:layout_height="wrap_content"
    android:onClick="chooseFragment"
    android:text="Fragment B" />
  <fragment
    android:name="fragment.fragmentdemo.FragmentA"
    android:id="@+id/fragment_placeholder"
    android:layout_width="match_parent"
    android:layout_height="match_parent" />
</LinearLayout>
```

In the layout, the <fragment> element defines an object of a *Fragment* class, in which **android:name** specifies the name of the class and **android:id** specifies the id of the *Fragment* object. *FragmentA* is the default *Fragment* but it can be replaced. So the id is just a place holder.

3. **Define Fragment Classes**:
   We create a simple class called *FragmentA* which displays a color background and a message:

   (a) In Eclipse IDE, click **File** > **New** > **Class**. Enter *fragment.fragmentdemo* and *FragmentA* for **Package:** and **Name:** respectively. Then click **Finish**.
   (b) Modify the file *src/fragment/fragmentdemo/FragmentA.java* to

```java
package fragment.fragmentdemo;
import android.app.Fragment;
import android.os.Bundle;
import android.view.LayoutInflater;
import android.view.View;
import android.view.ViewGroup;

public class FragmentA extends Fragment {
  @Override
  public View onCreateView(LayoutInflater inflater,
```

```
    ViewGroup container, Bundle savedInstanceState) {
    //Inflate the layout for this fragment
    return inflater.inflate(R.layout.fragment_a,container,false);
    }
  }
```

As we can see from the code, the class *FragmentA* extends the *Fragment* class and uses the **onCreateView** override method to create its user interface. The Android system calls this method, which returns a *View* component that is placed in the <fragment> element of the layout. The **inflate** method of *inflater* inflates a layout of an xml file and returns its view.

We smilarly create and define another class, *FragmentB*, which is almost identical to *FragmentA* except that we replace *fragment_a* by *fragment_b* in the first argument of **inflate**.

4. **Define Layout of Fragments**:
   Now we need to create and define the layouts for *FragmentA* and *FragmentB*:

   (a) In Eclipse, click **File** > **New** > Android XML File. The **New Android XML file** dialog shows up. Choose or enter *Layout*, *FragmentDemo* and *fragment_a* for **Resource Type**, **Project**, and **File** respectively. Then click **Finish**.
   (b) Modify the file *res/layout/fragment_a.xml* to the following to define the layout of *FragmentA*:
   ```
   <?xml version="1.0" encoding="utf-8"?>
   <LinearLayout xmlns:android=
            "http://schemas.android.com/apk/res/android"
     android:layout_width="match_parent"
     android:layout_height="match_parent"
     android:orientation="vertical"
     android:background="#ffffaa">
     <TextView
        android:id="@+id/textViewA"
        android:layout_width="match_parent"
        android:layout_height="match_parent"
        android:layout_weight="1"
        android:text="I am Fragment A"
        android:textSize="@dimen/font_size"
        android:textStyle="bold" />
   </LinearLayout>
   ```
   This layout defines a background with color "ffffaa", which has full red and green but less blue components. It displays the message "I am Fragment A" with bold font and text size specified in the file *dimens.xml*.
   (c) We similarly create another file, *fragment_b*.xml, that defines the layout for *FragmentB* that displays the message "I am Fragment B" with a different background color, which we set to "aaffff" that has less red component.
   (d) We can specify the dimensions of our layout in the file *dimens.xml*. In our example, we only need to specify the font size of text. To accomplish this, in Eclipse, click **File** > **New** > Android XML File. The **New Android XML file** dialog shows up. Choose or enter *Value*, *FragmentDemo* and *dimens* for **Resource Type**, **Project**, and **File** respectively. Then click **Finish**. Then modify the file *res/values/dimens.xml* to the following that specifies a large font size for text:
   ```
   <?xml version="1.0" encoding="utf-8"?>
   <resources>
     <dimen name="font_size">64sp</dimen>
   ```

```
                         </resources>
```

5. **Write Code for** *MainActivity*:
   We need to write the code for the class *MainActivity*, which is the entry point of the application. We modify the file *src/fragment/fragmentdemo/MainActivity.java* to the following:

```
package fragment.fragmentdemo;
import android.os.Bundle;
import android.app.Activity;
import android.app.Fragment;
import android.app.FragmentManager;
import android.app.FragmentTransaction;
import android.view.View;
public class MainActivity extends Activity {

  @Override
  protected void onCreate(Bundle savedInstanceState) {
    super.onCreate(savedInstanceState);
    setContentView(R.layout.activity_main);
  }

  public void chooseFragment(View view) {
     Fragment frag;
     FragmentManager fragManager = getFragmentManager();
     FragmentTransaction fragTransaction =
                         fragManager.beginTransaction();
     if(view == findViewById(R.id.buttonA))
         frag = new FragmentA();
     else
         frag = new FragmentB();
     fragTransaction.replace(R.id.fragment_placeholder, frag);
     fragTransaction.commit();
  }
}
```

As shown in the code, the class *FragmentTransaction* allows the application to add or replace the current fragment using the **add** or **replace** methods respectively. To commit the add or replace operation, we have to call the **commit** method as the code does. In this example, the current fragment is replaced by the chosen one when the user clicks on a button to choose the desired fragment. The first argument of the **replace** method is an integer identifier of the container whose fragment is to be replaced, and in our example, the id *fragment_placehoder* is specified in the <fragment> element in the activity_main layout.

6. **Run Application**:
   When we run the application, we will first see our default fragment, which is *FragmentA* as shown in Figure 3-9 (a) below. When we click on the *Fragment B* button, the layout of Figure 3-9 (b) will be displyed. Clicking on the *Fragment A* button will bring us back to the layout of Figure 3-9(a).

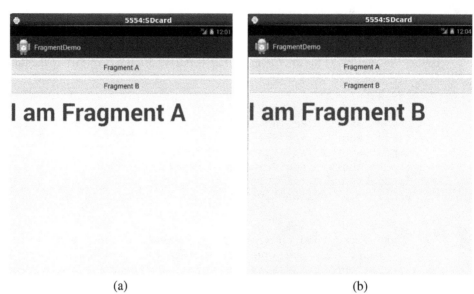

(a)   (b)

Figure 3-9 Fragments in Same Activity

3.5 Service

3.5.1 Android Services

In Android, a *Service* is an activity running in the background. It does not have any direct user interface and thus is not bound to the activity life cycle. It is convenient to use services to carry out communications with remote components, downloading or sending data. A service can be also used to do time-consuming operations in the background, such as image and speech processing, 3D graphics modeling and data analysis. Each service class must have a corresponding *<service>* declaration in *AndroidManifest.xml* of its package. A service can be started with *Context*.**startService**() and *Context*.**bindService**(). It can essentially take two forms:

1. **Started**: A service can be *started* by an application component, such as an activity, which calls **startService**(). Once started, it can run in the background to perform operations such as downloading or uploading files indefinitely, even if the component that started it has terminated. However, the service should stop itself when the operation is done,

2. **Bound**: A service can be *bound* to an application component, which calls **bindService**(). Once bound, a service allows the component to interact with it like sending requests, getting results, or doing interprocess communication (IPC). A service can be bound to multiple components at the same time, and the service is destroyed when all of the components have unbound.

A service is not a separate process. It runs by default as a component of the process that contains the main thread of the application, unless otherwise specified. Normally, a service is not a thread. It is not a means itself to do work off of the main thread.

A service is run with a higher priority than an invisible or inactive activity. It may be terminated by the Android system because of insufficient system resources. We can configure the system to restart it once sufficient resources are available.

Asynchronous communication techniques are commonly used in a service to perform resource intensive tasks. Often a service runs as a new thread to process the data in the background and terminates when the processing is finished.

Permissions of access to a service is declared in its manifest <service> element. Correspondingly, other applications have to declare a <**uses-permission**> element in their own manifest in order to start, stop, or bind to the service.

Since GINGERBREAD, when we use *Context*.**startService(Intent)**, we can also set *Intent.FLAG_GRANT_READ_URI_PERMISSION* and/or *Intent.FLAG_GRANT_WRITE_URI_PERMISSION* on the Intent, which will grant the *Service* temporary access to the Intent's specific URIs.

An Android system provides and runs predefined services, which can be used by any Android application that has the appropriate permissions. These system services are normally accessed via the **getSystemService**() method of a specific Manager class.

An application can also define its own services, which are started from other components such as activities, broadcast receivers, and other services. Custom services can be local or remote.

To create a service, we must define a class that extends *Service* (or one of its subclasses), and we have to override a few methods including the following callback methods, which are most important:

1. **onStartCommand**(): This method is called when another component, such as an activity, request to start the service by calling **startService**().
2. **onBind**(): It is called when another component wants to bind to service to perform a task such as RPC, by calling **bindService**(). In the implementation, we must provide an interface for a client to communicate with the service by return an *IBinder*.
3. **onCreate**(): It is called only when the service is first created.
4. **onDestroy**(): It is called when the service is not longer in use. Our service should implement this to release any resources such as registered listneers and receivers.

Figure 3-10 below shows the life cycles of an unbound service and a bound service. A bounded service can be rebound by calling **onRebind**() after it has been stopped.

3.5.2   Local Services

It is common that a *Service* is run as a secondary component along with other parts of an application, in the same process as the rest of the components. By default, all components of an **.apk** run in the same process unless otherwise stated explicitly.

To create a service, we need to declare it in AndroidManifest.xml. As an example, we want to define a local service called *ServiceLocal*. We have to add in the file *res/AndroidManifest.xml* an xml element similar to the following:

```
<application
  .....
  <service
    android:name="ServiceLocal"
    android:icon="@drawable/icon"
    android:label="@string/service_name">
  </service>
</application>
```

We should put an icon image file named *icon.png* in the appropriate *drawable* directory (e.g. *res/drawable-mdpi*, and add a couple of entries in the file *res/values/strings.xml* like the following:

```
<resources>
  .....
  <string name="service_name">Service Local</string>
  <string name="local_service_started">Local Service Started</string>
  <string name="local_service_label">Local Service Label</string>
</resources>
```

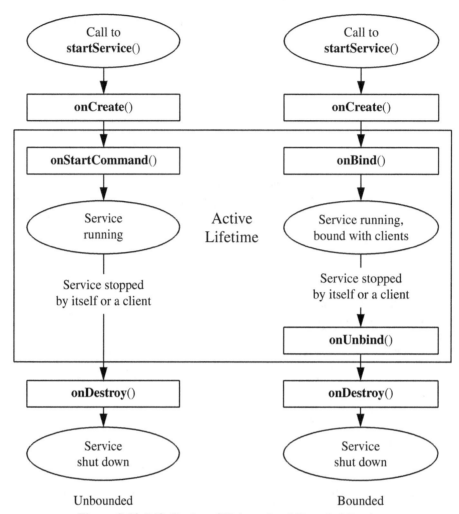

Figure 3-10 Life Cycles of Unbound and Bounded Services

To implement a service, we need to extend the *Service* class or one of its subclasses like the following:

```
public class ServiceLocal extends Service {

  @Override
  public int onStartCommand(Intent intent,int flags,int startId){
    ....
    return Service.START_NOT_STICKY;
  }

  // Class for clients to access.  Since this service is local, it always
  // runs in the same process as its clients.  So no need to deal with
  // Interprocess Communication (IPC).
  //
  public class LocalBinder extends Binder {
    ServiceLocal getService() {
      return ServiceLocal.this;
    }
  }
```

```
}
```

A service can be started by the **startService** method like the following:

```
Intent intent = new Intent(context, ServiceLocal.class);
// add extra data to the intent
intent.putExtra("Key", "Data to be used by service");
context.startService( intent );   //start service
```

Another way that we can start a service is to use the **bindService** method, which we will discuss later. It is a method of the class *ContextWrapper*, an extension of *Context*. The method allows us to communicate directly with the service.

If the service is not yet running when the **startService** method is called, a service object will be created and its **onCreate** method will be called. On the other hand, if the service is running when **startService** is called, its **onStartCommand** method is also called. The **onStartCommand** of a service is idempotent, allowing multiple calls without causing any harm to the tasks of the service.

The **onStartCommand**() method returns an **int**, which defines the restart behavior of the service if it is terminated by the Android platform. There are three common options of this returned **int**:

1. **START_STICKY**: The Service will be restarted automatically if for some reasons it is terminated. The *Intent* parameter passed to **onStartCommand**() should be null. This option is used for services that are independent of the *Intent* data, managing their own states by themselves.
2. **START_NOT_STICKY**: The Service will not be restarted automatically when it is terminated. It can be restarted by the **startService**() method.
3. **START_REDELIVER_INTENT**: This option is similar to **START_STICKY** except that the original *Intent* is redelivered to **onStartCommand**().

3.5.3   A Simple Local Service Example

We present in this section a simple example that illustrates how an activity binds to a local service. We implement a class called *ServiceLocal* to provide local service, which just returns a counter value. It extends the class *Service*, which is the base class for all services. The class *Toast* is used to flash messages on the screen. In general, a toast is a view containing a quick little message to be displayed on the screen.

In this appliction, the main activity presents a button on the screen. Whenever the button is pressed, a short message is displayed.

The following shows the steps of creating this application, assuming that we use Eclipse IDE to do the development. We call the project *ServiceLocal* with package name *service.servicelocal*.

1. Create project *ServiceLocal* from **File** > **New** > **Android Application** using names *ServiceLocal*, *ServiceLocal* and *service.serviclocal* for the names of **Application**, **Project** and **Package** respectively. Use defaults for other parameters, which generate the default main activity class file *MainActivity.java*, and the default layout file *activity_main.xml*.
2. Create class *ServiceLocal* from **File** > **New** > **Class**. Enter *ServiceLocal* for the class name. The Eclipse IDE generates the class file *ServiceLocal.java*. Modify this file to the following:

```
------------------------------------------------------------------
//ServiceLocal.java
package service.servicelocal;
import android.os.Binder;
import android.os.IBinder;
```

```
import android.util.Log;
import android.app.Service;
import android.widget.Toast;
import android.content.Intent;
import android.content.ComponentName;
import android.content.ServiceConnection;

public class ServiceLocal extends Service {
  private int counter = 0;

  public class LocalBinder extends Binder {
    ServiceLocal getService() {
      return ServiceLocal.this;
    }
  }

  int getCount() {
    // Some trivial task
    counter++;
    return counter;
  }

  @Override
  public int onStartCommand(Intent intent,int flags,int sId){
    Log.i("Service", "Received start id "+ sId + ": "+intent);
    //Return sticky so that this service continues to run until
    //it is explicitly stopped.
    return START_STICKY;
  }

  @Override
  public void onDestroy() {
    // Flash stopping message.
    Toast.makeText(this,"Service Stopped",Toast.LENGTH_SHORT).show();
  }
  @Override
  public IBinder onBind(Intent intent) {
    return iBinder;
  }
  // This object interacts with clients.
  private final IBinder iBinder = new LocalBinder();
}
```
----

3. Modify the main activity file *MainActivity.java* to the following. It defines the inner class *ServiceConnection* that establishes a connection to *ServiceLocal*. The method **bindServce**(), inherited from class *Context*, and called by **onCreate**(), binds the activity component to service *ServiceLocal*. This class also defines the **onClick** method, which is called when the button defined in *res/layout/activity_main.xml* is clicked; this method simply uses *Toast* to flash a brief message, indicating whether the service is bound successfully or not. If it is, the counter value of *ServiceLocal* is also displayed.

```
// MainActivity.java
package service.servicelocal;
```

```
import android.os.Bundle;
import android.view.Menu;
import android.view.View;
import android.os.IBinder;
import android.app.Activity;
import android.widget.Toast;
import android.content.Intent;
import android.content.Context;
import android.content.ComponentName;
import android.content.ServiceConnection;

public class MainActivity extends Activity {
  private ServiceLocal boundService;

  @Override
  protected void onCreate(Bundle savedInstanceState) {
    super.onCreate(savedInstanceState);
    setContentView(R.layout.activity_main);
    Intent intent= new Intent(this, ServiceLocal.class);
    bindService(intent, connection, Context.BIND_AUTO_CREATE);
  }

  private ServiceConnection connection = new ServiceConnection(){
   @Override
   public void onServiceConnected(ComponentName name,
                                                IBinder service){
     boundService =
              ((ServiceLocal.LocalBinder)service).getService();
     Toast.makeText(MainActivity.this, "Service connected!",
                              Toast.LENGTH_SHORT).show();
   }

   @Override
   public void onServiceDisconnected(ComponentName name) {
     boundService = null;
     Toast.makeText(MainActivity.this, "Service disconnected",
                     Toast.LENGTH_SHORT).show();
   }
  };

  public void onClick(View view) {
    if ( boundService != null ) {
      Toast.makeText(this, "Service bound " +
              boundService.getCount(),Toast.LENGTH_SHORT).show();
    } else
      Toast.makeText(this, "Service not bound ",
                              Toast.LENGTH_SHORT).show();
  }
}
```
----
4. Add the <service> element in the manifest description file *AndroidManifest.xml* like the following. It defines the service component.

```
<?xml version="1.0" encoding="utf-8"?>
```

```
<manifest xmlns:android="http://schemas.android.com/apk/res/android"
  package="service.servicelocal"
  android:versionCode="1"
  android:versionName="1.0" >
  ...........
  </activity>
  <service
      android:name="ServiceLocal">
  </service>
  </application>
</manifest>
```
----

5. Modify the layout description file *res/layout/activity_main.xml* to the following. The layout defines a button on the layout. When the button is clicked, the method **onClick**(), which is defined in *MainActivity.java* is called.

```
<LinearLayout xmlns:android =
              "http://schemas.android.com/apk/res/android"
    xmlns:tools="http://schemas.android.com/tools"
    android:layout_width="match_parent"
    android:layout_height="match_parent"
    android:paddingBottom="@dimen/activity_vertical_margin"
    android:paddingLeft="@dimen/activity_horizontal_margin"
    android:paddingRight="@dimen/activity_horizontal_margin"
    android:paddingTop="@dimen/activity_vertical_margin"
    tools:context=".MainActivity" >
    <Button
        android:id="@+id/button1"
        android:layout_width="wrap_content"
        android:layout_height="wrap_content"
        android:onClick="onClick"
        android:text="Click Here" >
    </Button>
</LinearLayout>
```

When we run the application and click the displayed button, we will see a message flashed on the screen similar to the one shown in Figure 3-11 below.

3.5.4 Remote Services

We refer to a service that is in a different process from its binding client as a **remote service**. We have seen in the previous section how local services can be created and used. A local service runs in the same process as the application that started it and thus the life of it depends on the life of the said application. On the other hand, a remote service runs in its own process, which can be in another machine. Therefore, communicating with a remote service is more complicated as it involves inter-process communication (IPC), and devices may be connected by networks. Like the traditional RPC (remote procedure call), the object that is passed between two processes needs to be marshaled. For this purpose, Android provides the AIDL (Android Interface Definition Language) tool to handle data marshaling and communication.

An interface definition language (IDL) is a specification language used to describe a software component's interface in a language-independent way. This enables communication between soft-

ware components that do not use the same programming language, such as communication between components written in C++ and components written in Java. Remote procedure call (RPC)
software commonly use IDLs are commonly used to bridge the components between two different
systems.

To bind a remote service process, we need to create an AIDL file, which looks similar to a Java
interface, but ends with the .*aidl* file extension. The service has to declare a service interface in
an AIDL file, which is used by the AIDL tool to automatically create a java interface specified
by it. The AIDL tool also generates a stub class that provides an abstract implementation of the
service interface methods. We have to extend this stub class to provide the real implementation of
the methods exposed through the interface. Also, the service clients need to invoke the **onBind**()
method in order to connect to the service. One can refer to its official site at

http://developer.android.com/guide/components/aidl.html
for the detailed documentation of AIDL.

We will discuss remote services again in Chapter 8.

Figure 3-11   Local Service

Chapter 4 Android Graphics and OpenGL ES 1.X

4.1 Graphics Classes

Android provides rich features for developers to create high-quality 2D and 3D graphics applications. Besides the conventional Java graphics interface, it supports OpenGL ES, an open source API meaning *Open Graphics Library for Embedded System*, which is widely used in 3D graphics modeling and creation of 3D scenes. We will discuss Android graphics programming with OpenGL ES in this chapter and Chapter 6. In this section, we discuss briefly basic graphics classes that we use often in our applications. For details of the classes, one can refer to the official Android developer site:

> http://developer.android.com/reference/packages.html

From the site, we can find all the Android APIs and all the API classes.

4.1.1 Class *View* and Subclasses

Class *View* is public and is a child of *Object*. It is used as a basis for building user interface components. A *View* object consists of a rectangular area on the screen to handle events and drawings. *View* is the parent of widgets for creating interactive user interface (UI) components such as buttons, and text fields. Its child *ViewGroup* is the parent of layouts, which are invisible containers holding other *Views*:

```
public class View  extends Object
   implements Drawable.Callback KeyEvent.Callback AccessibilityEventSource

java.lang.Object
   |--android.view.View

Known Direct Subclasses
   AnalogClock, ImageView, KeyboardView, MediaRouteButton, ProgressBar,
   Space, SurfaceView, TextView, TextureView, ViewGroup, ViewStub
```

The views in a window are all organized in a single tree. We can add views either from code or by defining a tree of views in XML layout files. Once we have created a tree of views, we typically wish to perform a few types of common operations:

1. **Set properties**: Set the properties of view such as setting the text of a *TextView*. We can also set the properties that are known at build time in the XML layout files.
2. **Set focus**: Set moving focus in response to user input. We can call **requestFocus**() to force focus to a specific view.
3. **Set up listeners**: Set up listeners to be notified when something interesting happens to the view, such as gaining or losing focus, or button clicking.
4. **Set visibility**: Hide or show views using **setVisibility**(int).

We can implement a custom view by implementing some of the following methods:

Category	Methods	Description
Creation	**onFinishInflate**()	Called after a view and all of its children have been inflated from XML.
Layout	**onMeasure**(int, int)	Called to determine the size requirements of this view and its children.
	onLayout(boolean, int,int,int,int)	Called upon this view's assigning a size and position to its children.
	onSizeChanged(int, int,int,int)	Called upon the changing of the view size.
Drawing	**onDraw**(android.graphics.Canvas)	Called upon the view's rendering its content.
Event processing	**onKeyDown**(int,KeyEvent) **onKeyUp**(int,KeyEvent) **onTrackballEvent**(MotionEvent)	Called upon occurence of a new hardware key event. Called upon occurence of a hardware key-up event. Called upon a trackball motion event.
	onTouchEvent(MotionEvent)	Called upon a touch screen motion event.
Focus	**onFocusChanged**(boolean, int,android.graphics.Rect)	Called upon the view gaining or losing focus.
	onWindowFocusChanged(boolean)	Called when the window that contains the view gains or loses focus.
Attaching	**onAttachedToWindow**() **onDetachedFromWindow**()	Called when the view is being attached to a window. Called when the view is begin detached from its window.
	onWindowVisibilityChanged(int)	Called when the visibility of the window that contains the view has changed.

A *View* object may have an integer ID associated with it. The ID is typically assigned in a layout XML file. It is used to find a specific view within the view tree. The following is a common pattern of using the ID:

1. Define a *Button* in the layout file and assign it a unique ID:

```
<Button
    android:id="@+id/my_button"
    android:layout_width="wrap_content"
    android:layout_height="wrap_content"
    android:text="@string/my_button_text"/>
```

2. From the **onCreate** method of an *Activity*, find the *Button*:

    Button myButton = (Button) findViewById(R.id.my_button);

4.1.2 Class *SurfaceView*

Class *SurfaceView* is a child of *View*. It provides a drawing surface embedded in a view hierarchy. A user can control the size and format of a *SurfaceView* object, but the class places the surface at the proper location on the screen:

```
java.lang.Object
  |- android.view.View
      |- android.view.SurfaceView

Known Direct Subclasses:
  GLSurfaceView, RSSurfaceView, VideoView
```

A surface object is ordered by its z-coordinate so that it is behind the window holding its *SurfaceView*. The *SurfaceView* object creates a hole in its window to display its surface. The transparent region that makes the surface visible depends on the layout positions in the view hierarchy.

We can access the underlying surface via the *SurfaceHolder* interface, which can be retrieved by calling **getHolder**(). The following is a summary of the class.

Public Methods

void **draw** (Canvas canvas)
It renders this view and its children to the given *Canvas*.
boolean **gatherTransparentRegion** (Region region)
It performs an optimization on the view hierarchy.
void **setSecure** (boolean isSecure)
It sets whether the content of the surface is to be viewed as secure, preventing it from appearing in screenshots or on non-secure displays.
void **setVisibility** (int visibility)
It sets whether the surface is visible or not.
Variable *visibility* is one of VISIBLE, INVISIBLE, or GONE.
void **setZOrderMediaOverlay** (boolean isMediaOverlay)
It sets whether the surface is overlayed on top of another surface.
void **setZOrderOnTop**(boolean onTop)
It sets whether the surface is overlayed on top of its window.
SurfaceHolder **getHolder**()
It returns the *SurfaceHolder* of the surface.

Protected Methods

void **dispatchDraw**(Canvas canvas)
It is called by **draw** to draw the child views.
void **onAttachedToWindow**()
It is called when the view is attached to a window.
void **onDetachedFromWindow**()
It is called when the view is detached from a window.
void **onMeasure**(int width, int height)
It measures the view to determine the width and the height.
void **onWindowVisibilityChanged**(int visibility)
It called when its window has changed its visibility.

Public Constructors

public **SurfaceView** (Context context)
public **SurfaceView** (Context context, AttributeSet attrs)
public **SurfaceView** (Context context, AttributeSet attrs, int defStyle)

4.1.3 Class *GLSurfaceView*

When we write an Android graphics application, we usually start by extending the class *GLSurfaceView*. It is a public class, a child of class *SurfaceView*, using the dedicated surface for rendering using OpenGL. It provides the following features:

1. Manages a surface that can be embedded in the Android view system.
2. Manages an EGL display, enabling OpenGL objects to be rendered on a surface.
3. Accepts a *Renderer* object provided by a user to do the actual rendering.
4. Renders on a dedicated thread to separate rendering from the tasks of an UI thread.
5. Supports both continuous and on-demand rendering.
6. Wraps, traces, and/or error-checks the OpenGL calls of the renderer.

The following are its relations with other related classes:

```
public class GLSurfaceView  extends SurfaceView
        implements SurfaceHolder.Callback

java.lang.Object
  |-- android.view.View
      |-- android.view.SurfaceView
          |-- android.opengl.GLSurfaceView
```

We typically use *GLSurfaceView* by extending it and overriding one or more of the *View* system input event methods. We often use the **set** methods to customize views.

We can call **setRenderer**(*Renderer*) to initialize *GLSurfaceView*. On the other hand, we can modify the default behavior of *GLSurfaceView* by calling one or more of the following methods prior to calling **setRenderer**:

> **setDebugFlags**(int)
> **setEGLConfigChooser**(boolean)
> **setEGLConfigChooser**(EGLConfigChooser)
> **setEGLConfigChooser**(int, int, int, int, int, int)
> **setGLWrapper**(GLWrapper)

By default *GLSurfaceView* creates a *PixelFormat.RGB_888* format surface. We can also call **getHolder().setFormat**(PixelFormat.TRANSLUCENT) to set a translucent surface, which is usually a 32-bit-per-pixel surface with 8 bits per component.

There are a few steps involved in setting up a *GLSurfaceView*.

Choosing an EGL Configuration

An Android device may support multiple *EGLConfig* rendering configurations, which may differ in the number of available data channels, and the number of bits allocated to each channel. Therefore, *GLSurfaceView* has to first choose what *EGLConfig* to use, and by default it chooses an *EGLConfig* that has an RGB_888 pixel format, with at least a 16-bit depth buffer and without any stencil buffer. We can always choose a different *EGLConfig* by calling one of the **setEGLConfig-Chooser** methods to override the default behavior.

Debug Behavior

We can optionally modify the *GLSurfaceView* behavior by calling one or more of the debugging methods, **setDebugFlags(int)** , and **setGLWrapper**(*GLSurfaceView.GLWrapper*), which may be called before and/or after **setRenderer**. Normally the methods are called before **setRenderer** so that they take effect immediately.

Setting a Renderer

Finally, we need to register a *GLSurfaceView.Renderer* by calling **setRenderer**(*GLSurfaceView.Renderer*). The renderer will do the actual OpenGL rendering.

Rendering Mode

Once we have setup the renderer, we can choose to draw continuously or on-demand by calling **setRenderMode(int)**. The default is continuous rendering.

Activity Life-cycle

A *GLSurfaceView* must be notified when the associated activity is paused or resumed. *GLSurfaceView* clients are required to call **onPause**() when the activity pauses and **onResume**() when the activity resumes. These calls let *GLSurfaceView* to pause and resume the rendering thread. They also allow *GLSurfaceView* to release and recreate the OpenGL display.

Handling events

To handle an event we normally extend *GLSurfaceView* and override the appropriate method. We may need to communicate with the *Renderer* object running in the rendering thread. We can do this using any standard Java thread communication techniques, or calling **queueEvent**(*Runnable*) as shown in the following example:

```
class MyGLSurfaceView extends GLSurfaceView {

   private MyRenderer myRenderer;

   public void start() {
     myRenderer = ...;
     setRenderer ( myRenderer );
   }

   public boolean onKeyDown ( int key, KeyEvent event ) {
     if ( key == KeyEvent.KEYCODE_DPAD_CENTER ) {
        queueEvent(new Runnable() {
        // Method  called on rendering thread:
        public void run() {
          myRenderer.handleDpadCenter();
        }});
        return true;
     }
     return super.onKeyDown ( key, event );
   }
}
```

4.2   OpenGL ES

The Android framework supports both the OpenGL ES 1.0/1.1 and OpenGL ES 2.0 APIs. OpenGL ES, where ES is short for embedded system, is a flavor of the OpenGL specification tailored for embedded devices. OpenGL ES is royalty-free and cross-platform. Its APIs have full-function support for 2D and 3D graphics on embedded systems such as mobile phones and appliances. OpenGL ES 1.X uses the traditional fixed-pipeline architecture and emphasizes hardware acceleration of the API. It offers enhanced functionality, good image quality and high performance. OpenGL ES 2.X is for programmable hardware. It emphasizes a programmable 3D graphics pipeline and allows the user to create shader and program objects. With ES 2.X, one can also write vertex and fragment shaders in the OpenGL ES Shading Language. On the other hand, OpenGL ES 2.0 does not support the fixed function transformation and fragment pipeline that OpenGL ES 1.X supports.

Since Android 1.0, the Android framework has supported the OpenGL ES 1.0 and 1.1 API specifications. Starting from Android 2.2 (API Level 8), the framework supports the OpenGL ES 2.0 API specification. One can find the API specifications at the site,

http://developer.android.com/guide/topics/graphics/opengl.html

However, earlier Android emulators do not support OpenGL ES 2.0. In this chapter, our discussions focus on OpenGL ES 1.X, which has certain limitations. In particular, it does not support direct vertex handling. For example, there are no **glBegin/glEnd** and **glVertex*** functions. Some constants such as GL_POLYGONS and GL_QUADS are missing. We will discuss ES 2.0 in Chapter 6.

4.3   OpenGL ES 1.X

We will discuss an example of using OpenGL ES 1.0 in Android, which was adopted from an example presented in the tutorial section of the Android developer site at

> *http://developer.android.com/resources/tutorials/opengl/opengl-es10.html*

4.3.1 Creating an Activity with GLSurfaceView

Before we start using OpenGL to create graphics in Android, we have to implement the class *GLSurfaceView*, which extends *SurfaceView*, and *GLSurfaceView.Renderer*, which is responsible for making OpenGL calls to render a frame. Typically, a *GLSurfaceView* client has a class implementing this interface, and calls **setRenderer**(*GLSurfaceView.Renderer*) to register the renderer with the GLSurfaceView. The renderer is handled by a separate thread, so that the main thread, which normally provides user interface is decoupled from the rendering performance. Clients typically have to communicate with the renderer via the main thread that interacts with the user.

We will use Android 4.3 (Level 18) in our example and use Eclipse IDE to create the activity *GLSurfaceView*:

1. In Eclipse, choose **File** > **New** > **Project** > **Android Application Project**.

2. Enter the following information for the *New Android Project*:

Project Name:	HelloES
Application Name:	HelloES
Package Name:	opengl.es10

   For other entries, use the defaults. Then click **Next** > **Next** > **Next**.

3. Choose *Blank Activity* and click **Next**.

4. Use the default names for *Blank Activity*:

Activity Name:	MainActivity
Layout Name:	activity_main
Navigation Type:	None

   Click **Finish** to create the project *HelloES*

5. Project **HelloES** should appear in *Package Explorer* of Eclipse. Choose **HelloES** > **src** > **opengl.es10** > **MainActivity.java** to open the file "MainActivity.java". Modify this file as follows:

```
package opengl.es10;

import android.app.Activity;
```

```
import android.os.Bundle;
import android.content.Context;
import android.opengl.GLSurfaceView;

public class MainActivity extends Activity {
  private GLSurfaceView mGLView;

  @Override
  public void onCreate(Bundle savedInstanceState) {
      super.onCreate(savedInstanceState);
      // Create a GLSurfaceView instance and set it
      // as the ContentView for this Activity.
      mGLView = new HelloESSurfaceView(this);
      setContentView(mGLView);
  }

  @Override
  protected void onPause() {
      super.onPause();
      // The following call pauses the rendering thread.
      mGLView.onPause();
  }

  @Override
  protected void onResume() {
      super.onResume();
      // The following call resumes a paused rendering thread.
      mGLView.onResume();
  }

  class HelloESSurfaceView extends GLSurfaceView {

      public HelloESSurfaceView(Context context){
          super(context);

          // Set the Renderer for drawing on the GLSurfaceView
          setRenderer(new HelloESRenderer());
      }
  }
}
```

Note that you should see an error indicator at *setRenderer(new HelloESRenderer()); .* This is because up to this point, we have not defined the class *HelloESRenderer.*

In the *MainActivity* class shown above, we use a single *GLSurfaceView* for its view; the class also implements callbacks for pausing and resuming activities. The *HelloESSurfaceView* class is responsible for setting the renderer to draw on the *GLSurfaceView.*

6. In Eclipse, choose **File** > **New** > **File** and enter "HelloESRenderer.java" for *File name* and click **Finish** to create a new file for the following class *HelloESRenderer*, which implements the *GLSurfaceView.Renderer* interface:

```
package opengl.es10;
import javax.microedition.khronos.egl.EGLConfig;
import javax.microedition.khronos.opengles.GL10;
import android.opengl.GLSurfaceView;
```

```
public class HelloESRenderer implements GLSurfaceView.Renderer {

  public void onSurfaceCreated(GL10 gl, EGLConfig config) {
    // Set the background frame color to blue
    gl.glClearColor(0.0f, 0.0f, 0.9f, 1.0f);
    // Enable use of vertex arrays
    gl.glEnableClientState(GL10.GL_VERTEX_ARRAY);
  }
  public void onDrawFrame(GL10 gl) {
    // Redraw background color
    gl.glClear(GL10.GL_COLOR_BUFFER_BIT | GL10.GL_DEPTH_BUFFER_BIT);
  }
  public void onSurfaceChanged(GL10 gl, int width, int height) {
    gl.glViewport(0, 0, width, height);
  }
}
```

7. Now you can run the application by choosing **Run > Run > Android Application** and click
OK. The Android emulator will start and will show a blue background screen. The code
above is mostly self-explained. The functions **glClear**(), **glClearColor**(), and **glViewport**()
are the standard OpneGL commands. (If you are not familiar with OpenGL commands, you
may refer to the book *An Introduction to 3D Computer Graphics, Stereoscopic Image, and
Animation in OpenGL and C/C++* by Fore June, for a brief quick introduction.) The only
non-OpenGL functions are the few used by Android to do the initialization, which include
the following:

  • **onSurfaceCreated**() is called once for setting up the *GLSurfaceView* environment.

  • **onDrawFrame**() is called whenever we redraw the *GLSurfaceView*. It is called to
    draw the current frame.

  • **onSurfaceChanged**() is called when the geometry of the **GLSurfaceView** changes.
    This is similar to the **glutPostRedisplay**() used in C programs.

4.3.2 Drawing a Triangle on GLSurfaceView

With the template code provided above, we should be able to make 2D or 3D graphics using
OpenGL ES 1.X commands. We discuss here how to draw a triangle.

By default OpenGL ES assumes a world coordinate system where the center of the *GLSurface-
View* frame is at $(0, 0, 0)$; the coordinates of the lower left corner and upper right corner are at
$(-1, -1, 0)$ and $(1, 1, 0)$ respectively. Therefore, as an example, we specify a triangle with the
following vertex coordinates:

$$(-0.6, -0.5, 0), (0.6, -0.5, 0), (0.0, 0.5, 0)$$

We will display this triangle with green color on the blue background. To accomplish this, we
modify the *HelloESRenderer* class to the following:

```
package opengl.es10;
import java.nio.*;
import javax.microedition.khronos.egl.EGLConfig;
import javax.microedition.khronos.opengles.GL10;
import android.opengl.GLSurfaceView;

public class HelloESRenderer implements GLSurfaceView.Renderer {
  private FloatBuffer triangle;
```

```
public void onSurfaceCreated(GL10 gl, EGLConfig config) {
    // Set the background frame color to blue
    gl.glClearColor(0.0f, 0.0f, 0.9f, 1.0f);
    // initialize the triangle vertex array
    initShapes();
    // Enable use of vertex arrays
    gl.glEnableClientState(GL10.GL_VERTEX_ARRAY);
}
public void onDrawFrame(GL10 gl) {
    // Redraw background color
    gl.glClear(GL10.GL_COLOR_BUFFER_BIT | GL10.GL_DEPTH_BUFFER_BIT);
    // Draw the triangle using green color
    gl.glColor4f(0.0f, 1.0f, 0.0f, 0.0f);
    gl.glVertexPointer(3, GL10.GL_FLOAT, 0, triangle);
    gl.glDrawArrays(GL10.GL_TRIANGLES, 0, 3);
}
public void onSurfaceChanged(GL10 gl, int width, int height) {
    gl.glViewport(0, 0, width, height);
}
private void initShapes(){
    float vertices[] = {  // (x, y, z) of triangle
        -0.6f, -0.5f, 0,
         0.6f, -0.5f, 0,
         0.0f,  0.5f, 0
    };
    // initialize vertex Buffer for triangle
    // argument=(# of coordinate values * 4 bytes per float)
    ByteBuffer vbb = ByteBuffer.allocateDirect(vertices.length * 4);
    // use the device hardware's native byte order
    vbb.order(ByteOrder.nativeOrder());
    // create a floating point buffer from the ByteBuffer
    triangle = vbb.asFloatBuffer();
    // add the coordinates to the FloatBuffer
    triangle.put(vertices);
    // set the buffer to read the first vertex coordinates
    triangle.position(0);
}
}
```

Figure 4-1   HelloES Graphics Output

(Do not forget to save the file by clicking the *save* icon, which is a small disk image.) We can recompile our graphics application by first clicking on the file **MainActivity.java** and then choosing **Run** in Eclipse. The Android emulator will run the application and we should see a green triangle displayed on a blue background as shown in Figure 4-1 above.

4.3.3 Setting Camera View and Transformations

Just as we do in a normal C program, we use **gluLookAt**() to set the camera view and position. The modelview transformation and projection transformation functions of basic OpenGL programming also apply here. As an example, we modify the functions **onDrawFrame**() and **on-SurfaceChange**() of the class *HelloESRenderer* as follows to include projection and modelview transformations; our camera is at $(0, 0, 5)$ viewing along the negative z direction. We also scale the triangle by a factor of 3 along the y-direction and rotate it about the z-axis by 30°. (Note again that we first scale, then rotate.)

```
import android.opengl.GLU;
....
public void onDrawFrame(GL10 gl) {
 // Redraw background color
 gl.glClear(GL10.GL_COLOR_BUFFER_BIT|GL10.GL_DEPTH_BUFFER_BIT);
 // Set GL_MODELVIEW transformation mode
 gl.glMatrixMode(GL10.GL_MODELVIEW);
 gl.glLoadIdentity();  //reset the matrix to its default state

 // When using GL_MODELVIEW, you must set the view point.
 //   camera at (0, 0, 5) look at (0,0,0), up = (0, 1, 0)
 GLU.gluLookAt(gl, 0, 0, 5, 0f, 0f, 0f, 0f, 1.0f, 0.0f);
 //rotate about z-axis for 30 degrees
 gl.glRotatef(30, 0, 0, 1);
 //magnify triangle by x3 in y-direction
 gl.glScalef ( 1, 3, 1);
 // Draw the triangle
 gl.glColor4f(0.0f, 1.0f, 0.0f, 0.0f);
 gl.glVertexPointer(3, GL10.GL_FLOAT, 0, triangle);
 gl.glDrawArrays(GL10.GL_TRIANGLES, 0, 3);
 }

public void onSurfaceChanged(GL10 gl, int width, int height){
 gl.glViewport(0, 0, width, height);
 float aratio = (float) width / height;  //aspect ratio
  float l, r, b, t, n, f;     //left,right,bottom,top,near,far
  b = -1.5f; t = 1.5f; n = 3.0f; f = 7.0f;
  l =  b * aratio; r = t * aratio;
  gl.glMatrixMode(GL10.GL_PROJECTION);//set projection mode
  gl.glLoadIdentity();                   // reset the matrix
  gl.glFrustumf( l, r, b, t, n, f);    //apply projection matrix
 }
```

We also need to include the header statement "import android.opengl.GLU;" at the beginning of the file as we need to use the function **GLU.gluLookAt**(). After making the modifications, we can run the program **MainActivity.java** again. The output of the program is shown in Figure 4-2 below.

Figure 4-2   HelloES Output with Projection and Modelview Transformations

4.4   Animation and Event Handling

We can make use of the methods (functions) provided by the Android class *SystemClock* to create animated graphics. The class consists of core timekeeping facilities. To use the methods. we have to import the class by adding the header statement,

> **import android.os.SystemClock**;

There are three clocks we can use to keep time. Each method returns a **long** data type:

1. **SystemClock.currentTimeMillis**() gives the current time and date expressed in milliseconds since the epoch. This clock can be set by the user or the phone network.

2. **SystemClock.uptimeMillis**() gives the active time lapse in milliseconds since the system was booted. This clock stops when the process is in a blocked or a sleep state like waiting for an I/O event or executing **Thread.sleep()**.

3. **SystemClock.elapsedRealtime**() gives the counts in milliseconds since the system was booted, including the time when the process is blocked or in a sleep state.

There are several ways to control timing events in an animation process:

1. **Thread.sleep**(*millis*) and **Object.wait**(*millis*) are standard blocking functions that can be used to generate desired time delays. When these functions are executed, the **uptimeMillis**() clock stops. The thread can be woken up by the function **Thread.interrupt**().

2. **SystemClock.sleep**(*millis*) is a utility function very similar to **Thread.sleep**(*millis*), except that it ignores **InterruptedException**.

3. We can use the *Handler* class to schedule asynchronous callbacks at an absolute or relative time. A handler object uses the **uptimeMillis**() clock to keep time. It requires an event loop to wait for an event to happen.

4. We can use the *AlarmManager* class to access the system alarm services such as triggering one-time or recurring events when the thread is in a blocked state.

As an example, let us rotate the triangle of Figure 4-2 discussed above for 6° every second. To accomplish this, all we need to do is to add to the class *HelloESRenderer* a data member *angle* of type float:

公 public float angle = 0.0f;

Then we make the following modifications to the code of its member function **onDrawFrame**():

```
public void onDrawFrame(GL10 gl) {
  ....
  gl.glLoadIdentity();   // reset the matrix to its default state
  GLU.gluLookAt(gl, 0, 0, 5, 0f, 0f, 0f, 0f, 1.0f, 0.0f);
  SystemClock.sleep ( 1000 );  //delay for 1 second
  angle += 6;          //increment angle by 6 degrees
  //rotate triangle about z-axis
  gl.glRotatef(angle, 0.0f, 0.0f, 1.0f);
  //magnify triangle by x3 in y-direction
  gl.glScalef ( 1, 3, 1);
  // Draw the triangle
  .....
}
```

When we run the modified program, we will see the triangle of Figure 4-2 rotating anticlockwise 6° every second.

If we want the triangle to interact with us rather than rotating automatically, we need to expand our implementation of *GLSurfaceView* to override the **onTouchEvent**() function to listen for touch events. Since we have defined above the data member *angle* of the *HelloESRenderer* class to be public, the member is exposed to other classes. We just need to modify the *HelloESSurfaceView* class to process touch events and pass the data to the renderer. To accomplish this, we have to include the import statement,

        import android.view.MotionEvent;

In the **onDrawFrame**() function, we just comment out the time delay and increment statements as the *angle* value is determined by touch events:

```
public void onDrawFrame(GL10 gl) {
  ....
  // SystemClock.sleep ( 1000 );  //delay for 1 second
  // angle += 6;

  gl.glRotatef(angle, 0.0f, 0.0f, 1.0f);
}
```

Then we modify the *HelloESSurfaceView* class (in the file "MainActivity.java") as follows. We set the *renderer* member so that we have a handle to pass in rotation input and set the render mode to RENDERMODE_WHEN_DIRTY, which means that the method **onDrawFrame**() is not called unless something calls **requestRender**() explicitly for rendering. Consequently, setting rendering to this mode forbids the renderer to refresh automatically. We also override the **onTouchEvent**() method to listen for touch events and pass the parameters to our renderer:

```
class HelloESSurfaceView extends GLSurfaceView {
  private final float TOUCH_SCALE_FACTOR = 180.0f / 320;
  private HelloESRenderer renderer;
  private float previousX;
  private float previousY;

  public HelloESSurfaceView(Context context){
    super(context);
    // set the renderer member
    renderer = new HelloESRenderer();
    setRenderer(renderer);
```

```
    // Render the view only when there is a change; onDrawFrame
    // is not called unless requestRender() is called explicitly
    setRenderMode(GLSurfaceView.RENDERMODE_WHEN_DIRTY);
  }
  @Override
  public boolean onTouchEvent(MotionEvent e) {
    // MotionEvent reports input details from the touch screen
    // and other input controls. Here, we are only interested
    // in events where the touch position has changed.

    float x = e.getX();
    float y = e.getY();

    switch (e.getAction()) {
      case MotionEvent.ACTION_MOVE:

      float dx = x - previousX;
      float dy = y - previousY;

      // reverse direction of rotation above the mid-line
      if (y > getHeight() / 2)
        dx = dx * -1 ;

      // reverse direction of rotation to left of the mid-line
      if (x < getWidth() / 2)
        dy = dy * -1 ;

        renderer.angle += (dx + dy) * TOUCH_SCALE_FACTOR;
        requestRender();
    }

    previousX = x;
    previousY = y;
    return true;
  }
}
```

As we have set the render mode to *GLSurfaceView.RENDERMODE_WHEN_DIRTY*, the scene will be rendered only when there is a change in the scene. When we run the application, we should see the green triangle again. If we drag our mouse and move its cursor around the center in an anticlockwise direction, the triangle will rotate in a clockwise direction. Conversely, if we drag the mouse clockwise, the triangle rotates anticlockwise.

In summary, these sections give us an introduction of creating 2D and 3D graphics in the Android platform using OpenGL. We can find a lot more examples and resources of creating graphics in Android at its official site and associated links at

```
http://developer.android.com/guide/topics/graphics/opengl.html
```

4.5 Rendering a 3D Color Cube

In these few sections, we extend the example of the previous section where we rotate a 2D triangle when we drag the mouse. First, we discuss rendering a color cube, which can be rotated by dragging the mouse. Second, we discuss putting textures on the cube. In the process, we will discuss other related but stand-alone graphics topics.

4.5.1 Color Cube

A cube consists of 8 vertices and 6 faces, each of which is a square. OpenGL ES 1.X does not support primitives of GL_QUAD or GL_POLYGON. It only renders triangles. So to render any polygon other than a triangle, we have to first decompose it into triangles.

Any polygon has two faces: a front face and a back face. Whether a face is front or back depends on our winding convention, the way we order the vertices of the polygon. In general we want to specify the winding in a way that the back faces of an object are those facing the interior of the object and front faces are those facing the exterior. The winding of a front face could be clockwise or counterclockwise and can be specified by the command **gl.glFrontFace()**. For example,

> gl.glFrontFace (GL10.GL_CCW);

specifies that a face is a front face if the vertices of the triangle is ordered in the counter-clockwise (CCW) direction, and it is a back face if the vertices are ordered in the clockwise (CW) direction. In our discussion, we always consider a face with counter-clockwise winding to be a front face.

In practice, if an object is opaque, we do not want to display any of its back faces as they are facing the interior of the object. We can suppress rendering back faces using the commands,

> gl.glEnable(GL10.GL_CULL_FACE);
> gl.glCullFace (GL10.GL_BACK);

Now consider a cube whose center is at the origin with length 2. The coordinates of the vertices of the face (square) at $z = 1$ are given by

$$v_4 = (-1, -1, 1),\ v_5 = (1, -1, 1),\ v_6 = (1, 1, 1),\ v_7 = (-1, 1, 1)$$

The front face of the square is specified by $v_4 v_5 v_6 v_7$ which are CCW and its back face is specified by $v_4 v_7 v_6 v_5$ which are CW when we observe the face from a point at $z > 1$. The square can be decomposed into two triangles as shown in Figure 4-3. When we make the decomposition, we must be careful that the windings of the triangles are consistent with that of the face considered.

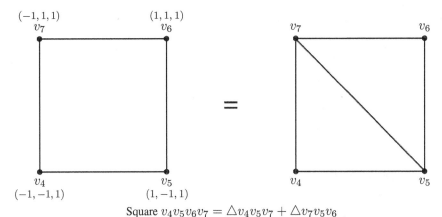

Square $v_4 v_5 v_6 v_7 = \triangle v_4 v_5 v_7 + \triangle v_7 v_5 v_6$

Figure 4-3. Decomposing a square into 2 triangles

In Figure 4-3, the vertices of a polygon are always specified in counterclockwise order.

Suppose we call this application and project *cube*. We follow the steps discussed in Section 4.3.1 to create an activity with *GLSurfaceView*. The file *MainActivity.java* of the previous section is slightly modified to the code shown in Listing 4-1 below.

Program Listing 4-1 *MainActivity.java* for Rendering Cube

```java
package opengl.cube;

import android.app.Activity;
import android.os.Bundle;
import android.content.Context;
import android.opengl.GLSurfaceView;
import android.view.MotionEvent;

public class MainActivity extends Activity {
  private GLSurfaceView mGLView;

  @Override
  public void onCreate(Bundle savedInstanceState) {
    super.onCreate(savedInstanceState);
    mGLView = new CubeSurfaceView(this);
    setContentView(mGLView);
  }
  @Override
  protected void onPause() {
    super.onPause();
    // The following call pauses the rendering thread.
    mGLView.onPause();
  }
  @Override
  protected void onResume() {
    super.onResume();
    // The following call resumes a paused rendering thread.
    mGLView.onResume();
  }

  class CubeSurfaceView extends GLSurfaceView {
    private final float TOUCH_SCALE_FACTOR = 180.0f / 320;
    private CubeRenderer renderer;
    private float previousX;
    private float previousY;

    public CubeSurfaceView(Context context){
      super(context);
      // set the renderer member
      renderer = new CubeRenderer();
      setRenderer(renderer);
      // Render the view only when there is a change
      setRenderMode(GLSurfaceView.RENDERMODE_WHEN_DIRTY);
    }
    @Override
    public boolean onTouchEvent(MotionEvent e) {
      // MotionEvent reports input details from the touch screen
      // and other input controls. Here, we are only interested
      // in events where the touch position has changed.
      float x = e.getX();
      float y = e.getY();
```

```
      switch (e.getAction()) {
        case MotionEvent.ACTION_MOVE:
          float dx = x - previousX;
          float dy = y - previousY;

          // reverse direction of rotation above the mid-line
          if (y > getHeight() / 2)
              dx = dx * -1 ;
          // reverse direction of rotation to left of the mid-line
          if (x < getWidth() / 2)
              dy = dy * -1 ;
          renderer.angle += (dx + dy) * TOUCH_SCALE_FACTOR;
          requestRender();
        }
        previousX = x;
        previousY = y;
        return true;
      }
    }
  }
```

As we can see from Listing 4-1, the class *CubeSurfaceView* extends *GLSurfaceView* and creates an object of the *CubeRenderer* class, which is discussed below, to render a color cube.

Listing 4-2 shows the complete code of the file *CubeRenderer.java*, which contains the code of the class *CubeRenderer* that implements *GLSurfaceView.Renderer*, and the code of the class *Cube* that has the attributes of a cube with length 2 and center at the origin of the coordinate system.

The methods **onSurfaceChanged** and **onDrawFrame** are basically the equivalent of the GLUT functions **glutReshapeFunc** and **glutDisplayFunc**. The former is called when there is a change in surface size like the case when the phone switches between landscape and portrait modes. The latter is called each time the cube is rendered.

The class *Cube* uses two *FloatBuffer* objects to store vertex and color data and a *ByteBuffer* to store the face indices. To understand the code, we may also refer to the comments of it, which give more detailed explanations of the processing of the data.

Program Listing 4-2   *CubeRenderer.java*

```
package opengl.cube;
import java.nio.ByteBuffer;
import java.nio.ByteOrder;
import java.nio.FloatBuffer;
import javax.microedition.khronos.egl.EGLConfig;
import javax.microedition.khronos.opengles.GL10;
import android.opengl.GLSurfaceView;
import android.opengl.GLU;
import android.os.SystemClock;
import android.view.MotionEvent;

public class CubeRenderer implements GLSurfaceView.Renderer {
  public float angle = 0.0f;        //rotation angle
  private Cube cube = new Cube();
```

```
public void onSurfaceCreated(GL10 gl, EGLConfig config) {
  // Set the background frame color to grey, opaque
  gl.glClearColor(0.5f, 0.5f, 0.5f, 1.0f);
  gl.glEnable( GL10.GL_CULL_FACE ); //Enable culling faces
  gl.glCullFace ( GL10.GL_BACK );   //don't render back faces
}

public void onDrawFrame(GL10 gl) {
  // Redraw background color
  gl.glClear(GL10.GL_COLOR_BUFFER_BIT | GL10.GL_DEPTH_BUFFER_BIT);
  // Set GL_MODELVIEW transformation mode
  gl.glMatrixMode(GL10.GL_MODELVIEW);
  gl.glLoadIdentity();   // Reset the matrix to identity matrix
  // Move objects away from view point to observe
  gl.glTranslatef(0.0f, 0.0f, -10.0f);
  // Rotate about a diagonal of cube
  gl.glRotatef(angle, 1.0f, 1.0f, 1.0f);
  cube.draw(gl);         // Draw the cube
  gl.glLoadIdentity();   // Reset transformation matrix
}
@Override
public void onSurfaceChanged(GL10 gl, int width, int height) {
  gl.glViewport(0, 0, width, height);
  gl.glMatrixMode(GL10.GL_PROJECTION);
  gl.glLoadIdentity();  // Reset projection matrix
  // Setup viewing volume
  GLU.gluPerspective(gl,45.0f,(float)width/(float)height,0.1f,100.0f);
  gl.glViewport(0, 0, width, height);

  gl.glMatrixMode(GL10.GL_MODELVIEW);
  gl.glLoadIdentity();  // Reset transformation matrix
}
}

class Cube {
  private FloatBuffer vertexBuffer;
  private FloatBuffer colorBuffer;
  private ByteBuffer  indexBuffer;

  // Coordinates of 8 vertices of 6 cube faces
  private float vertices[] = {
    -1.0f, -1.0f, -1.0f,    1.0f, -1.0f, -1.0f,
     1.0f,  1.0f, -1.0f,   -1.0f,  1.0f, -1.0f,
    -1.0f, -1.0f,  1.0f,    1.0f, -1.0f,  1.0f,
     1.0f,  1.0f,  1.0f,   -1.0f,  1.0f,  1.0f };
  // Colors of vertices
  private float colors[] = {
    0.0f, 1.0f, 0.0f, 1.0f,    0.0f, 1.0f, 0.0f, 1.0f,
    1.0f, 0.5f, 0.0f, 1.0f,    1.0f, 0.5f, 0.0f, 1.0f,
    1.0f, 0.0f, 0.0f, 1.0f,    1.0f, 0.0f, 0.0f, 1.0f,
    0.0f, 0.0f, 1.0f, 1.0f,    1.0f, 0.0f, 1.0f, 1.0f };

  // indices of 12 triangles (6 squares) in GL_CCW
  //  referencing vertices[] array coordinates
  private byte indices[] = {
```

```
        5, 4, 0,    1, 5, 0,    6, 5, 1,    2, 6, 1,
        7, 6, 2,    3, 7, 2,    4, 7, 3,    0, 4, 3,
        6, 7, 4,    5, 6, 4,    1, 0, 3,    2, 1, 3 };

    public Cube() {
        // initialize vertex Buffer for cube
        // argument=(# of coordinate values * 4 bytes per float)
        ByteBuffer byteBuf = ByteBuffer.allocateDirect(vertices.length * 4);
        byteBuf.order(ByteOrder.nativeOrder());
        // create a floating point buffer from the ByteBuffer
        vertexBuffer = byteBuf.asFloatBuffer();
        // add the vertices coordinates to the FloatBuffer
        vertexBuffer.put(vertices);
        // set the buffer to read the first vertex coordinates
        vertexBuffer.position(0);

        // Do the same to colors array
        byteBuf=ByteBuffer.allocateDirect(colors.length*4);
        byteBuf.order(ByteOrder.nativeOrder());
        colorBuffer = byteBuf.asFloatBuffer();
        colorBuffer.put(colors);
        colorBuffer.position(0);
        // indices are integers
        indexBuffer = ByteBuffer.allocateDirect(indices.length);
        indexBuffer.put(indices);
        indexBuffer.position(0);
    }

    // Typical drawing routine using vertex array
    public void draw(GL10 gl) {
        //Counterclockwise order for front face vertices
        gl.glFrontFace(GL10.GL_CCW);

        //Points to the vertex buffers
        gl.glVertexPointer(3, GL10.GL_FLOAT, 0, vertexBuffer);
        gl.glColorPointer(4, GL10.GL_FLOAT, 0, colorBuffer);

        //Enable client states
        gl.glEnableClientState(GL10.GL_VERTEX_ARRAY);
        gl.glEnableClientState(GL10.GL_COLOR_ARRAY);
        //Draw vertices as triangles
        gl.glDrawElements(GL10.GL_TRIANGLES, 36, GL10.GL_UNSIGNED_BYTE,
                                    indexBuffer);
        //Disable client state
        gl.glDisableClientState(GL10.GL_VERTEX_ARRAY);
        gl.glDisableClientState(GL10.GL_COLOR_ARRAY);
    }
}
```

In Listing 4-2 above, the **draw** method of class *Cube* is a typical OpenGL drawing routine using vertex array:

1. **gl.glVertexPointer** tells the renderer where to read the vertices coordinates and of what data type they are. The first parameter is the number of coordinates of a vertex and it is 3 here for

the (x, y, z) 3D coordinates. The second parameter tells that data type of each coordinate value is float. The third parameter, referred to as *stride*, is the offset between neighboring vertices in the array. A value of 0 indicates that array is tightly packed, not containing other data such as color values other than the vertex coordinates. The last parameter points to a buffer, *vertexBuffer* in our example, where the vertex coordinates are held.

2. **gl.glColorPointer** tells the renderer where to read the color data of the vertices. It works similarly to **gl.glVertexPointer**. The first parameter is 4 because a color tuple (r, g, b, a) consists of four values representing red, green, blue and alpha (transparency).

3. **gl.glEnableClientState** enables OpenGL to use a vertex array for rendering.

4. **gl.glDrawArrays** tells OpenGL to draw the primitive. In our code, the first parameter, GL10.GL_TRIANGLES tells the renderer to draw the vertices held in the vertex buffer as triangles. The second parameter specifies the number (*count*) of vertices. In our example, we have 6 faces. Each face has 2 triangles and each triangle has 3 vertices. Therefore, the total number of vertices is

$$count = 6 \times 2 \times 3 = 36$$

The third parameter specifies the type of values in the array specified by the fourth parameter which is a pointer pointing to the location where the indices of vertex data are stored.

5. We may think of *glEnableClientState* and *glDisableClientState* as *begin ... end* statements in a program.

When we compile and run the app, we will see a color cube which may appear 2D as the viewing point is right in front of it. We will see its 3D shape when we drag the mouse, which rotates it. Figure 4-4 below shows an output of the app.

Figure 4-4   Color Cube

4.5.2 Rendering a Square Only

If we want to render a square only, we can define a class *Square* similar to the class *Cube* presented in Listing 4-2, except that we use the primitive GL_TRIANGLE_STRIP and method **gl.glDrawArrays** rather than **gl.glDrawElements** to render the two triangles. A triangle strip is a series of connected triangles, two in our case. In this method, we only have to define four vertices for a square. Using the square shown in Figure 4-3 as an example, OpenGL first draws the triangle using vertices in the order of $v_4v_5v_7$, then it takes the last vertex v_7 from the previous triangle and uses the last side v_7v_5 of it as the basis for the new triangle which will be drawn in the order $v_7v_5v_6$. Listing 4-3 shows the code of class *Square*.

Program Listing 4-3   Class *Square*

```
class Square {
  private FloatBuffer vertexBuffer;    //buffer holding the vertices
  private float vertices[] = {         //Figure 4-3
    -1.0f, -1.0f,  1.0f,        // v4 - bottom left
     1.0f, -1.0f,  1.0f,        // v5 - bottom right
    -1.0f,  1.0f,  1.0f,        // v6 - top left
     1.0f,  1.0f,  1.0f         // v7 - top right
  };

  public Square() {
    ByteBuffer byteBuffer=ByteBuffer.allocateDirect(vertices.length*4);
    byteBuffer.order(ByteOrder.nativeOrder());
    vertexBuffer = byteBuffer.asFloatBuffer();
    vertexBuffer.put(vertices);
    vertexBuffer.position(0);
  }

  public void draw(GL10 gl) {
     gl.glFrontFace(GL10.GL_CCW);
     gl.glColor4f(1.0f, 1.0f, 1.0f, 1.0f);
     gl.glVertexPointer(3, GL10.GL_FLOAT, 0, vertexBuffer);
     gl.glEnableClientState(GL10.GL_VERTEX_ARRAY);

     gl.glDrawArrays(GL10.GL_TRIANGLE_STRIP, 0, vertices.length / 3);

     gl.glDisableClientState(GL10.GL_VERTEX_ARRAY);
  }
}
```

The only other changes to render the square using the class *CubeRenderer* is to add the data member declaration statement

        private Square square = new Square();

to the class and to replace *cube.draw()* by *square.draw()*. Upon running the code, we should see a white square over a grey background. Again we can drag the mouse to rotate the square.

4.5.3 Rendering a Rotating Cube

If we want to render a cube that rotates by itself, we simply do **not** set the render mode to *RENDERMODE_WHEN_DIRTY*. Then the method **onDrawFrame**(), which renders a frame, will be called automatically at a certain frame rate. We just need to increment the rotation angles in this method, assuming that each time **onDrawFrame** is called, the transformation matrix is first reset to the identity matrix. The following code, which can be part of the file *MainActivity.java* shows such a renderer.

```
----------------------------------------------------------------------
class CubeRenderer1 implements Renderer
{
  GL10 gl;
  Cube cube = new Cube();
  private float anglex;
  private float anglez;
  private final int nfaces = 12;
  //@Override
  //Refresh automatically as RENDERMODE_WHEN_DIRTY is not used
  public void onDrawFrame(GL10 gl)
  {
        gl.glClear(GL10.GL_COLOR_BUFFER_BIT | GL10.GL_DEPTH_BUFFER_BIT);
        gl.glEnableClientState(GL10.GL_VERTEX_ARRAY);
        gl.glEnableClientState(GL10.GL_COLOR_ARRAY);
        gl.glMatrixMode(GL10.GL_MODELVIEW);
        gl.glLoadIdentity();
        gl.glTranslatef(0.0f, 0.0f, -3.0f);
        gl.glRotatef( anglex, 1.0f, 0.0f, 0.0f );   // Rotate about  x-axis
        gl.glRotatef( anglez, 0.0f, 0.0f, 1.0f);    // Rotate about z-axis
        cube.draw(gl);
        anglex += 1.0f;
        anglez += 2.0f;
        gl.glDisableClientState(GL10.GL_VERTEX_ARRAY);
        gl.glDisableClientState(GL10.GL_COLOR_ARRAY);
  }


  public void onSurfaceChanged(GL10 gl, int width, int height)
  {
        gl.glViewport(0, 0, width, height);
        float ratio = (float) width / height;
        gl.glMatrixMode(GL10.GL_PROJECTION);
        gl.glLoadIdentity();
        gl.glFrustumf(-ratio, ratio, -1, 1, 1, 10);
  }

  public void onSurfaceCreated(GL10 gl, EGLConfig config)
  {
      gl.glDisable(GL10.GL_DITHER);
      gl.glHint(GL10.GL_PERSPECTIVE_CORRECTION_HINT, GL10.GL_FASTEST);
      gl.glClearColor(1, 1, 1, 0);
      gl.glEnable(GL10.GL_CULL_FACE);
      gl.glShadeModel(GL10.GL_SMOOTH);
      gl.glEnable(GL10.GL_DEPTH_TEST);
  }
}
----------------------------------------------------------------------
```

The renderer can be called in the **onCreate**() method. Since we do not use DIRTY mode, the thread will automatically invoke **onDrawFrame**() at a certain frame rate.

```
----------------------------------------------------------------------
public class MainActivity extends Activity {
    @Override
    protected void onCreate(Bundle savedInstanceState) {
```

```
        super.onCreate(savedInstanceState);

        // Create our Preview view and set it as the content of our
        // Activity

        mGLSurfaceView = new GLSurfaceView(this);
        CubeRenderer1 renderer = new CubeRenderer1();
        mGLSurfaceView.setRenderer(renderer);
        setContentView(mGLSurfaceView);
    }
```

4.6   Rendering a 3D Texture Cube

4.6.1 Displaying Images

Before discussing putting textures on the surfaces of an object, we discuss very **briefly** how to display images.

Android runs on a variety of devices with different screen sizes and resolutions, and supports the three common image formats PNG, JPG, and GIF. Images are saved in the directory *res/layout/drawable*.

As an example, let's create a project called *displayimage* and package *graphics.displayimage* using Eclipse IDE with its *Blank Activity* as we did above. Under the directory *res*, we can find the drawable subdirectories:

    drawable-hdpi
    drawable-ldpi
    drawable-mdpi
    drawable-xhdpi
    drawable-xxhdpi

which correspond to different screen sizes and resolutions. In the naming convention of the subdirectories, letter 'h' refers to high resolution, 'm' to medium, 'l' to low, and 'x' to extra. So *xhdpi* means extra high resolution. Image file names should be lowercase and contain only letters, numbers, and underscores. Figure 4-5, obtained from the official Android web site, illustrates how Android roughly maps actual sizes and pixel densities to generalized sizes and resolutions.

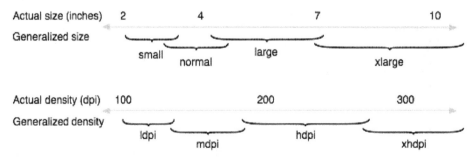

Figure 4-5   Android Screen Sizes and Resolutions

Supporting various screen resolutions allows us to create images at different dpi (dots per inch) to enhance the appearance of our application.

In our example, we want to display an image saved in the file *galaxy.jpg*, which is downloaded from the NASA web site and is an image of the galaxy. To achieve this, we first copy this file to the directory *res/drawable-hdpi*, which also contains the icon file *ic_launcher.png*. (Alternatively, we can create a directory named *drawable* inside *res* and put the image file there.) Then we add the below *ImageView* layout component, the base element used for displaying images, to the *RelativeLayout* component of the file *activity_main.xml*, which is in the directory *res/layout*, after the *TextView*:

```
<ImageView
    android:id="@+id/galaxy_image"
    android:src="@drawable/galaxy"
    android:layout_width="fill_parent"
    android:layout_height="fill_parent" />
```

In the file *MainActivity.java*, which is generated by Eclipse and contains the class *MainActivity*, we add an image import statement and in the method **onCreate** the *ImageView* statement:

```
import android.widget.ImageView;

public class MainActivity extends Activity {
  @Override
  protected void onCreate(Bundle savedInstanceState) {
    super.onCreate(savedInstanceState);
    setContentView(R.layout.activity_main);
    //Added statement for displaying image
    ImageView image = (ImageView) findViewById(R.id.galaxy_image);
  }
  ....
}
```

When we compile and run the program, we will see the *galaxy* image displayed on the Android screen as shown in Figure 4-6 (a) below.

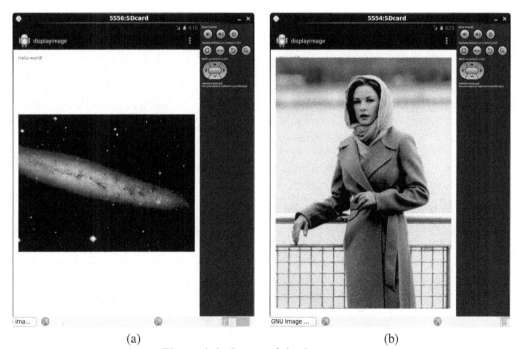

(a)   (b)

Figure 4-6 Output of *displayimage*

If we want to change to another image, say, *catherine.jpg*, we can use the **setImageResource** method of the class *ImageView* to load this new image. So we add a statement in the file *MainActivity.java*:

```
public class MainActivity extends Activity {
  @Override
  protected void onCreate(Bundle savedInstanceState) {
    super.onCreate(savedInstanceState);
    setContentView(R.layout.activity_main);
    //Added statement for displaying image
    ImageView image = (ImageView) findViewById(R.id.galaxy_image);
    //Change to another image
    image.setImageResource(R.drawable.catherine);
  }
}
```

The output is shown in Figure 4-6 (b).

Alternatively, we can use bitmap to change the display of an image:

```
protected void onCreate(Bundle savedInstanceState) {
  super.onCreate(savedInstanceState);
  setContentView(R.layout.activity_main);
  ImageView image = (ImageView) findViewById(R.id.galaxy_image);
  Bitmap bitmap = BitmapFactory.decodeResource(this.getResources(),
      R.drawable.catherine);
  image.setImageBitmap( bitmap );
}
```

In the code, the *BitmapFactory* class creates a bitmap object with the image *catherine.jpg*, which is saved in the directory *res/drawable-hdpi* (or in *res/drawable*). We use the method **ImageView.setImageBitmap()** to update the *ImageView* component.

4.6.2 Rendering Texture Square

Texture mapping is the mapping of a separately defined graphics image, a picture, or a pattern to a surface. The technique helps us to combine pixels with geometric objects to generate complex images without building large geometric models. For example, we can apply texture mapping to 'glue' an image of a brick wall to a polygon and to draw the entire wall as a single polygon.

To apply texture to a surface, we need to load up an image and tell the OpenGL renderer that the image will be used as a texture. We also need to tell the renderer where exactly onto our square we want to "glue" it.

We use texture coordinates to specify the image, which is normalized to size 1×1. That is, any point on the image lies within the range $(0, 1) \times (0, 1)$. However, an Android system considers the upper left corner to be $(0, 0)$ and the lower right corner to be $(1, 1)$. On the other hand, we have set the lower left corner of our square to $(-1, -1, 1)$ and upper right corner to $(1, 1, 1)$. This situation is illustrated in Figure 4-7 below.

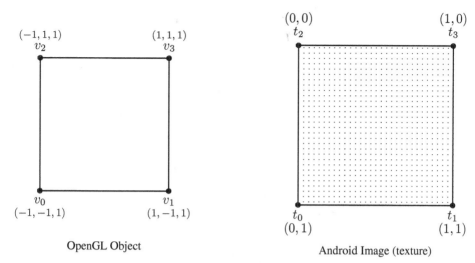

Figure 4-7. Vertex Coordinates and Texture Coordinates

OpenGL Object

Android Image (texture)

We want to make the mapping of the texture image to the square object vertices in the following way:

$$t_0(0,1) \longrightarrow v_0(-1,-1,1)$$
$$t_1(1,1) \longrightarrow v_1(1,-1,1)$$
$$t_2(0,0) \longrightarrow v_2(-1,1,1)$$
$$t_3(1,0) \longrightarrow v_3(1,1,1)$$

Therefore, we define and initilialize two arrays, one for vertex coordinates and one for texture coordinates in the class *Square*:

```
class Square {
    private FloatBuffer vertexBuffer;     // buffer holding vertices coord
    private FloatBuffer textureBuffer;    // buffer holding texture coord
    private float vertices[] = {          // vertex coordinates
        -1.0f, -1.0f,  1.0f,              // v0 - bottom left
         1.0f, -1.0f,  1.0f,              // v1 - bottom right
        -1.0f,  1.0f,  1.0f,              // v2 - top left
         1.0f,  1.0f,  1.0f               // v3 - top right
    };
    private float texture[] = {           // texture coordinates
        0.0f, 1.0f,                       // bottom left      (t0)
        1.0f, 1.0f,                       // bottom right     (t1)
        0.0f, 0.0f,                       // top left         (t2)
        1.0f, 0.0f,                       // top right        (t3)
    };
    ....
}
```

The above code also shows that we have added the variable *textureBuffer*, which works in a way similar to the *vertexBuffer*.

We modify the *Square* constructor to initialize the buffering of texture data; we will just reuse the variable *byteBuffer*. Also, we define another integer array, *texHandles* to hold the handle to the texture that we will create, and add another method, **initTexture**, which will be called from the renderer in the **onSurfaceCreated** method. The **initTexture** method initializes the OpenGL texture commands.

```
class Square {
    ....
```

```
    private int[] texHandles = new int[1];  //holds handle to textures

  public Square() {
    ByteBuffer byteBuffer = ByteBuffer.allocateDirect(vertices.length*4);
    byteBuffer.order(ByteOrder.nativeOrder());
    vertexBuffer = byteBuffer.asFloatBuffer();
    vertexBuffer.put(vertices);
    vertexBuffer.position(0);

    byteBuffer = ByteBuffer.allocateDirect(texture.length * 4);
    byteBuffer.order(ByteOrder.nativeOrder());
    textureBuffer = byteBuffer.asFloatBuffer();
    textureBuffer.put(texture);
    textureBuffer.position(0);
  }

  public void initTexture(GL10 gl, Context context) {
    // loading texture
    Bitmap bitmap=BitmapFactory.decodeResource(context.getResources(),
         R.drawable.catherine);
    // generate one texture handle
    gl.glGenTextures(1, texHandles, 0);
    // ...and bind it to our array
    gl.glBindTexture(GL10.GL_TEXTURE_2D, texHandles[0]);
    // create nearest filtered texture
    gl.glTexParameterf(GL10.GL_TEXTURE_2D,
                       GL10.GL_TEXTURE_MIN_FILTER,GL10.GL_NEAREST);
    gl.glTexParameterf(GL10.GL_TEXTURE_2D,
                       GL10.GL_TEXTURE_MAG_FILTER, GL10.GL_LINEAR);
    //Use Android GLUtils to specify a 2D texture image from bitmap
    GLUtils.texImage2D(GL10.GL_TEXTURE_2D, 0, bitmap, 0);
    // Clean up
    bitmap.recycle();
  }
  ....
}
```

The **initTexture** method generates a texture handle, binds it to a 2D texture array, loads the image *catherine.jgp* from the the directory *res/drawable-hdpi*. The loaded image will be used as the texture for subsequent operations.

The **draw** method of *Square* is slightly modified to incorporate operations of the texture:

```
class Square {
  ....
  public void draw(GL10 gl) {
    // Vertices of a front face are in counterclockwise order
    gl.glFrontFace(GL10.GL_CCW);
    gl.glColor4f(1.0f, 1.0f, 1.0f, 1.0f);
    // bind the previously generated texture
     gl.glBindTexture(GL10.GL_TEXTURE_2D, texHandles[0]);

    gl.glVertexPointer(3, GL10.GL_FLOAT, 0, vertexBuffer);
    gl.glTexCoordPointer(2, GL10.GL_FLOAT, 0, textureBuffer);
    gl.glEnableClientState(GL10.GL_VERTEX_ARRAY);
    gl.glEnableClientState(GL10.GL_TEXTURE_COORD_ARRAY);
```

```
        gl.glDrawArrays(GL10.GL_TRIANGLE_STRIP, 0, vertices.length / 3);

        gl.glDisableClientState(GL10.GL_VERTEX_ARRAY);
        gl.glDisableClientState(GL10.GL_TEXTURE_COORD_ARRAY);
    }
}
```

The renderer class now looks like the following:

```
public class SquareRenderer implements GLSurfaceView.Renderer {

    public float angle = 0.0f;
    private Square square = new Square();
    private Context context;

    public SquareRenderer ( Context context0 )
    {
        context = context0;
    }

    public void onSurfaceCreated(GL10 gl, EGLConfig config) {
        // Set the background frame color to grey
        gl.glClearColor(0.5f, 0.5f, 0.5f, 1.0f);
        // Do not render back faces
        gl.glEnable( GL10.GL_CULL_FACE );
        gl.glCullFace ( GL10.GL_BACK );
        square.initTexture(gl, context);
        gl.glEnable(GL10.GL_TEXTURE_2D);
    }
    .....
}
```

When we run the app, we'll see the output of Figure 4-8; the image *catherine.jpg* shown in Figure 4-6 (b) has been glued on a square.

Figure 4-8   Square with Texture

4.6.3 Rendering Texture Cube

To render a cube with texture, we simply put a texture image on each of the 6 faces (squares) of the cube. So it is a straightforward extension of rendering a texture square discussed above.

Since we need to handle 6 images, it is more convenient to reference the images using resource ids. The method **getResources().getIdentifier** of the class *Context* returns the integer ID of an image file in a resource directory. To use this method in our program, we need to add the following import statement:

        import android.content.res.Resources;

Suppose we have put 6 different image files (in .png or .jpg format) in the directory *res/drawable-hdpi*. We can use the following code to obtain their ids:

```
int nFaces = 6;
int rids[] = new int[nFaces];  //resource ids
//Image filenames, omitting extension (.jpg or .png)
String img[] = {"catherine", "lu", "galaxy", "lu1", "lu2", "zhouxun"};
for ( int i = 0; i < nFaces; i++ ){
  rids[i] = context.getResources().getIdentifier( img[i] , "drawable",
          context.getPackageName());
  .....
}
```

The initialization of texture operations, the loading of an image and the rendering of a face with texture are the same as what we did in rendering a square discussed above except that now we need 6 texture handles, 6 vertex buffers and 6 texture buffers. Listing 4-3 shows the code for the modified *cube* class.

Program Listing 4-3   Class *Cube* with Texture

```
class Cube {
  //6 faces
  private final int nFaces = 6;

  private FloatBuffer vertexBuffer[] = new FloatBuffer[nFaces];
  // buffer holding the texture coordinates
  private FloatBuffer textureBuffer[] = new FloatBuffer[nFaces];
  private int[] texHandles = new int[nFaces];

  // Coordinates of 6 cube faces
  private float vertices[][] = {
      { -1.0f, -1.0f, 1.0f,  1.0f, -1.0f,  1.0f,
        -1.0f,  1.0f, 1.0f,  1.0f,  1.0f,  1.0f},      //front
      {  1.0f, -1.0f,-1.0f, -1.0f, -1.0f, -1.0f,
         1.0f,  1.0f,-1.0f, -1.0f,  1.0f, -1.0f},      //back
      { -1.0f, -1.0f,-1.0f, -1.0f, -1.0f,  1.0f,
        -1.0f,  1.0f,-1.0f, -1.0f,  1.0f,  1.0f},      //left
      {  1.0f, -1.0f, 1.0f,  1.0f, -1.0f, -1.0f,
         1.0f,  1.0f, 1.0f,  1.0f,  1.0f, -1.0f},      //right
      { -1.0f, -1.0f,-1.0f,  1.0f, -1.0f, -1.0f,
        -1.0f, -1.0f, 1.0f,  1.0f, -1.0f,  1.0f},      //bottom
      { -1.0f,  1.0f, 1.0f,  1.0f,  1.0f,  1.0f,
        -1.0f,  1.0f, -1.0f, 1.0f,  1.0f, -1.0f} };    //top
```

```
private float texture[][] = {
   // Mapping texture coordinates for the vertices
   { 0.0f, 1.0f, 1.0f, 1.0f, 0.0f, 0.0f, 1.0f, 0.0f},
   { 0.0f, 1.0f, 1.0f, 1.0f, 0.0f, 0.0f, 1.0f, 0.0f},
   { 0.0f, 1.0f, 1.0f, 1.0f, 0.0f, 0.0f, 1.0f, 0.0f},
   { 0.0f, 1.0f, 1.0f, 1.0f, 0.0f, 0.0f, 1.0f, 0.0f},
   { 0.0f, 1.0f, 1.0f, 1.0f, 0.0f, 0.0f, 1.0f, 0.0f},
   { 0.0f, 1.0f, 1.0f, 1.0f, 0.0f, 0.0f, 1.0f, 0.0f} };

public Cube() {
   // initialize vertex Buffer for each  cube face
   // argument=(# of coordinate values * 4 bytes per float)
   for ( int i = 0; i < nFaces; i++ )  // do for 6 faces
   {
     ByteBuffer byteBuf=ByteBuffer.allocateDirect(vertices[i].length*4);
     byteBuf.order(ByteOrder.nativeOrder());
     // create a floating point buffer from the ByteBuffer
     vertexBuffer[i] = byteBuf.asFloatBuffer();
     // add the coordinates to the FloatBuffer
     vertexBuffer[i].put(vertices[i]);
     // set the buffer to read the first vertex coordinates
     vertexBuffer[i].position(0);

     byteBuf = ByteBuffer.allocateDirect(texture[i].length * 4);
     byteBuf.order(ByteOrder.nativeOrder());
     textureBuffer[i] = byteBuf.asFloatBuffer();
     textureBuffer[i].put(texture[i]);
     textureBuffer[i].position(0);
   }
}

public void initTexture(GL10 gl, Context context) {
   // loading texture
   // generate 6 texture pointers
   gl.glGenTextures(nFaces, texHandles, 0);
   // get resource ids of images in res/drawable-hdpi
   int rids[] = new int[nFaces];  //resource ids
   // image file names
   String img[] = {"catherine","lu","galaxy","lu1","lu2","zhouxun"};
   // Initialize texture feature for 6 (nFaces) faces
   for ( int i = 0; i < nFaces; i++ ){
     rids[i] = context.getResources().getIdentifier( img[i],"drawable",
                    context.getPackageName());
     // loading texture
     Bitmap bitmap =
        BitmapFactory.decodeResource(context.getResources(),rids[i]);
     gl.glBindTexture(GL10.GL_TEXTURE_2D, texHandles[i]);
     // create nearest filtered texture
     gl.glTexParameterf(GL10.GL_TEXTURE_2D,GL10.GL_TEXTURE_MIN_FILTER,
        GL10.GL_NEAREST);
     gl.glTexParameterf(GL10.GL_TEXTURE_2D, GL10.GL_TEXTURE_MAG_FILTER,
        GL10.GL_LINEAR);
     //Use Android GLUtils to specify a two-dimensional texture image
     GLUtils.texImage2D(GL10.GL_TEXTURE_2D, 0, bitmap, 0);
```

```
      //cleanup
      bitmap.recycle();
    }
  }


  // Typical drawing routine using vertex array
  public void draw(GL10 gl) {
    // Vertices of a front face are in counterclockwise order
    gl.glFrontFace(GL10.GL_CCW);

    for ( int i = 0; i < nFaces; i++) {
      gl.glBindTexture(GL10.GL_TEXTURE_2D, texHandles[i]);
      gl.glVertexPointer(3, GL10.GL_FLOAT, 0, vertexBuffer[i]);
      gl.glTexCoordPointer(2, GL10.GL_FLOAT, 0, textureBuffer[i]);
      gl.glEnableClientState(GL10.GL_VERTEX_ARRAY);
      gl.glEnableClientState(GL10.GL_TEXTURE_COORD_ARRAY);

      gl.glDrawArrays(GL10.GL_TRIANGLE_STRIP, 0, vertices[i].length / 3 );
      gl.glDisableClientState(GL10.GL_VERTEX_ARRAY);
      gl.glDisableClientState(GL10.GL_TEXTURE_COORD_ARRAY);
    }
  }
}
```

We slightly modify the method **onDrawFrame** of the class *CubeRenderer* to display three cubes at the same time so that we can see the six different faces when we drag the mouse to rotate them:

```
public class CubeRenderer implements GLSurfaceView.Renderer
{
  public float angle = 0.0f;
  private Cube cube = new Cube();
  private Context context;

  public CubeRenderer ( Context context0 ) {
     context = context0;
  }

  public void onSurfaceCreated(GL10 gl, EGLConfig config) {
      // Set the background frame color to grey
      gl.glClearColor(0.5f, 0.5f, 0.5f, 1.0f);
      // Do not render back faces
      gl.glEnable( GL10.GL_CULL_FACE );
      gl.glCullFace ( GL10.GL_BACK );
      cube.initTexture(gl, context);
      gl.glEnable(GL10.GL_TEXTURE_2D);
  }

  public void onDrawFrame(GL10 gl) {
    // Redraw background color
    gl.glClear(GL10.GL_COLOR_BUFFER_BIT | GL10.GL_DEPTH_BUFFER_BIT);
    // Set GL_MODELVIEW transformation mode
    gl.glMatrixMode(GL10.GL_MODELVIEW);
    gl.glLoadIdentity();   // Reset the matrix to identity matrix

    // Move objects away from view point to observe
```

```
    gl.glTranslatef(-1.0f, 2.0f, -10.0f);
    // Rotate about a diagonal of cube
    gl.glRotatef(angle, 1.0f, 1.0f, 0.0f);
    // Draw the cube
    cube.draw(gl);

    gl.glLoadIdentity(); //reset matrix, draw another cube
    gl.glTranslatef(0.0f, 0.0f, -10.0f);
    gl.glRotatef(angle, 0.0f, 1.0f, 1.0f);
    cube.draw(gl);

    gl.glLoadIdentity(); //reset matrix, draw another cube
    gl.glTranslatef(1.0f, -2.0f, -10.0f);
    gl.glRotatef(angle, -1.0f, -1.0f, 0.0f);
    cube.draw(gl);
    gl.glLoadIdentity();      // Reset matrix
  }
  . . . . .
}
```

Figure 4-10 Texture Cubes

When we run the app, we should see on the screen 3 cubes with texture images on the faces. If we drag the mouse, we should see the cubes rotate and appear like those showniFigure 4-10 above.

Interested readers may download the complete code of this app from the website, *http://www.forejune.com/android/*

4.7   Rendering a Rotating Cube

Rotating a cube is similar to rotating a triangle that we have discussed in Section 4.4.   As an example, let us rotate the 3D color cube discussed in Section 4.5 along a diagonal of the cube for 1° every 0.1 second.   To accomplish this, we first do **not** set the render mode to *GLSurface-View.RENDERMODE_WHEN_DIRTY* so that the frames will be updated automatically.   Second, we let the thread sleep for 0.1 second and then increment a rotation angle by 1° in the method **onDrawFrame()** of the class *CubeRenderer*:

```
public void onDrawFrame(GL10 gl)
{
   // Redraw background color
   gl.glClear(GL10.GL_COLOR_BUFFER_BIT | GL10.GL_DEPTH_BUFFER_BIT);
   // Set GL_MODELVIEW transformation mode
   gl.glMatrixMode(GL10.GL_MODELVIEW);
   gl.glLoadIdentity();   // Reset the matrix to identity matrix

   SystemClock.sleep ( 100 );  //delay for 0.1 second
   angle += 1;       //increment angle by 6 degrees

   // Move objects away from view point to observe
   gl.glTranslatef(0.0f, 0.0f, -10.0f);
   // Rotate about a diagonal of cube
   gl.glRotatef(angle, 1.0f, 1.0f, 1.0f);
   // Draw the cube
   cube.draw(gl);
}
```

When we run the app, we will see a color cube rotating on the screen. Figure 4-11 below shows two frames of it.

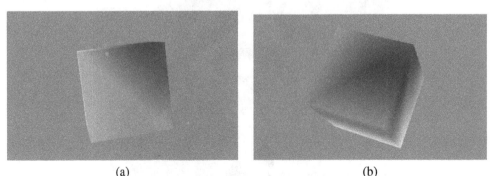

(a)   (b)

Figure 4-11   Two Frames of a Rotating Cube

Chapter 5   File I/O and JNI

Since Android uses Java as its programming language, it inherits plenty of the Java classes for accessing files and I/O resources, though many of the Java I/O fields and methods are not needed in practice and might have made the language less attractive. In addition, Android defines other means of specifying and accessing resources. We have seen that Android generates the resource directory *res*, which contains other files and subdirectories to define layouts, resources, assets, and parameters, often in *xml* format. The URL

http://developer.android.com/reference/android/content/Context.html

that describes the functionalities of the class *Context*, presents a lot of methods for accessing I/O resources.

Android also supports JNI (Java Native Interface) for Java programs to interact with native code written in C/C++. JNI is vendor-neutral and has support for loading code from dynamic shared libraries, which can be efficient.

5.1   Read Raw Data From File

If we do not want to specify our data in the *xml* format but to keep them as raw data, we can create our own subdirectories and files under the *res* directory. Let us consider a very simple example to illustrate the technique. Suppose in our example, we want to read in the data saved in a file, say *res/raw/hello*, as unformated strings. We call our project and application *ReadRaw*, and the package, *data.readraw*. Suppose like what we did before, we have used the defaults of the Eclipse Android settings to create the project. We continue to do the following in Eclipse IDE:

1. **Create Directory** *res/raw*: Click **File** > **New** > **Folder**. Select the **parent folder** to be *ReadRaw/res* and enter *raw* for **Folder name**. Then click **Finish**, which creates the directory *res/raw*.
2. **Create File** *res/raw/hello*: Click **File** > **New** > **File**. Select the **parent folder** to be *ReadRaw/res/raw* and enter *hello* for **File name**. Then click **Finish**, which creates the file *res/raw/hello*. You may enter any text in *hello*. For example, we enter *Android The Beautiful!* in the file and save it.
3. **Modify** *MainActivity.java*: Modify the main program *MainActivity.java* to the following code, which simply reads in the data in the file *res/raw/hello* and prints it out as a string.

```
package data.readraw;

import java.io.IOException;
import java.io.InputStream;
import android.app.Activity;
import android.os.Bundle;
import android.util.Log;
import android.os.Build;

public class MainActivity extends Activity {

    @Override
    protected void onCreate(Bundle savedInstanceState) {
```

```
super.onCreate(savedInstanceState);
setContentView(R.layout.activity_main);
String str = null;
InputStream inputStream = null;
try {
  inputStream = getResources().openRawResource(R.raw.hello);
  byte[] reader = new byte[inputStream.available()];
  while (inputStream.read(reader) != -1) {}
  str = new String ( reader );
  System.out.println ( str );
}  catch(IOException e) {
  Log.e(Tag", e.getMessage());
}
}
}
```

In the code, **getResources**() is an abstract method declared in the class *Context*. It returns a *Resources* instance for the application's package. Note that our class *MainActivity* extends *Activity*, which extends the class *ContextThemeWrapper*; one of the intermediate classes in the class hierarchy *android.view.ContextThemeWrapper* provides an implementation for the method **getResources**. The returned *Resources* object calls its method **OpenRawResources** to open a data stream for reading a raw resource, which in the example is specified by the resource name *R.raw.hello* and will be translated to an integer indentifier by the Android tools. The code creates a byte array, named *reader*, large enough to hold all the data of the input data stream using the *InputStream* class method **available**(). The raw bytes read into the array *reader* is converted to a string usng the *String* constructor and is printed out as a log message.

When we run the application, we will see the message *Android The Beautiful!* appeared in the *Text* column of the Eclipse IDE **LogCat** output.

5.2   Read and Write Files

5.2.1   Read Assets and Display Files

For each application, Android tools generate an *assets* directory for users to put customized resources there. In contrast to the *res* directory, which is accessible from *R.class*, *assets* behaves like a file system, In the *res* directory, each file is assigned an integer identifier, which can be accessed easily through **R.id.***res_id*, providing convenient ways to access images, sounds, icons, xml files and some commonly used resources. On the other hand, the *assets* directory provides users more freedom to put any file there, which can be then accessed like a file in a Java file system. Android does not generate IDs for assets content, and thus we need to specify relative paths and names for files inside the directory *assets*.

The Android public final class *AssetManager*, which extends class *Object* provides access to an application's raw asset files. The class presents a lower-level API that allows one to open and read any raw files lying inside the **Assets** directory or its subdirectories. The APIs could read the raw asset files that have been bundled with the application as a simple stream of bytes.

To illustrate the technique, we again consider a simple example that reads data from an asset file as raw streams. We use the **getAssets**() method of public class *Resources* to obtain an *AssetManager* object, from which we use its **open**() method to open the asset file as an input stream. Suppose we have used Eclipse IDE defaults to create the the project and application *ReadAsset*, and we call the package *data.readasset*, and the asset file *hello_world.txt*. We do the following to finish building the project that reads data from the asset file and prints out its data as a string:

1. **Create File** *assets/hello_world.txt*: Click **File > New > File**. Select the **parent folder** to be *ReadAsset/assets* and enter *hello_world.txt* for **File name**. Then click **Finish**, which creates the file *assets/hello_world.txt*. You may enter any text in *hello_world.txt*. For example, we enter *Hello World, Democracy the Beautiful!* in the file and save it.
2. **Modify** *MainActivity.java*: Modify the main program *MainActivity.java* to the following code, which simply reads the data from the file *assets/hello_world.txt* as a simple stream and prints it out as a string.

```
package data.readassest;

import java.io.IOException;
import java.io.InputStream;
import android.os.Bundle;
import android.app.Activity;
import android.content.res.AssetManager;

public class MainActivity extends Activity {
  @Override
  protected void onCreate(Bundle savedInstanceState) {
    super.onCreate(savedInstanceState);
    setContentView(R.layout.activity_main);

    try{
      InputStream inputStream=this.getAssets().open("hello_world.txt");
      int nBytes = inputStream.available();
      byte data[] = new byte[nBytes];
      String str = "";

      //read all data from file "hello_world.txt"
      while( inputStream.read(data) != -1);

      str = new String ( data );
      System.out.println ( str );
      inputStream.close();
    } catch(IOException e) {
      e.printStackTrace();
    }
  }
}
```

In the code, the statement
   InputStream inputStream = this.getAssets().open("hello_world.txt");
finds the file location and opens it as an input stream. The code finds the number of bytes the file has using the method **available**() of the class *InputStream*. It then allocates memory for an array, reads the data as bytes to the array, converts the bytes to a string using a constructor of the class *String* and prints out the string. When we run the application, we should see the text *Hello World, Democracy the Beautiful!* appear in the *Text* column of the entry with **Tag** *System.out* of the Eclipse IDE **LogCat** output.

We can also make use of the *AssetManager* class to display files, including subdirectories in the *assets* directory. We can use the **list**() method of *AssetManager* to find all the files inside the *assets* directory. The method takes a string as the input parameter, which specifies a relative path like *docs/home.html* within *assets*; it returns a *String* array of all the assets at the given path.

Suppose in our project, in addition to the file *hello_world.txt*, we have created a subdirectory, *dir1*, inside *assets* and another subdirectory, *dir2* under *dir1*. We create another file, called *demo.txt* inside *assets/dir1/dir2*. The following code shows using this method to display all assets files and directories:

```
package data.displayasset;

import java.io.File;
import android.util.Log;
import android.os.Bundle;
import java.io.IOException;
import android.app.Activity;
import android.content.res.AssetManager;

public class MainActivity extends Activity {
  @Override
  protected void onCreate(Bundle savedInstanceState) {
    super.onCreate(savedInstanceState);
    setContentView(R.layout.activity_main);
    final AssetManager mgr = getAssets();
    displayFiles(mgr, "");
  }

  void displayFiles (AssetManager mgr, String path) {
    try {
      String list[] = mgr.list(path);
      if (list != null)
        for (int i=0; i<list.length; ++i) {
          if ( path.length() >  0 ) {
            Log.v("Assests:", path + "/" + list[i]);
            displayFiles(mgr, path  + "/" + list[i] );
          }else{
            Log.v("Assests:", path  + list[i]);
            displayFiles(mgr, path  + list[i] );
          }
        }
      else
        Log.v("List:", "empty!");
    } catch (IOException e) {
      Log.v("List error:", "can't list" + path);
    }
  }
}
```

In the code, the method **displayFiles**() is called recursively to display all the assets files and directories. Initially, the empty string is passed in as the *path* parameter for the **list**() method of the class *AssetManager*, which returns the files and directories in the root directory of the asset file system. A directory name is then appended to *path* to search for the next level recursively. At deeper levels the symbol '/' is added to construct a path in the hierarchical form *dir1/dir2*. Figure 5-1 shows a screen shot of a portion of the Eclipse IDE, showing the project of the outputs at *LogCat* when the program is executed. As one can see from the outputs, besides the files in the *assets* directory, the system also consists of other assets such as images, and sounds.

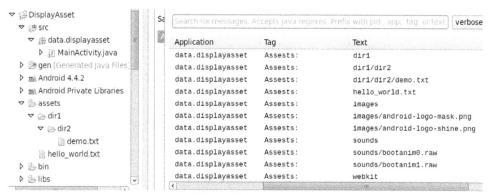

Figure 5-1 Assets

5.2.2   Write to Files

We can easily use a Java class of file I/O to save data in a file. The interested question is: *where is the written file located?* To answer this question, let us again consider a simple example, in which we write some text to a file named *sampleFile.txt*, and read it back, printing the text on the **LogCat** output. Suppose we call the project of this example *WriteFile*. The following is the complete code of the *MainActivity* of *WriteFile*:

```
----------------------------------------------------------------------
package data.writefile;

import java.io.FileInputStream;
import java.io.FileOutputStream;
import java.io.InputStreamReader;
import java.io.OutputStreamWriter;
import java.io.IOException;
import android.app.Activity;
import android.os.Bundle;
import android.util.Log;
import android.view.Menu;

public class MainActivity extends Activity {
  @Override
  protected void onCreate(Bundle savedInstanceState) {
    super.onCreate(savedInstanceState);
    setContentView(R.layout.activity_main);
    try {
      final String helloString = new String("Hello, Friend!");
      FileOutputStream fos = openFileOutput("sampleFile.txt",
                                   MODE_WORLD_READABLE);
      OutputStreamWriter osw = new OutputStreamWriter( fos );

      // Write the string to the file
      osw.write ( helloString );

      // Flush out anything in buffer
      osw.flush();
      osw.close();

      // Read the file back...
```

```
FileInputStream fis = openFileInput ( "sampleFile.txt" );
InputStreamReader isr = new InputStreamReader ( fis );

// Prepare a char-Array that to read data back
char[] inputBuffer = new char[fis.available()];

// Fill the Buffer with data from the file
isr.read(inputBuffer);

// Transform the chars to a String
String readString = new String(inputBuffer);

// Check if we read back the same chars that we had written out
boolean writeReadEqual = helloString.equals ( readString );
Log.i( "String read:", readString );
Log.i( "File Reading:", "success = " + writeReadEqual );

} catch (IOException ioe)  { ioe.printStackTrace(); }
  }
}
```

In the code, we use the methods **openFileOutput**() and **openFileInput**() of the class *Context*, which are implemented in *ContextWrapper*, to access files. For **openFileOutput**, the first parameter is file name and the second is access mode, which specifies who has the right to access the file. In the example, the mode is *MODE_WORLD_READABLE* implying that everyone can access the file.

When we run this code in Eclipse IDE, we will see in the **LogCat** a portion of the output similar to following:

Application	Tag	Text
data.writefile	String read:	Hello, Friend!
data.writefile	File Reading:	success = true

The log indicates that we have successfully written the data to the file *sampleFile.txt* and read the data back. However, if we examine the directory tree of the project *WriteFile*, we will not find in any of the subdirectories. This is because the file has been saved somewhere else, in an emulated file system, which is compressed and is in the path of our home directory. We can find this out by issuing a listing command such as

$ ls ~/.android/

In this command, the symbol '~' means home directory and the dot '.' preceding a directory name means that the directory is hidden. This command displays the files, including directories under *.android*, similar to the following:

```
adbkey           androidwin.cfg  debug.keystore    repositories.cfg
adbkey.pub       avd             default.keyset    sites-settings.cfg
adb_usb.ini      cache           modem-nv-ram-5554
androidtool.cfg ddms.cfg         modem-nv-ram-5556
```

Suppose we examine deeper directories:

$ ls /.android/avd/*avd_name*/

This command would list files with names like the following:

```
cache.img       emulator-user.ini      sdcard.img       userdata-qemu.img
cache.img.lock  hardware-qemu.ini      sdcard.img.lock  userdata-qemu.img.lock
config.ini      hardware-qemu.ini.lock userdata.img
```

Our data file *sampleFile.txt* is saved in the compressed file image *userdata-qemu.img*. (We can verify this by a command like **strings userdata-qemu.img | grep sampleFile**, which would display *sampleFile.txt*.) The compressed image can be decompressed by the Android extra utility *simg2img*. Alternatively, we can extract the data files using the Android *adb* command with the **pull** option. (The command *adb –help* lists all options of the utility *adb*.) We can first make a directory, say *uncompressed* inside our project:

```
$ mkdir uncompressed
$ cd uncompressed
```

While extracting the data, the emulator should be running. To check the device status, we can issue the command,

$ adb devices

which lists the attached devices, displaying a message similar to the following:

```
List of devices attached
emulator-5554 device
```

Now we can extract the data using the command,

$ adb pull data

If we use *ls* to list the files in *uncompressed*, we will see the following list:

```
anr  backup        data  nativebenchmark  property  tombstones
app  dalvik-cache  misc  nativetest       system
```

Our file *sampleFile.txt* is in the path *data*, which can be displayed by:

$ ls data/data.writefile/files/

We can use the *cat* command to see its content:

$ cat data/data.writefile/files/sampleFile.txt

which displays the message

```
Hello, Friend!
```

which is indeed the text we have written to *sampleFile.txt* in our applicaiton.
   For more information about internal storage, one can refer to the site:

```
http://developer.android.com/guide/topics/data/data-storage.html#filesInternal
```

5.2.3 External Storage

Normally, an Android device supports a shared external storage that we can store data. It can be a removable storage media such as an SD card. Files saved in the external storage are world-readable. They can be accessed and modified by the user if the USB mass storage has been enabled to transfer files on a computer.
   In order to read or write files on the external storage, the application must acquire system permissions *READ_EXTERNAL_STORAGE* or *WRITE_EXTERNAL_STORAGE*, which can be done by adding the permission statements in the manifest file *AndroidManifest.xml* like the following:

```
<manifest ...>
  <uses-permission android:name="android.permission.WRITE_EXTERNAL_STORAGE" />
  ...
</manifest>
```

External storage will become unavailable if the user removes the media. There is no enforcing security on files that we save in the external storage; any application can read or write the files and the user can remove them.

We can setup external storage in the emulator by clicking in the Eclipse IDE:

Window > Android Virtual Device Manager > Android Virtual Devices

Then we choose our AVD and click **Edit**, which displays an I/O panel showing the information of our AVD. In the entry **SD Card**, we may check **Size** and enter 200 for 200 MB storage.

5.3   Android JNI

5.3.1   Installing Android NDK

The Java Native Interface (JNI) is a programming framework that enables Java code running in a Java Virtual Machine (JVM) to interface with native applications that may be specific to a hardware and operating system platform. Through JNI, Java programs can call libraries written in other languages such as C/C++ and assembly.

In Android, two key data structures, *JavaVM* and *JNIEnv* are defined by JNI. They are essentially pointers to pointers to function tables. The *JavaVM* structure provides *invocation interface* functions, which allow us to create and destroy a *JavaVM* object. Though in principle a process can have multiple *JavaVM* objects, Android only allows one per process. The *JNIEnv* structure provides most of the JNI functions and our native functions all receive a *JNIEnv* object as the first argument. It is used for thread-local storage and thus we cannot share a *JNIEnv* object threads.

To use the JNI, we must first install the Android NDK, which can be downloaded from the site: *https://developer.android.com/tools/sdk/ndk/index.html*
We have to unzip and unpack the package. Suppose we unpack it into the directory
   /apps/android/android-ndk-r10
To associate ths package with the Eclipse IDE, click **Window > Preferences > Android > NDK**. Then enter the root directory of the NDK for **NDK Location** (e.g. */apps/android/android-ndk-r10*), and click **Apply > OK**. (You may need to restart Eclipse.)

5.3.2   A Simple Example of JNI

We present a simple example here to illustrate how an Android Java program can call a routine written in C/C++ through JNI. Suppose we call our project and application *JniDemo* and the package *data.jnidemo*. As usual, we have created the project using Eclipse and the default main program is *MainActivity.java*. The steps of writing a C program and calling its function are exaplained below. In our example, our C program (*sum-jni.c*) has a function named **sum(int** n **)**, which adds the integers from 1 to n and returns the sum of them.

1. Add folder *jni*: Click **File > New >** Folder. Enter *JniDemo* for the parent folder name and *jni* for the folder name. Then click **Finish** to create the folder named *jni*.
2. Add *Android.mk* inside folder *jni*: Click **File > New >** File. Enter *JniDemo/jni* for the parent folder name and *Android.mk* for the file name and click **Finish** to create the file.

This file acts as a *Makefile* for linking Java and C programs. We write it with the followng statements:

```
LOCAL_PATH := $(call my-dir)
include $(CLEAR_VARS)
LOCAL_MODULE    := sum-jni
LOCAL_SRC_FILES := sum-jni.c
include $(BUILD_SHARED_LIBRARY)
```

This *Makefile* says that our C file, which contains the C routines is named *sum-jni.c*.

3. Create a Java source wrapper, *SumWrapper.java*: Click **File** > **Class**. Enter *JniDemo/src* for **Source Foler** and *SumWrapper* for **Name**. Click **Finish** to create the class. Modify the file to the following:

```
package data.jnidemo;

public class SumWrapper
{
  // Declare native method public to expose it
  public static native int sum ( int n );

  public static int getSum ( int n) {
    int s = sum ( n );   //call native method
    return s;
  }
  // Load library
  static {
    System.loadLibrary( "sum-jni");   // C-file is sum-jni.c
  }
}
```

This wrapper's job is to load the library, and expose any functions in the C program we will use in other Java programs.

4. Create the C header: We compile the source *SumWrapper.java* to obtain its class file and use it to create a C header file, which contains the function prototypes of the native methods. We do this in a terminal via the javac command, assuming our workspace is in the directory */workspace*:

```
$ cd /workspace/JniDemo/src #change into the source directory
$ javac -d /tmp data/jnidemo/SumWrapper.java
```

The switch *-d* specifies an output directory, and here we simply put the class in the directory */tmp*. We can list the class with the command *ls /tmp/data/jnidemo/*, which will display the file name *SumWrapper.class*. The C header file can be created by the commands:

```
$ cd /tmp
$ javah -jni data.jnidemo.SumWrapper
```

This creates the C header file *data_jnidemo_SumWrapper.h* in the directory */tmp*, which looks like the following:

```
/* DO NOT EDIT THIS FILE - it is machine generated */
#include <jni.h>
/* Header for class data_jnidemo_SumWrapper */
```

```
#ifndef _Included_data_jnidemo_SumWrapper
#define _Included_data_jnidemo_SumWrapper
#ifdef __cplusplus
extern "C" {
#endif
/*
 * Class:     data_jnidemo_SumWrapper
 * Method:    sum
 * Signature: (I)I
 */
JNIEXPORT jint JNICALL Java_data_jnidemo_SumWrapper_sum
  (JNIEnv *, jclass, jint);
#ifdef __cplusplus
}
#endif
#endif
```

5. Create C source code: Using the prototype generated by *javah*, we can implement our C source code. We first create the file *sum-jni.c* inside the directory *jni* by clicking **File > New > File** and entering file name *sum-jni.c*. Modify this file to the following:

```
#include <jni.h>
JNIEXPORT jint JNICALL Java_data_jnidemo_SumWrapper_sum
  (JNIEnv * je, jclass jc, jint n)
{
  int i, sum = 0;

  for ( i = 1; i <= n; i++ )
    sum += i;

  return sum;
}
```

6. Build a shared library: We use the *ndk-build* script to build a shared library from *sum-jni.c*. Suppose we have installed the Android NDK in the directory */apps/android/android-nkk-r10*. To compile, we first go to the project directory */workspace/JniDemo/jni/*, which we created earlier, then run the *ndk-build* script provided by the Android NDK:

$ cd /workspace/JniDemo/jni/
$ /apps/android/android-ndk-r10/ndk-build

The script makes use of the information in *jni/Android.mk* to create the dynamic-linked library *libsum-jni.so* from *sum-jni.c* and install it in the directory *libs/armeabi* of the project. (i.e. */workspace/JniDemo/libs/armeabi*) The script generates the following messages, reflecting what it has done:

```
[armeabi] Compile thumb :sum-jni <= sum-jni.c
[armeabi] SharedLibrary :libsum-jni.so
[armeabi] Install        :libsum-jni.so=>libs/armeabi/libsum-jni.so
```

7. Modify *MainActivity.java*: Modify the default main program to the following:

```
package data.jnidemo;
```

```
import android.app.Activity;
import android.os.Bundle;
import android.util.Log;

public class MainActivity extends Activity {
  @Override
  protected void onCreate(Bundle savedInstanceState) {
    super.onCreate(savedInstanceState);
    setContentView(R.layout.activity_main);
    int n = 10;
    int s = SumWrapper.getSum( n );
    Log.v ( "Sum of", String.format ("1 to %d = %d",n,s));
  }
}
```

This main program deos not do much. It simply calls the *SumWrapper*'s **getSum**(n) method, which calls the native method **sum**(n) to calculate the sum $1 + 2 + ... + n$. It sends the result to the *LogCat*.

8. Run the program: We run the progam as usual, clicking **Run** > **Run**. The emulator will not show any output but the Eclipse LogCat will show the sum output. Figure 5-2 shows a caputred image of the Eclipse environment when running the program; we can see from it the file struture and log output of the project.

Figure 5-2 A Simple JNI Example

5.3.3   A Simple JNI Example with UI

We can easily add a UI to the above example. Suppose we call this new project *JniDemo1*, and have gone through the above steps. To create a UI we first modify *res/layout/activity_main.xml* to:

```
<?xml version="1.0" encoding="utf-8"?>
  <LinearLayout xmlns:android="http://schemas.android.com/apk/res/android"
    android:layout_width="fill_parent"
    android:layout_height="fill_parent"
    android:orientation="vertical" >
    <LinearLayout
```

```
    android:id="@+id/linearLayout0"
    android:layout_width="match_parent"
    android:layout_height="wrap_content"
    android:layout_marginLeft="12pt"
    android:layout_marginRight="12pt"
    android:layout_marginTop="4pt" >

  <TextView
    android:id="@+id/info"
    android:layout_width="match_parent"
    android:layout_height="wrap_content"
    android:layout_marginLeft="6pt"
    android:layout_marginRight="6pt"
    android:layout_marginTop="4pt"
    android:gravity="center_horizontal"
    android:text="Enter a postive number:"
    android:textSize="12pt" >
  </TextView>
</LinearLayout>

<LinearLayout
    android:id="@+id/linearLayout1"
    android:layout_width="match_parent"
    android:layout_height="wrap_content"
    android:layout_marginLeft="12pt"
    android:layout_marginRight="12pt"
    android:layout_marginTop="4pt" >

  <EditText
    android:id="@+id/n"
    android:layout_width="match_parent"
    android:layout_height="wrap_content"
    android:layout_marginRight="6pt"
    android:layout_weight="1"
    android:inputType="numberDecimal" >
  </EditText>

  <Button    android:id="@+id/getsum"
    android:layout_width="wrap_content"
    android:layout_height="wrap_content"
    android:text="Get Sum"
    android:textSize="10pt"
    android:onClick="onClick"/>
</LinearLayout>

<TextView
    android:id="@+id/sum"
    android:layout_width="match_parent"
    android:layout_height="wrap_content"
    android:layout_marginLeft="6pt"
    android:layout_marginRight="6pt"
    android:layout_marginTop="4pt"
    android:gravity="center_horizontal"
    android:textSize="12pt" >
</TextView>
```

```
</LinearLayout>
```

In this layout, we define an *EditText* for the user to enter an integer. We define a *Button* named *getsum* for the user to click upon that calls the summing routine. The result is didsplayed in *TextView sum*.

We also need to modify *MainActivity.java* to the following:

```
package data.jnidemo1;

import android.os.Bundle;
import android.view.View;
import android.widget.*;
import android.app.Activity;
import android.text.TextUtils;

public class MainActivity extends Activity
{

  private EditText n;
  private TextView sum;
  private Button getsum;

  @Override
  protected void onCreate(Bundle savedInstanceState) {
  super.onCreate(savedInstanceState);
  setContentView(R.layout.activity_main);
  n = (EditText) findViewById(R.id.n);
  getsum = (Button) findViewById(R.id.getsum);
  sum = (TextView) findViewById(R.id.sum);
  TextView info = (TextView) findViewById(R.id.info);
  }

  // @Override
  public void onClick(View view) {
    // check if the fields are empty
    if (TextUtils.isEmpty(n.getText().toString()) )
       return;

    // read numbers from EditText
    String str = n.getText().toString();

    int n1 = Integer.parseInt( str );
    int s = SumWrapper.getSum( n1 );

    // display result
    str = "Sum of 1 to " + str + " is ";
    str += Integer.toString ( s );;
    sum.setText ( str );
  }
}
```

The method **onClick**() is called when the user clicks on the *Button getsum*. It reads the integer entered and saves it in *EditText n*. The *EditText n* is converted to a *String*, which in turn is converted to an integer. The method then calls **getSum**() of the class *SumWrapper*, which in turn calls the native routine **sum** to calculate the sum of the integers from 1 to n. The returned result is displayed by *TextView sum*.

When we run the program we will see a UI like that of Figure 5-3(a). Figure 5-3(b) shows the UI after we have entered the number 100 and clicked the button.

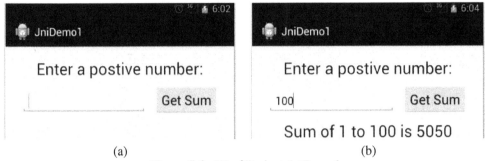

(a)   (b)

Figure 5-3   UI of Project *JniDemo1*

Chapter 6   Graphics with OpenGL ES 2.X

6.1   Programmable Pipeline

As we have mentioned in Chapter 4, OpenGL ES is an application programming interface (API) for advanced 3D graphics targeted for embedded devices such as cell phones, digital health kits, and tablets. It consists of well-defined subsets of desktop OpenGL, including profiles for floating-point and fixed-point systems and the EGL specification for portability that binds native windowing systems. (EGL (Embedded Graphics Library) is a native platform graphics interface between Khronos rendering APIs such as OpenGL ES or OpenVG and the underlying native window system.) The API is created and maintained by the Khronos Group, which is a member-funded industry consortium founded in January 2000, focusing on the creation of open standard and royalty-free APIs for embedded devices.

OpenGL ES 1.X is based on the traditional fixed pipeline graphics architecture, in which the functionality of each processing stage is fixed. It offers acceleration, image quality and performance. OpenGL ES 2.X supports fully programmable pipeline architecture, a trend in graphics hardware, for creating 3D graphics. In ES 2.X, one can use the OpenGL Shading Language (glsl) to write vertex shaders and fragment shaders. For details of the APIs, one can refer to the Web site,

http://www.khronos.org/opengles/2_X/

Android supports both OpenGL ES 1.X and OpenGL ES 2.X. Figure 6-1 below shows the traditional fixed function pipeline architecture of OpenGL used by OpenGL ES 1.X.

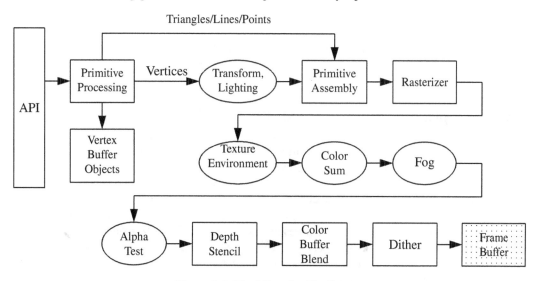

Figure 6-1. Fixed Function Pipeline

OpenGL ES 2.X does not support this fixed pipeline architecture. Its programmable pipeline replaces the fixed function transformation and fragment pipeline of OpenGL 1.X as shown in Figure 6-2 below.

OpenGL ES 2.0 is defined relative to the OpenGL 2.0 specification, emphasizing a programmable 3D graphics pipeline that allows users to create shader and program objects and to write vertex and fragment shaders using OpenGL Shading Language (glsl). It combines a glsl version for programming vertex and fragment shaders that has been adapted for embedded platforms, with a streamlined API from OpenGL ES 1.1 with the fixed functionality replaced by shader programs. This helps minimize the cost and power consumption of advanced programmable graphics subsystems.

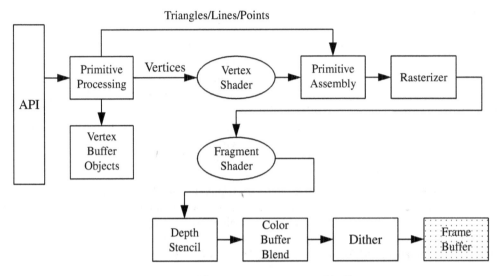

Figure 6-2. ES 2.X Programmable Pipeline

6.2   OpenGL Shading Language (GLSL)

Before we discuss using OpenGL ES 2.X to write graphics applications in Android, we give a brief introduction to OpenGL Shading Language (glsl), a C-like language with some C++ features designed for 3D graphics programming. It is part of OpenGL and thus can be naturally integrated with OpenGL programs with ease. The language is mainly used for processing numerics, but not for strings or characters.

6.2.1   OpenGL Shaders Execution Model

We can consider a driver as a piece of software that manages the access of a hardware. In this sense, we can view OpenGL libraries as drivers because they manage shared access to the underlying graphics hardware and applications communicate with graphics hardware by calling OpenGL functions. An OpenGL shader is embedded in an OpenGL application and may be viewed as an object in the driver to access the hardware. We use the command **glCreateShader**() to allocate within the OpenGL driver the data structures needed to store an OpenGL shader. The source code of a shader is provided by an application by calling **glShaderSource**() and we have to provide the source code as a **null-terminated** string to this function. Figure 6-3 below shows the steps to create a shader program for execution.

As shown in Figure 6-2, there are two kinds of shaders, the vertex shaders and the fragment shaders. A **vertex shader** (program) is a shader running on a **vertex processor**, which is a programmable unit that operates on incoming vertex values. This processor usually performs traditional graphics operations including the following:

1. vertex transformation

2. normal transformation and normalization
3. texture coordinate generation
4. texture coordinate transformation
5. lighting
6. color material application

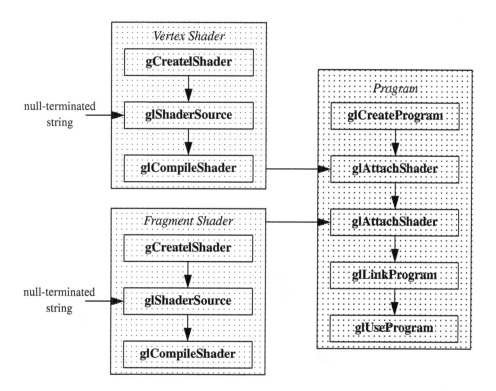

Figure 6-3 Shader Program Development

The following is an example of a simple "pass-through" vertex shader which does not do anything.

```
//A simple pass-through vertex shader
void main()
{
  gl_Position=gl_ProjectionMatrix*gl_ModelViewMatrix*gl_Vertex;
}
```

A shader program must pass a null-terminated string to the OpenGL function **glShaderSource**(), which is then compiled and linked with the rest of the application by other glsl commands as shown in Figure 6-3.

A **fragment shader** is a shader running on a **fragment processor**, which is a programmable unit that operates on fragment values. A fragment is a pixel plus its attributes such as color and transparency. A fragment shader is executed after the rasterization. Therefore a fragment processor operates on each fragment rather than on each vertex. It usually performs traditional graphics operations including:

1. operations on interpolated values
2. texture access

3. texture application
4. fog effects
5. color sum
6. pixel zoom
7. scaling
8. color table lookup
9. convolution
10. color matrix operations

The following is an example of a simple fragment shader, which sets the color of each fragment for render.

```
//A simple fragment shader
void main()
{
  gl_FragColor = gl_FrontColor;
}
```

6.2.2   OpenGL Shading Language API

Figure 6-3 above shows the development steps of a glsl shader program. The following table lists the OpenGL functions involved in the process.

Table 6-1   OpenGL Commands for Embedding Shaders

glCreateShader()	Creates one or more shader objects.
glShaderSource()	Provides source codes of shaders.
glCompileShader()	Compiles each of the shaders.
glCreateProgram()	Creates a program object.
glAttachShader()	Attach all shader objects to the program.
glLinkProgram()	Link the program object.
glUseProgram()	Install the shaders as part of the OpenGL program.

The following discusses the usual steps to develop an OpenGL shader program.

1. **Creating a Shader Object**

   We first create an empty shader object using the function **glCreateShader**, which has the following prototype:

   Gluint **glCreateShader** (GLenum *shaderType*)
   Creates an empty shader.
   shaderType specifies the type of shader to be created. It can be either GL_VERTEX_SHADER or GL_FRAGMENT_SHADER.
   Return: A non-zero integer handle for future reference.

   ---

2. **Providing Source Code for the Shader**

   We pass the source code to the shader as a null-terminated string using the function **glShaderSource** which has the prototype:

   ---

   void **glShaderSource** (GLuint *shader*, GLsizei *count*, const GLchar **string*, const GLint *lengthp)

Defines a shader's source code.

shader is the shader object created by glCreateShader().

string is the array of strings specifying the source code of the shader.

count is the number of strings in the array.

lengthp points to an array specifying the lengths of the strings. If NULL, the strings are NULL-terminated.

The source code can be hard-coded as a string in the OpenGL program or it can be saved in a separate file and read into an array as a null-terminated string, which ends with the null character '\0'.

3. Compiling Shader Object

We use the function **glCompileShader** to compile the shader source code to object code. This function has the following prototype.

---

void **glCompileShader** (GLuint *shader*)

Compiles the source code strings stored in the shader object *shader*.

The function **glShaderInfoLog** gives the compilation log.

---

4. Linking and Using Shaders

Each shader object is compiled independently. To create a shader program, we need to link all the shader objects to the OpenGL application. These are done within the C/C++ application using the functions **glCreateProgram, glAttachShader, glLinkProgram**, and **glUseProgram**, which have the prototypes listed below. These are done while we are running the C/C++ application. Performing the steps of compiling and linking shader objects are simply making C function calls.

GLuint **glCreateProgram** (void)

Creates an empty program object and returns a non-zero integer handle for future reference.

void **glAttachShader** (GLuint *program*, GLuint *shader*)

Attaches the shader object specified by *shader* to the program object specified by *program*.

void **glLinkProgram** (GLuint *program*)

Links the program objects specified by *program*.

void **glUseProgram** (GLuint *program*)

Installs the program object specified by *program* as part of current rendering state.

If *program* is 0, the programmable processors are disabled, and fixed functionality is used for both vertex and fragment processing.

---

5. Cleaning Up

At the end, we need to release all the resources taken up by the shaders. The clean up is done by the commands,

```
void glDeleteShader ( GLuint shader ),
void glDeleteProgram ( GLuint program ),
void glDetachShader ( GLuint program, GLuint shader ).
```

Listing 6-1 below is a complete example of a shader program; the OpenGL application is the C/C++ program *shaderdemo.cpp*, which does the shader creation, reading shader source code, shader compilation and shader linking. The shader source codes are hard-coded in the program. In compiling *shaderdemo.cpp*, we need to link the GL extension library by "-lGLEW". If we compile "shaderdemo.cpp" to the executable "shaderdemo", we can run the shader program by typing "./shaderdemo" and press 'Enter'.

Program Listing 6-1   Complete Example of a Shader Program

shaderdemo.cpp

```
/*
 shaderdemo.cpp
 Sample program showing how to write GL shader programs.
*/
#include <stdlib.h>
#include <stdio.h>
#include <string.h>
#include <GL/glew.h>
#include <GL/glut.h>

using namespace std;

/*
  Global handles for the currently active program object,
  with its two shader objects
*/
GLuint programObject = 0;
GLuint vShader = 0;
GLuint fShader = 0;
static GLint win = 0;

// String defining vertex shader
char vertexStr[] = "                          \
 //a minimal vertex shader  \n    \
 void main(void)                   \
 {                                 \
   gl_Position = gl_ModelViewProjectionMatrix * gl_Vertex; \
 }                                 \
";

// String for fragment shader
char fragmentStr[] = "                        \
 //a minimal fragment shader \n   \
 void main(void)                   \
 {                                 \
   gl_FragColor = vec4( 1, 0, 0, 1); \
 }                                 \
";
```

```
int readShaderSource( char str[],  GLchar **shader )
{
   // Allocate memory to hold the source of our shaders.
   int shaderSize;

   shaderSize = strlen ( str );

   if ( shaderSize <= 0 ){
       printf("Shader string  empty\n" );
       return 0;
   }
   // Allocate memory for shader
   *shader = (GLchar *) malloc( shaderSize + 1);

   // Read the source code
   strcpy ( *shader, str );

   return 1;
}

int installShaders(const GLchar *vertex, const GLchar *fragment)
{
   GLint  vertCompiled, fragCompiled;  // status values
   GLint  linked;

   // Create a vertex shader object and a fragment shader object
   vShader = glCreateShader(GL_VERTEX_SHADER);
   fShader = glCreateShader(GL_FRAGMENT_SHADER);

   // Load source code strings into shaders, compile and link
   glShaderSource(vShader, 1, &vertex, NULL);
   glShaderSource(fShader, 1, &fragment, NULL);

   glCompileShader(vShader);
   glGetShaderiv(vShader, GL_COMPILE_STATUS, &vertCompiled);
   glCompileShader( fShader );
   glGetShaderiv( fShader, GL_COMPILE_STATUS, &fragCompiled);

   if (!vertCompiled || !fragCompiled)
       return 0;

   // Create a program object and attach the two compiled shaders
   programObject = glCreateProgram();
   glAttachShader( programObject, vShader);
   glAttachShader( programObject, fShader);

   // Link the program object
   glLinkProgram(programObject);
   glGetProgramiv(programObject, GL_LINK_STATUS, &linked);

   if (!linked)
       return 0;
   // Install program object as part of current state
   glUseProgram(programObject);
```

```
      return 1;
}

int init(void)
{
  const char *version;
  GLchar *vShaderSource, *fShaderSource;
  int loadstatus = 0;

  version = (const char *) glGetString(GL_VERSION);
  if (version[0] != '2' || version[1] != '.') {
    printf("This program requires OpenGL 2.x, found %s\n", version);
    exit(1);
  }
  readShaderSource( vertexStr, &vShaderSource );
  readShaderSource( fragmentStr, &fShaderSource );
  loadstatus = installShaders(vShaderSource, fShaderSource);

  return loadstatus;
}

static void reshape(int width, int height)
{
  glViewport(0, 0, width, height);
  glMatrixMode(GL_PROJECTION);
  glLoadIdentity();
  glFrustum(-1.0, 1.0, -1.0, 1.0, 5.0, 25.0);
  glMatrixMode(GL_MODELVIEW);
  glLoadIdentity();
  glTranslatef(0.0f, 0.0f, -15.0f);
}

void cleanUp(void)
{
  glDeleteShader ( vShader );
  glDeleteShader ( fShader );
  glDeleteProgram ( programObject );
  glutDestroyWindow ( win );
}

static void idle(void)
{
  glutPostRedisplay();
}

static void keyPressed ( unsigned char key, int x, int y )
{
  switch(key) {
  case 27:
    cleanUp();
    exit(0);
    break;
  }
  glutPostRedisplay();
```

```
  }

void display(void)
{
  GLfloat vec[4];

  glClear(GL_COLOR_BUFFER_BIT | GL_DEPTH_BUFFER_BIT);
  glClearColor( 1.0, 1.0, 1.0, 0.0 ); //get white background color
  glColor3f( 0, 1, 0 ); //green, have no effect if shader is loaded
  glLineWidth ( 3 );
  glutWireSphere(2.0, 12, 6);
  glutSwapBuffers();
  glFlush();
}

int main(int argc, char *argv[])
{
  int success = 0;

  glutInit(&argc, argv);
  glutInitWindowPosition( 0, 0);
  glutInitWindowSize(200, 200);
  glutInitDisplayMode(GLUT_RGB | GLUT_DOUBLE | GLUT_DEPTH);
  win = glutCreateWindow(argv[0]);
  glutReshapeFunc(reshape);
  glutKeyboardFunc ( keyPressed );
  glutDisplayFunc(display);
  glutIdleFunc(idle);
  // Initialize the "OpenGL Extension Wrangler" library
  glewInit();
  success = init();
  if ( success )
    glutMainLoop();
  return 0;
}
```

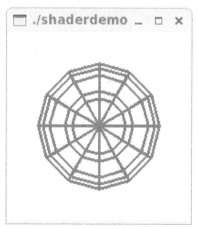

Figure 6-4 Output of Shader Program *shaderdemo.cpp*

6.2.3   Data Types in GLSL

There are four main data types in GLSL: **float, int, bool**, and **sampler**. Vector types are available for the first three types:

vec2, vec3, vec4	2D, 3D and 4D floating point vector
ivec2, ivec3, ivec4	2D, 3D and 4D integer vector
bvec2, bvec3, bvec4	2D, 3D and 4D boolean vectors

For floats there are also matrix types:

mat2, mat3, mat4	$2 \times 2, 3 \times 3, 4 \times 4$ floating point matrix

Samplers are types used for representing textures:

sampler1D, sampler2D, sampler3D	1D, 2D and 3D texture
samplerCube	Cube Map texture
sampler1Dshadow, sampler2Dshadow	1D and 2D depth-component texture

Attributes, Uniforms and Varyings

GLSL shaders have three different input-output data types for passing data between vertex and fragment shaders, and the OpenGL application. The data types are **uniform, attribute** and **varying**. They must be declared as global (visible to the whole shader object). The variables have the following properties:

1. **Uniforms** : These are read-only variables (i.e. A shader object can only read the variables but cannot change them.). Their values do not change during a rendering. Therefore, Uniform variable values are assigned outside the scope of **glBegin/glEnd**. Uniform variables are used for sharing data among an application program, vertex shaders, and fragment shaders.

2. **Attributes**: These are also read-only variables. They are only available in vertex shaders. They are used for variables that change at most once per vertex in a vertex shader. There are two types of attribute variables, user-defined and built-in. The following are examples of user-defined attributes:

   attribute float x;
   attribute vec3 velocity, acceleration;

   Built-in variables include OpenGL state variables such as color, position, and normal; the following are some examples:

   gl_Vertex
   gl_Color

3. **Varyings**: These are read/write variables, which are used for passing data from a vertex shader to a fragment shader. They are defined on a per-vertex basis but are interpolated over the primitive by the rasterizer. They can be user-defined or built-in.

Built-in Types

The following tables list some more of the GLSL built-in types.

Table D-2   Built-in Attributes (for Vertex Shaders)

gl_Vertex	4D vector representing the vertex position
gl_Normal	3D vector representing the vertex normal
gl_Color	4D vector representing the vertex color
gl_MultiTexCoord$n$	4D vector representing the texture coordinate of texture n

Table D-3   Built-in Uniforms (for Vertex and Fragment Shaders)

gl_ModelViewMatrix	4×4 Matrix representing the model-view matrix
gl_ModelViewProjectionMatrix	4×4 Model-view-projection matrix
gl_NormalMatrix	3×3 Matrix used for normal transformation

Table D-4   Built-in Varyings (for Data Sharing between Shaders)

gl_FrontColor	4D vector representing the primitives front color
gl_BackColor	4D vector representing the primitives back color
gl_TexCoord[n]	4D vector representing the n-th texture coordinate
gl_Position	4D vector representing the final processed vertex position (vertex shader only)
gl_FragColor	4D vector representing the final color written in the frame buffer (fragment shader only)
gl_FragDepth	float representing the depth written in the depth buffer (fragment shader only)

GLSL has many built in functions, including

1. trigonometric functions: **sin, cos, tan**
2. inverse trigonometric functions: **asin, acos, atan**
3. mathematical functions: **pow, log2, sqrt, abs, max, min**
4. geometrical functions: **length, distance, normalize, reflect**

The following is an example of using various data types; it consists of a vertex shader and a fragment shader for defining a modified Phong lighting model.

Program Listing 6-2   Shaders for Modified Phong Lighting

(a) Vertex Shader: phong.vert

```
//phong.vert
varying vec3 N;   //normal direction
varying vec3 L;   //light source direction
varying vec3 E;   //eye position

void main(void)
{
   gl_Position =gl_ModelViewMatrix*gl_Vertex;
   vec4 eyePosition = gl_ModelViewProjectionMatrix*gl_Vertex;
   vec4 eyeLightPosition = gl_LightSource[0].position;

   N = normalize( gl_NormalMatrix*gl_Normal );
   L = eyeLightPosition.xyz - eyePosition.xyz;
   E = -eyePosition.xyz;
}
```

(b) Fragment Shader: phong.frag

```
//phong.frag
varying vec3 N;
varying vec3 L;
varying vec3 E;

void main()
{
  vec3 norm = normalize(N);
  vec3 lightv = normalize(L);
  vec3 viewv = normalize(E);
  vec3 halfv = normalize(lightv + viewv);
  float f;
  if(dot(lightv, norm)>= 0.0) f =1.0;
  else f = 0.0;

  float Kd = max(0.0, dot(lightv, norm));
  float Ks = pow(max(0.0, dot(norm, halfv)), gl_FrontMaterial.shininess);
  vec4 diffuse = Kd * gl_FrontMaterial.diffuse*gl_LightSource[0].diffuse;
  vec4 ambient = gl_FrontMaterial.ambient*gl_LightSource[0].ambient;
  vec4 specular = f*Ks*gl_FrontMaterial.specular*gl_LightSource[0].specular;
  gl_FragColor = ambient + diffuse + specular;
}
```

6.3 Android Graphics with ES 2.0

6.3.1 Drawing a Triangle

The *android.opengl.GLES20* package provides the interface to OpenGL ES 2.0, which supports OpenGL Shader Library APIs. In earlier days, android emulator did not support this feature and one had to use a real android device to test its code in the development process. However, newer emulator versions begin to support ES 2.0.

To use the OpenGL ES 2.0 API, we have to add the following declaration in the manifest file, *AndroidManifest.xml*:

```
<uses-feature android:glEsVersion="0x00020000" android:required="true" />
```

If our application uses texture compression, we also need to declare which compression formats we support so that devices that do not support theses formats will not run the application:

```
<supports-gl-texture android:name="GL_OES_compressed_ETC1_RGB8_texture" />
<supports-gl-texture android:name="GL_OES_compressed_paletted_texture" />
```

The following steps walk you through the process of creating an android glsl application, which simply draws a magenta triangle. Suppose we use Eclipse IDE in the development process. We call our project and application *Glsl1*, and the package *opengl.glsl1*. In the example, the vertex and fragment shaders are hard-coded as null-terminated strings in the program:

1. In Eclipse IDE, click **File > New > Android Application Project** (You may need to click **Poject ..** first if your Eclipse has been setup differently.). The *New Android Application* diaglog shows up.

2. Enter *Glsl1, Glsl1*, and *opengl.glsl1* for the names of application, project, and package respectivley. You may use defaults for other features for selection. Then click **Next** > **Next** > **Next** and **Next**.

3. You may use the default names *MainActivity* and *activity_main* for the names of Activity and Layout. Then click **Finish** to create the project *Glsl1*.

4. In the base directory *Glsl1*, you can find the xml file, *AndroidManifest.xml*, which presents essential information about the app to the Android system. Add the following statement to this file:
   <uses-feature android:glEsVersion="0x00020000" android:required="true" />
   which tells the system that the app requires OpenGL ES 2.0. You may add the statement before the < *application* > element in the file.

5. Modify the main program *MainActivity.java* in the subdirectory *src/opengl/glsl1* to the following, which along with comments is self-explained:

```
---------------------------------------------------------------------------
package opengl.glsl1;

import android.app.Activity;
import android.content.Context;
import android.opengl.GLSurfaceView;
import android.os.Bundle;

public class MainActivity extends Activity {

  private GLSurfaceView glView;

  @Override
  protected void onCreate(Bundle savedInstanceState) {
    super.onCreate(savedInstanceState);
    // Create a GLSurfaceView instance and set it
    // as the ContentView for this Activity.
    glView = new MyGLSurfaceView(this);
    setContentView(glView);
  }
}


class MyGLSurfaceView extends GLSurfaceView {

  public MyGLSurfaceView(Context context){
    super(context);
    // Create an OpenGL ES 2.0 context
    setEGLContextClientVersion ( 2 );
  public MyGLSurfaceView(Context context){
    super(context);
    // Create an OpenGL ES 2.0 context
    setEGLContextClientVersion ( 2 );
    // Render the view only when there is a change in the drawing data
    // Set the Renderer for drawing on the GLSurfaceView
    setRenderer(new MyRenderer());
  }
}
---------------------------------------------------------------------------
```

6. Create a new class by clicking **File** > **New** > **Class**. Enter *MyRenderer* for the name and use defaults for other entries. This creates the class file *src/opengl/glsl1/MyRenderer.java*. Modify this file to the following:

```
--------------------------------------------------------------------
package opengl.glsl1;

import android.opengl.GLES20;
import android.opengl.GLSurfaceView;
import javax.microedition.khronos.egl.EGLConfig;
import javax.microedition.khronos.opengles.GL10;

public class MyRenderer implements GLSurfaceView.Renderer {

  private Triangle triangle;
  public void onSurfaceCreated(GL10 unused, EGLConfig config) {
    // Set the background frame color
    GLES20.glClearColor(0.9f, 0.9f, 0.9f, 1.0f);
    // construct a triangle object
    triangle = new Triangle();
  }

  public void onDrawFrame(GL10 unused) {
    // Redraw background color
    GLES20.glClear(GLES20.GL_COLOR_BUFFER_BIT);
    triangle.draw();
  }

  public void onSurfaceChanged(GL10 unused, int width, int height) {
     GLES20.glViewport(0, 0, width, height);
  }
}
--------------------------------------------------------------------
```

This class renders a *Triangle* object, which is defined in the next step.

7. Create another new class by clicking **File** > **New** > **Class**. Enter *Triangle* for the name and use defaults for other entries. This creates the class file *src/opengl/glsl1/Triangle.java*. Modify this file to the following:

```
--------------------------------------------------------------------
package opengl.glsl1;

import java.nio.ByteBuffer;
import java.nio.ByteOrder;
import java.nio.FloatBuffer;

import android.opengl.GLES20;

public class Triangle {
  // Source code of vertex shader
  private final String vsCode =
    "attribute vec4 vPosition;" +
        "void main() {" +
    " gl_Position = vPosition;" +
```

```
"}";

  // Source code of fragment shader
  private final String fsCode =
    "precision mediump float;" +
    "uniform vec4 vColor;" +
    "void main() {" +
    "  gl_FragColor = vColor;" +
      "}";

private int program;
private int vertexShader;
private int fragmentShader;
private FloatBuffer vertexBuffer;
private int vertexCount = 3;

  // number of coordinates per vertex in this array
  static final int COORDS_PER_VERTEX = 3;
  static float triangleCoords[] = {    // in counterclockwise order:
     0.0f,   0.9f, 0.0f, // top vertex
    -0.5f,   0.1f, 0.0f, // bottom left
     0.5f,   0.1f, 0.0f  // bottom right
  };

  // Set color of displaying object
  // with red, green, blue and alpha (opacity) values
  float color[] = { 0.9f, 0.1f, 0.9f, 1.0f };

  // Create a Triangle object
  Triangle(){
    // create empty OpenGL ES Program, load, attach, and link shaders
    program = GLES20.glCreateProgram();
    vertexShader = loadShader(GLES20.GL_VERTEX_SHADER, vsCode);
    fragmentShader = loadShader(GLES20.GL_FRAGMENT_SHADER, fsCode);
    // add the vertex shader to program
    GLES20.glAttachShader(program, vertexShader);
    // add the fragment shader to program
    GLES20.glAttachShader(program, fragmentShader);
    GLES20.glLinkProgram(program); //creates ES program executables
    GLES20.glUseProgram( program); //use shader program

    //initialize vertex byte buffer for shape coordinates with
    // paramters (number of coordinate values * 4 bytes per float)
    //use the device hardware's native byte order
    ByteBuffer bb=ByteBuffer.allocateDirect(triangleCoords.length*4);
    bb.order ( ByteOrder.nativeOrder() );

    // create a floating point buffer from the ByteBuffer
    vertexBuffer = bb.asFloatBuffer();
    // create a floating point buffer from the ByteBuffer
    vertexBuffer = bb.asFloatBuffer();
    // add the coordinates to the FloatBuffer
    vertexBuffer.put(triangleCoords);
    // set the buffer to read the first coordinate
    vertexBuffer.position(0);
```

```
    } //Triangle Constructor

    public static int loadShader (int type, String shaderCode ) {

        // create a vertex shader type (GLES20.GL_VERTEX_SHADER)
        // or a fragment shader type (GLES20.GL_FRAGMENT_SHADER)
        int shader = GLES20.glCreateShader(type);

        // pass source code to the shader and compile it
        GLES20.glShaderSource(shader, shaderCode);
        GLES20.glCompileShader(shader);

        return shader;
    }

    public void draw() {
        // Add program to OpenGL ES environment
        GLES20.glUseProgram(program);

        //get handle to vertex shader's attribute variable vPosition
        int positionHandle=GLES20.glGetAttribLocation(program,
                                                        "vPosition");

        // Enable a handle to the triangle vertices
        GLES20.glEnableVertexAttribArray(positionHandle);

        // Prepare the triangle coordinate data
        GLES20.glVertexAttribPointer(positionHandle, COORDS_PER_VERTEX,
                            GLES20.GL_FLOAT, false, 0, vertexBuffer);

        // get handle to fragment shader's uniform variable vColor
        int colorHandle=GLES20.glGetUniformLocation(program, "vColor");

        // Set color for drawing the triangle
        GLES20.glUniform4fv(colorHandle, 1, color, 0);

        // Draw the triangle
        GLES20.glDrawArrays(GLES20.GL_TRIANGLES, 0, vertexCount);

        // Disable vertex array
        GLES20.glDisableVertexAttribArray(positionHandle);
    }
}
```

This class draws a color triangle using a vertex shader and a fragment shader. The color is defined in the class by the array color[] and its values are passed to the fragment shader via the uniform variable vColor, which is a **vec4** defined in the fragment shader. The coordinates of the vertices of the triangle are defined by the array triangleCoords[] and stored in the byte buffer vertexBuffer. These values are passed to the vertex shader via the attribute variable *vPosition*, which is a **vec4** defined in the vertex shader.

The strings *vsCode* and *fsCode* defines the vertex shader and the fragment shader respectively. If we remove the quotes and the operator + in defining the strings, we can see that the codes of our vertex shader and fragment shader are:

```
// Source code of vertex shader
attribute vec4 vPosition;
void main() {
    gl_Position = vPosition;
}

// Source code of fragment shader
precision mediump float;
uniform vec4 vColor;
void main() {
    gl_FragColor = vColor;
}
```

Note that the keyword **precision** is used to specify the precision of any floating-point or integer-based variable. Keywords **lowp**, **mediump**, and **highp** are used to specifiy low, medium, and high precisions respectively.

8. Run the application by clicking *Run* > **Run** > **Android Application** > **OK**. We should see an output like the one shown in Figure 6-5, displaying a magneta triangle over a grey background. The color of the triangle is passed from the array variable *color* in the graphics application to the fragment shader **uniform** variable *vColor*, which sets the triangle color.

Figure 6-5   Output of Project *Glsl1*

Not all avd emulator configurations can run OpenGL ES 2.X. Figure 6-6 shows one of the avd configurations that we have used and works, which requires API level 16. It seems that for the emulator to work, a high screen resolution device needs to be chosen.

AVD Name:	avd-4.1.2
Device:	Nexus 7 (7.02", 1200 × 1920: xhdpi)
Target:	Android 4.1.2 - API Level 16
CPU/ABI:	ARM (armeabi-v7a)
Keyboard:	☑ Hardware keyboard present
Skin:	No skin
Front Camera:	None
Back Camera:	None
Memory Options:	RAM: 1024 VM Heap: 32
Internal Storage:	200 MiB
SD Card:	⦿ Size: 200 MiB
	○ File: Browse...
Emulation Options:	☐ Snapshot ☑ Use Host GPU

Figure 6-6 An avd Emulator Configuration That Runs ES 2.X

6.3.2 Shaders in Files

In the above example, we have hard-coded the shaders in the class *Triangle*. It will be difficult to comprehend the hard-coded code when the shaders become complex. A better way to write the shaders is to handle them separately, saving them in separate files; we then read the codes from the files as null-terminated strings, passing them as input parameters to the function **glShader-Source**(). We discuss this method here, repeating the above example except that we save the shaders in raw data format that we have discussed in Chapter 5.

Suppose we call the project of this example *GlslRaw* and we have created all the classes of the project *Glsl1* above and have added the *uses-features* element to the file *AndroidManifest.xml* to use ES 2.0. The following are the additional steps required to finish this project. Besides reading the shader codes from the raw files, the main difference from before is that we pass the context handle of the main activity to the rendering class so that the class can access the raw files.

1. Click **File > New > Folder**. Enter *GlslRaw/res* for parent folder and *raw* for folder name. Click **Finish** to create the directory *res/raw*.

2. Click on the folder *raw* in the Package Explorer. Then click **File > New > File**. Enter *vshader* to create the file *res/raw/vshader*, which will be our vertex shader program. Similarly, create another file, *res/raw/fshader*, which will be our fragment shader program.

3. Write *vshader* with the vertex shader code:

```
// Source code of vertex shader
attribute vec4 vPosition;
void main() {
  gl_Position = vPosition;
}
```

4. Write *fshader* with the fragment shader code:

```
// Source code of fragment shader
precision mediump float;
uniform vec4 vColor;
void main() {
  gl_FragColor = vColor;
}
```

5. The only change to the above file *MainActivity.java* is to pass the context to the renderer by modifying the **setRenderer** statement to:
   setRenderer(new MyRenderer (*context*));

6. The file *MyRenderer.java* is almost the same as above. We use a new constructor to save the context of the thread that creates the object and pass this context handle to the *Triangle* object to access the raw files:

```
public class MyRenderer implements GLSurfaceView.Renderer {
   private Triangle triangle;
   private Context context;

   public MyRenderer( Context context0 ) {
      context = context0;
   }

   public void onSurfaceCreated(GL10 unused, EGLConfig config) {
      // Set the background frame color
      GLES20.glClearColor(0.9f, 0.9f, 0.9f, 1.0f);
      // construct a triangle object
      triangle = new Triangle( context );
   }
   . . . . .
}
```

7. The main change to *Triangle.java* is to read the vertex and fragment shaders codes from the files *res/raw/vshader* and *res/raw/fshader* respectively. Other features remain the same as above:

```
public class Triangle
{
 private static String LOG_APP_TAG = "io_tag";
 private Context context;
 private String vsCode = null;
 private String fsCode = null;
 private int program;
 private int vertexShader;
 private int fragmentShader;
```

```
.....

// Constructor
Triangle( Context context0){
 context = context0;
 // get shader codes from res/raw/vshader and res/raw/fshader
 vsCode = getShaderCode( GLES20.GL_VERTEX_SHADER );
 fsCode = getShaderCode( GLES20.GL_FRAGMENT_SHADER );
 program = GLES20.glCreateProgram(); // create empty OpenGL ES Program

 vertexShader = loadShader(GLES20.GL_VERTEX_SHADER, vsCode );
 fragmentShader = loadShader(GLES20.GL_FRAGMENT_SHADER, fsCode );
 GLES20.glAttachShader ( program, vertexShader );
 GLES20.glAttachShader(program, fragmentShader);
 GLES20.glLinkProgram(program);
 GLES20.glUseProgram( program);
 .....
}

// get shader code from file
protected String getShaderCode( int type ) {
 InputStream inputStream = null;
 String str = null;
 try {
  if ( type == GLES20.GL_VERTEX_SHADER )
   inputStream=context.getResources().openRawResource(R.raw.vshader);
  else
   inputStream=context.getResources().openRawResource(R.raw.fshader);
   byte[] reader = new byte[inputStream.available()];;
   while (inputStream.read(reader) != -1) {}
   str = new String ( reader );
 } catch(IOException e) {
    Log.e(LOG_APP_TAG, e.getMessage());
 }
 return   str;
}
.....
}
```

When we run the application, we will get the same output as the previous example, which is shown in Figure 6-5.

From now on we will always put our shaders in the files *res/raw/vshader* and *res/raw/fshaer*.

6.3.3 Animation

We can easily do animation using glsl by passing a time parameter from the main OpenGL program to the shaders. The time parameter can be used to control the positions, orientations and other attributes of the graphics objects.

We consider a simple example where we display a color triangle expanding, shrinking, flipping and changing color. Suppose we call this project *GlslAnimate*, and have created or modified all the files used in the above project *GlslRaw*, including *MainActivity.java, MyRenderer.java, Triangle.java, vshader, fshader*, and *AndroidManifest.xml* except that now our package name is *opengl.glslanimate*. We need to do some modifications to the files to accomplish animation:

1. The file *MainActivity.java* is the same as before; we do not need to make any modification besides changing the package name.

2. For *MyRenderer*, we need to pass the elapsed time between rendering frames to the vertex shader to animate any desired motion. We use the method **elapsedRealtime**() of the class *SystemClock* discussed in Chapter 4 to obtain the time. This method returns a **long** that represents the time in milliseconds since the bootup of the device. We subtract this time value from the value when the *GLSurfaceView* is created and pass the difference to the *draw* method of the *Triangle* class, which in turn passes it to the vertex shader. The following is the complete code for this class:

```
// MyRenderer.java
package opengl.glslanimate;

import android.content.Context;
import android.os.SystemClock;
import android.opengl.GLES20;
import android.opengl.GLSurfaceView;
import javax.microedition.khronos.egl.EGLConfig;
import javax.microedition.khronos.opengles.GL10;

public class MyRenderer implements GLSurfaceView.Renderer {
  private Triangle triangle;
  private Context context;
  private long t0;

  public MyRenderer( Context context0 ) {
    context = context0;
  }

  public void onSurfaceCreated(GL10 unused, EGLConfig config) {
    // Set the background frame color
    GLES20.glClearColor(0.9f, 0.9f, 0.9f, 1.0f);
    // construct a triangle object
    triangle = new Triangle( context );
    t0 = SystemClock.elapsedRealtime();   //initial time
  }

  public void onDrawFrame ( GL10 unused ) {
    // Redraw background color
    GLES20.glClear(GLES20.GL_COLOR_BUFFER_BIT);
    SystemClock.sleep ( 100 );  // delay 0.1 s
    long t = SystemClock.elapsedRealtime() - t0;
    triangle.draw( t );
  }

  public void onSurfaceChanged(GL10 unused,int width,int height) {
    GLES20.glViewport(0, 0, width, height);
  }
}
```

3. For the *Triangle* class, only the **draw** method has been added the variable *deltaTHandle* to pass the elapsed time value to the vertex shader. The following is the new **draw** method: small

```
public class Triangle
{
 .....
 public void draw( long t ) {
  // Add program to OpenGL ES environment
  GLES20.glUseProgram(program);

  // get handle to vertex shader's vPosition member
  int positionHandle = GLES20.glGetAttribLocation(program,
                                                 "vPosition");
  // Enable a handle to the triangle vertices
  GLES20.glEnableVertexAttribArray( positionHandle);

  // Prepare the triangle coordinate data
  int vertexStride = 0;
  GLES20.glVertexAttribPointer(positionHandle,COORDS_PER_VERTEX,
          GLES20.GL_FLOAT, false, vertexStride, vertexBuffer);
  // get handle to fragment shader's vColor member
  int colorHandle=GLES20.glGetUniformLocation(program,"vColor");
  // get handle to vertex shader's uniform variable deltaT
  int deltaTHandle=GLES20.glGetUniformLocation(program,"deltaT");
  // Set color for drawing the triangle
  GLES20.glUniform4fv(colorHandle, 1, color, 0);
  // set value for deltaT of vertex shader
  GLES20.glUniform1f( deltaTHandle, (float) t );
  // Draw the triangle
  GLES20.glDrawArrays(GLES20.GL_TRIANGLES, 0, vertexCount);

  // Disable vertex array
  GLES20.glDisableVertexAttribArray(positionHandle);
 }
}
```

4. The vertex shader in *res/raw/vshader* receives the value of the uniform variable *deltaT* from the **draw** method of the *Triangle* class of the application. It makes use of the *sin* function to obtain a multiplication factor s that changes between -1 and 1. This factor is multiplied to the vertex positions of the triangle and thus the triangle expands and shrinks according to the value of s. When s changes sign (e.g from positive to negative), the triangle flips over. It is defined as a global **varying** variable, so that its value can be passed to the fragment shader for other uses. The following is the complete code of the vertex shader:

```
// vshader
precision mediump float;
uniform float deltaT;     //value from application program
attribute vec4 vPosition; //value from application program
varying float s;          //value also used in fragment shader
void main(void)
{
   s =  sin ( 0.001 * deltaT );  // scaling factor
   vec4 vPosition1 = vPosition * vec4 ( s, s, s, 1.0 );
   gl_Position = gl_ModelViewProjectionMatrix * vPosition1;
}
```

As *s* changes sinusoidally, the **vec4** variable *vPosition1* that defines the final vertex positions also changes. This *s* value is also passed to the fragment shader to define the drawing color.

5. The fragment shader *fshader* takes the value of the varying variable *s* calculated in the vertex shader. It changes the color of the triangle from cyan to magenta when *s* changes from positive to negative and vice versa. The complete code is shown below:

```
// fshader
 precision mediump float;
 varying float s;
 void main(void)
 {
   if ( s > 0 )
     gl_FragColor = vec4( 0, 1, 1, 1);
   else
     gl_FragColor = vec4( 1, 0, 1, 1);
 }
```

Figure 6-7 shows two frames of the output.

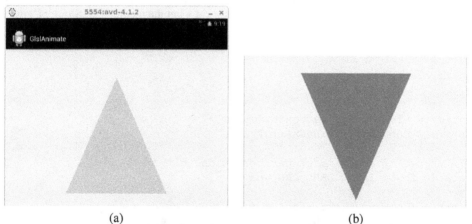

(a)   (b)
Figure 6-7   Two Sample Frames of Animated Triangle

6.3.4   Drawing a Square

We have discussed in Chapter 4 that OpenGL ES polygon drawing primitives only support the drawing of triangles. To draw any other kind of polygon, we have to decompose the polygon into triangles. This is true even if we use shaders to draw the polygon. As an example, suppose we want to draw a square like the one shown in Figure 6-8 below.

To draw the square, we first draw the triangle $v_0 v_1 v_3$ and then draw $v_3 v_1 v_2$, ordering the vertices in a counter-clockwise direction. We will use the function **glDrawElements**() to perform this task. All we need to do is to supply the vertex coordinates and an array that contains the vertex indices.

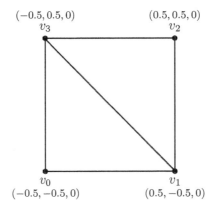

$$\text{Square } v_0v_1v_2v_3 = \triangle v_0v_1v_3 + \triangle v_3v_1v_2$$

Figure 6-8. A Square Consisting of Two Triangles

Suppose we name the project that draws the square of Figure 6-8 *GlslSquare*. The files needed are almost the same as those of the project *GlslRaw* except that we replace the *Triangle* class by the *Square* class. The following is the code of the *Square* class but the methods **getShaderCode**() and **loadShader**(), and some data members are not listed as they are identical to that of the *Triangle* class discussed above.

```
public class Square
{
    .....
    private FloatBuffer vertexBuffer;
    private ShortBuffer indexArray;

    // number of coordinates per vertex in this array
    static final int COORDS_PER_VERTEX = 3;

    static float squareCoords[] = {
            -0.5f, -0.5f, 0.0f, // v0 - bottom left
             0.5f, -0.5f, 0.0f, // v1 - bottom right
            -0.5f,  0.5f, 0.0f, // v2 - top left
             0.5f,  0.5f, 0.0f  // v3 - top right
    };

    // draw in the order v0, v1, v2, v2, v1, v3
    private short drawOrder[] = { 0, 1, 2, 2, 1, 3 };
    float color[] = { 0.9f, 0.1f, 0.9f, 1.0f };

    // Constructor
    Square( Context context0){
      context = context0;

      // get shader codes from res/raw/vshader and res/raw/fshader
      vsCode = getShaderCode( GLES20.GL_VERTEX_SHADER );
      fsCode = getShaderCode( GLES20.GL_FRAGMENT_SHADER );
      program = GLES20.glCreateProgram();

      vertexShader = loadShader (GLES20.GL_VERTEX_SHADER, vsCode );
      fragmentShader = loadShader (GLES20.GL_FRAGMENT_SHADER, fsCode );
```

```
GLES20.glAttachShader ( program, vertexShader );
GLES20.glAttachShader(program, fragmentShader);
GLES20.glLinkProgram(program);
GLES20.glUseProgram( program);

// initialize vertex byte buffer for shape coordinates
ByteBuffer bb = ByteBuffer.allocateDirect(
                    squareCoords.length * 4);
bb.order(ByteOrder.nativeOrder());
vertexBuffer = bb.asFloatBuffer();
vertexBuffer.put(squareCoords);
vertexBuffer.position(0);
// initialize byte buffer for the draw list
ByteBuffer bbOrder = ByteBuffer.allocateDirect(
                    drawOrder.length * 2);
bbOrder.order(ByteOrder.nativeOrder());
indexArray = bbOrder.asShortBuffer();
indexArray.put(drawOrder);
indexArray.position(0);
} // Square Constructor

public void draw () {
  // Add program to OpenGL ES environment
  GLES20.glUseProgram(program);

  int positionHandle = GLES20.glGetAttribLocation(program, "vPosition");
  GLES20.glEnableVertexAttribArray( positionHandle);

  int vertexStride = 0;
  GLES20.glVertexAttribPointer( positionHandle, COORDS_PER_VERTEX,
              GLES20.GL_FLOAT, false, vertexStride, vertexBuffer);

  int colorHandle = GLES20.glGetUniformLocation(program, "vColor");
  GLES20.glUniform4fv(colorHandle, 1, color, 0);
  // Draw the square
  GLES20.glDrawElements( GLES20.GL_TRIANGLES, drawOrder.length,
              GLES20.GL_UNSIGNED_SHORT, indexArray );

  // Disable vertex array
  GLES20.glDisableVertexAttribArray(positionHandle);
}
.....
}
```

In the code, *indexArray* contains the vertex indices specified by *drawOrder*, the *length* of which gives the total number of indices and is equal to 6 in the example, representing the two triangles that form the square. The method **glDrawElements**() draws these two triangles, connecting the vertices in the order given by *indexArray*.

Besides replacing the *Triangle* class by the *Square* class in *MyRenderer*, we adjust the display aspect ratio as we want to display a square on the rectangular Android screen. Also we want to display the square at the upper part of the screen. So we set the viewport in the method **onSurfaceChanged**:

```
public void onSurfaceChanged(GL10 unused, int width, int height) {
  float ratio = (float) width / height;
```

```
    GLES20.glViewport(0,  height/3, width,  (int) (height * ratio) );
}
```

The vertex shader and the fragment shader are the same as those for displaying a triangle:

```
// vshader: Source code of vertex shader
attribute vec4 vPosition;
void main() {
   gl_Position = vPosition;
}

// fshader: Source code of fragment shader
precision mediump float;
uniform vec4 vColor;
void main() {
    gl_FragColor = vColor;
}
```

Figure 6-9 below shows the output of this project.

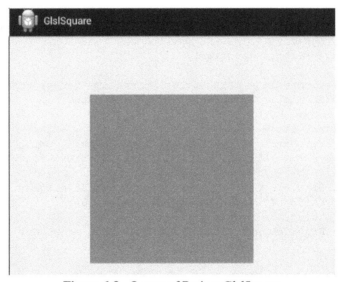

Figure 6-9 Output of Project *GlslSquare*

6.3.5 Drawing a Color Square

In the above example, we draw a square with a single color by passing the color through a **uniform** variable to the fragment shader. Suppose now we want to draw the square with a unique color at each vertex of the square. We cannot pass the colors directly to the fragment shader any more because we need to associate a color with a vertex. To accomplish this, we can pass a color value as a vertex attribute to the vertex shader, which then passes the color value to the color shader through a **varying** variable. The following are the shader codes:

```
// vshader
precision mediump float;
attribute vec4 vPosition;  // value from application program
attribute vec4 sourceColor;
varying vec4 vColor;        // value to be sent to fragment shader
```

```
void main(void)
{
  vColor = sourceColor;
  gl_Position = vPosition;
}

// fshader
varying vec4 vColor;

void main() {
  gl_FragColor = vColor;
}
```

We just need to make minor changes to the class *Square*. All we need to do is to define an array called *colors* to specify the RGBA color at each vertex of the square. We then treat the array *colors* in the way we do to the vertex coordinates array *vertexArray*. Each color is passed to the **varying** variable *sourceColor* of the vertex shader. The following is the modified portion of the code of *Square*:

```
public class Square
{
  .....
  private FloatBuffer vertexBuffer, colorBuffer;
  private ShortBuffer indexArray;

  static float squareCoords[] = {
    -0.5f, -0.5f, 0.0f,  // v0 - bottom left
     0.5f, -0.5f, 0.0f,  // v1 - bottom right
    -0.5f,  0.5f, 0.0f,  // v2 - top left
     0.5f,  0.5f, 0.0f   // v3 - top right
  };

  static float colors[] = {
    1.0f, 0.0f, 0.0f, 1.0f,   // v0 red
    0.0f, 1.0f, 0.0f, 1.0f,   // v1 green
    0.0f, 0.0f, 1.0f, 1.0f,   // v2 blue
    1.0f, 1.0f, 0.0f, 1.0f    // v3 yellow
  };
  private short drawOrder[] = { 0, 1, 2, 2, 1, 3 };

  // Constructor
  Square( Context context0){
    .....
    // initialize vertex byte buffer for shape coordinates
    ByteBuffer bb = ByteBuffer.allocateDirect(squareCoords.length * 4);
    bb.order(ByteOrder.nativeOrder());
    // do the same for colors
    ByteBuffer bbc = ByteBuffer.allocateDirect( colors.length * 4 );
    bbc.order(ByteOrder.nativeOrder());
    // create a floating point buffer from the ByteBuffer
    vertexBuffer = bb.asFloatBuffer();
    // add the coordinates to the FloatBuffer
    vertexBuffer.put(squareCoords);
    // set the buffer to read the first coordinate
```

```
      vertexBuffer.position(0);

      // do the same for colors
      colorBuffer = bbc.asFloatBuffer();
      colorBuffer.put( colors );
      colorBuffer.position(0);

      // initialize byte buffer for the draw list
      ByteBuffer bbOrder = ByteBuffer.allocateDirect(drawOrder.length * 2);
      bbOrder.order(ByteOrder.nativeOrder());
      indexArray = bbOrder.asShortBuffer();
      indexArray.put(drawOrder);
      indexArray.position(0);
   } // Square Constructor

 public void draw() {
      // Add program to OpenGL ES environment
      GLES20.glUseProgram(program);

      // get handle to vertex shader's vPosition and sourceColor
      int positionHandle=GLES20.glGetAttribLocation(program,"vPosition");
      int colorHandle=GLES20.glGetAttribLocation(program,"sourceColor");

      GLES20.glEnableVertexAttribArray( positionHandle );
      GLES20.glEnableVertexAttribArray( colorHandle );
      GLES20.glVertexAttribPointer( positionHandle, 3,
           GLES20.GL_FLOAT, false, 0, vertexBuffer);
      GLES20.glVertexAttribPointer ( colorHandle, 4,
            GLES20.GL_FLOAT, false, 0, colorBuffer);
       // Draw the square
       GLES20.glDrawElements( GLES20.GL_TRIANGLES, drawOrder.length,
                    GLES20.GL_UNSIGNED_SHORT, indexArray );

      // Disable vertex arrays
      GLES20.glDisableVertexAttribArray( positionHandle );
      GLES20.glDisableVertexAttribArray( colorHandle );
   }
   .....
 }
```

When we run the program, we will see a color square like the one shown in Figure 6-10 below.

6.3.6 Temperature Shaders

As an application to the above example, color square, we use colors to represent temperatures with red meaning hot and blue meaning cold. A warm temperature is a mixture of red and blue. We can imagine that the square is a metallic sheet with each corner connected to a heat or a cooling source. We can express smoothly the surface temperature as a mixture of red and blue. In the example, we assume that the lowest temperature is 0 and the highest is 50.

To accomplish this we pass the temperature value at each square vertex via the **attribute** array variable *vertexTemp* to the vertex shader. The shader normalizes it to a value between 0 and 1 before passing the value to the fragment shader via the **varying** variable *temperature*.

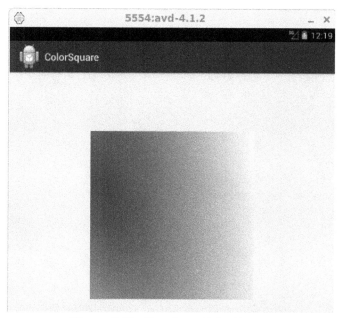

Figure 6-10   Drawing a Color Square

The following is the vertex shader code:

```
// vshader
precision mediump float;
attribute vec4 vPosition;    // value from application program
attribute float vertexTemp;  // from application program
varying float temperature;   // value to be sent to fragment shader

void main(void)
{
  // normalize temperature to  [0, 1]
  temperature = ( vertexTemp - 0 ) / 50;
  gl_Position = vPosition;
}
```

The application also passes the blue color that represents the coldest temperature and the red color that represents the hottest temperature to the fragment shader via the **uniform** variables *coldColor* and *hotColor* respectively. Knowing these two colors, the fragment shader gets the normalized temperature value from the vertex shader and calculates a color for it with use of the glsl built-in funciton **mix**:

```
// fshader
uniform vec3 coldColor;
uniform vec3 hotColor;
varying float temperature;   // from vshader, value in [0,1]
void main() {
  vec3 color = mix ( coldColor, hotColor, temperature );
  gl_FragColor = vec4 ( color, 1 );
}
```

The application just needs to define the data for those quantities and gets handles to the **attribute** and **uniform** variables of the shaders to pass the data to them. The following is the modified portion of the *Square* class that does the job:

```
public class Square
{
 .....
 private FloatBuffer vertexBuffer, vertexTempBuffer;
 private ShortBuffer indexArray;

 static float squareCoords[] = {
   -0.5f, -0.5f, 0.0f,  // v0 - bottom left
    0.5f, -0.5f, 0.0f,  // v1 - bottom right
   -0.5f, 0.5f,  0.0f,  // v2 - top left
    0.5f, 0.5f,  0.0f   // v3 - top right
 };
 // Temperature at each vertex
 static float vertexTemp[] = {
    5.0f,              // v0 cold
   12.0f,              // v1 cool
   22.0f,              // v2 warm
   40.0f               // v3 hot (upper right)
 };

  private short drawOrder[] = { 0, 1, 2, 2, 1, 3 };

  // Constructor
 Square( Context context0){
   .....
   // initialize vertex byte buffer for square coordinates
   ByteBuffer bb = ByteBuffer.allocateDirect(squareCoords.length * 4);
   bb.order(ByteOrder.nativeOrder());
   // do the for vertexTemp
   ByteBuffer bbc = ByteBuffer.allocateDirect( vertexTemp.length * 4 );
   bbc.order(ByteOrder.nativeOrder());

   vertexBuffer = bb.asFloatBuffer();
   vertexBuffer.put(squareCoords);
   vertexBuffer.position(0);

   vertexTempBuffer = bbc.asFloatBuffer();
   vertexTempBuffer.put( vertexTemp );
   vertexTempBuffer.position(0);

   // initialize byte buffer for the draw list
   ByteBuffer bbOrder = ByteBuffer.allocateDirect(drawOrder.length * 2);
   bbOrder.order(ByteOrder.nativeOrder());
   indexArray = bbOrder.asShortBuffer();
   indexArray.put(drawOrder);
   indexArray.position(0);

 } // Square Constructor

 public void draw() {
   // Add program to OpenGL ES environment
   GLES20.glUseProgram(program);

   // get handle to vertex shader's vPosition, vertexTemp, ....
   int positionHandle = GLES20.glGetAttribLocation(program,"vPosition");
```

```
int vertexTempHandle=GLES20.glGetAttribLocation(program,"vertexTemp");
int coldColorHandle =GLES20.glGetUniformLocation(program,"coldColor");
int  hotColorHandle = GLES20.glGetUniformLocation(program,"hotColor");
GLES20.glUniform3f (coldColorHandle, 0.0f, 0.0f, 1.0f);// blue = cold
GLES20.glUniform3f (hotColorHandle, 1.0f, 0.0f, 0.0f); // red = hot

GLES20.glEnableVertexAttribArray( positionHandle );
GLES20.glEnableVertexAttribArray( vertexTempHandle );
GLES20.glVertexAttribPointer( positionHandle, 3,
      GLES20.GL_FLOAT, false, 0, vertexBuffer);
// pass temperature at each vertex to vertex shader
GLES20.glVertexAttribPointer ( vertexTempHandle, 1,
      GLES20.GL_FLOAT, false, 0, vertexTempBuffer);
 // Draw the square
 GLES20.glDrawElements ( GLES20.GL_TRIANGLES, drawOrder.length,
          GLES20.GL_UNSIGNED_SHORT, indexArray );
 // Disable vertex arrays
 GLES20.glDisableVertexAttribArray( positionHandle );
 GLES20.glDisableVertexAttribArray( vertexTempHandle );
}
. . . . .
}
```

Figure 6-11 below shows the output of this example.

Figure 6-11   Output of Temperature Shaders

6.4 Drawing 3D Objects

6.4.1 Introduction

So far the rendering objects we have considered are two dimensional. If we want to render 3D objects, we need to define a 3D viewing volume, which is referred to as a frustum. Figure 6-12 below shows a typical setup of such a view-frustum, which is bounded by a near plane at $z = -n$, and a far plane at $z = -f$. In the figure, the point O is the origin of the coordinate system, and is the observation point (i.e. location of the camera or eye). The observer looks along the negative $z-$axis. So the near plane is at a distance of n from O and the far plane is f from O. The notations l, r, b, and t denote left, right, bottom and top respectively. So the left boundary of the near plane is at $x = l$, and the right boundary at $x = r$. The bottom and top boundaries of the near plane are at $y = b$ and $y = t$ respectively. Ultimately, all 3D objects inside the frustum are projected onto the near plane, which is viewed by an observer at point O.

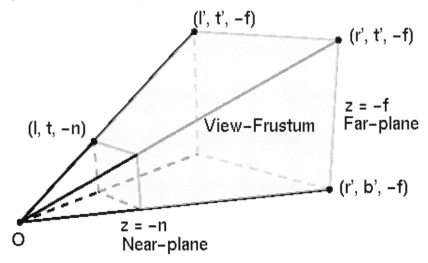

Figure 6-12 Frustum-shaped Viewing Volume

In 3D graphics, both a point and an Euclidean vector can be represented by a 3-tuple (x, y, z). Though they have the same representation and appear to be the same, a point and a vector are different elements. A point represents a location; it does not have any direction or magnitude. On the other hand, a vector indicates a direction but does not specify any location; a vector also has a magnitude (length). For convenience, people use homogeneous coordinates to represent both a vector and a point by introducing the fourth coordinate w:

$$A = \begin{pmatrix} x \\ y \\ z \\ w \end{pmatrix} \tag{6.1}$$

In (6.1), A is a vector when $w = 0$, and is a point when $w = 1$. This is consistent with our common intuition about points and vectors. When we add a vector to another vector, we get a new vector as the sum of the w components, which are 0, is 0. When we add a point ($w = 1$) to a vector ($w = 0$), we get a point as the sum of the w components, 0 and 1, is 1. In summary we have,

```
vector + vector    = vector
vector - vector    = vector
vector + point     = point
vector - point     = invalid
point  - vector    = point
point  - point     = vector
point  + point     = invalid
constant x vector  = vector
```

We can form a linear combination of points:

$$A = c_1 P_1 + c_2 P_2 + ... + c_n P_n \tag{6.2}$$

where P_i denotes a point and c_i is a coefficient constant. Whether the result A is a valid point or not depends on the sum of the coefficients

$$S = c_1 + c_2 + ... + c_n \tag{6.3}$$

If $S = 0$, A is a vector. If $S = 1$, A is a valid point and (6.2) is referred to as an affine combination of points. Otherwise A is invalid. Conversely, an Euclidean vector can always be expressed as a linear combination of points.

As a point is represented by a 4×1 matrix as shown in Equation (6.1), any transformation operation on it, such as a rotation, a translation or a scaling, can represented by a 4×4 matrix. For example, if M is a 4×4 matrix, and P and Q are points, the equation $Q = MP$ represents that the point P is transformed to the point Q under the transformation matrix M. We may also write this explicitly as

$$Q = \begin{pmatrix} x' \\ y' \\ z' \\ 1 \end{pmatrix} = MP = \begin{pmatrix} m_{00} & m_{01} & m_{02} & m_{03} \\ m_{10} & m_{11} & m_{12} & m_{13} \\ m_{20} & m_{21} & m_{22} & m_{23} \\ m_{30} & m_{31} & m_{32} & m_{33} \end{pmatrix} \begin{pmatrix} x \\ y \\ z \\ 1 \end{pmatrix} \tag{6.4}$$

Transformations such as translations, rotations, and scalings that change the view of a 3D object are referred to as model-view transformations. These transformation are reversible. For example, we rotate a point about the $z-$axis by 30° to get to a new location. We can go back to the original position by rotating the new point about the $z-$axis in the opposite direction by 30°.

At the end, a 3D point is projected on to the near-plane screen, which is two dimensional; this is called projection transformation. In principle, such a transformation is not reversible as going from 3D to 2D will lose information in the process. However, to make a transformation matrix of projection compatible with that of model-view, people have expressed the projection matrix in a way that it is reversible (i.e., its inverse exists). The trick is to store the depth component (the z value) in a separate buffer and handle it separately. The z component recovered by the inverse of the project matrix will be discarded. So in OpenGL, all transformation matrices are 4×4.

In OpenGL ES 2.0, we need to pass the 4×4 matrix M to the vertex shader to perform the 3D transformation. In declaring a variable, we usually use *mv* to refer to **model-view** and *mvp* to refer to **model-view projection**.

6.4.2 Drawing a Tetrahedron

A tetrahedron is composed of four triangular faces, three of which meet at each vertex and thus it has four vertices. It may be the simplest kind of 3D objects.

A tetrahedron can be considered as a pyramid, which is a polyhedron with a flat polygon base and triangular faces connecting the base to a common point. A tetrahedron simply has a triangular base, so a tetrahedron is also known as a **triangular pyramid**.

A **regular tetrahedron** is one in which all four faces are equilateral triangles. The vertices coordinates of a regular tetrahedron with edge length 2 centered at the origin are

$$(1, 0, \frac{-1}{\sqrt{2}}), \quad (-1, 0, \frac{-1}{\sqrt{2}}), \quad (0, 1, \frac{1}{\sqrt{2}}), \quad (0, -1, \frac{1}{\sqrt{2}}) \tag{6.5}$$

We illustrate many basic techniques of drawing 3D objects with OpenGL ES 2.0 through an example of drawing a regular tetrahedron. One main feature is to pass the resulted 4×4 model-view projection matrix to the vertex shader. The matrix transforms a point accordingly and projects it onto a 2D plane.

Suppose we call our project and application *Tetrahedron*. The structure of our project is the same as those discussed above, where the shaders are saved in the files *res/raw/vshader*, and *res/raw/fshader*. Just like before, we have three classes, *MainActivity*, *MyRenderer*, and *Tetrahderon*. The class *MainActivity* is the same as what we have used above .

MyRenderer

The main change to the class *MyRenderer* is that we need to define our viewing environment and caculates the model-view projection transformation matrix, which will be passed to the vertex shader for displaying the vertices of the 3D object properly.

We calculate the data for a projection transformation in the **onSurfaceChanged**() method. This is done using the method **frustumM** of the class *Matrix*, which stores 4×4 matrices in column-major order. The method has prototype,

```
public static void frustumM (float[] m, int offset, float left,
        float right, float bottom, float top, float near, float far)
```

The method defines a viewing frustum as shown in Figure 6-12 above. The second parameter, *offset*, is the offset into float array *m* where the projection matrix data are written. The parameters, *left*, *right*, *bottom*, and *top* define the boundaries of the near-plane, *near* and *far* are the distances from the observation point (*O* in Figure 6-12) to the near-plane and the far-plane respectively. Based on these parameters, OpenGL ES calculates a 4×4 matrix and saves it in the array *m*, the first parameter of the method.

The following is what we use in our *tetrahedron* example,

```
Matrix.frustumM( projectionMatrix, 0, -1, 1, -1, 1, 2, 10);
```

Projecting a 3D object on a plane is like taking a photo of the object. How the 3D object appears on the projection screen depends on the way the camera views the 3D object. We can define the camera view transformation using the **setLookAtM**() method of the class *Matrix*. The method calculates a 4×4 matrix for a specified setup. It has the following prototype:

```
public static void setLookAtM (float[] m, int offset, float eyeX,
        float eyeY, float eyeZ, float centerX, float centerY,
        float centerZ, float upX, float upY, float upZ)
```

The point $(eyeX, eyeY, eyeZ)$ specifies the location of the observation point (eye), and the point (*centerX, centerY, centerZ*) is the view center, the point at which the viewer is looking at. The vector (*upX, upY, upZ*) denotes the up direction of the camera. The method calculates the 4×4 viewing matrix and writes it to the array *m*.

After we have obtained the projection matrix and the viewing matrix, we can multiply them together to form a single matrix, which can be passed to the vertex shader to draw the object. The multiplication can be done by the *Matrix* method **multiplyMM**:

```
public static void multiplyMM (float[] result, int resultOffset,
        float[] lhs, int lhsOffset, float[] rhs, int rhsOffset)
```

The array *lhs* holds the 4×4 left-hand side matrix while *rhs* holds the right-hand side matrix. The product of these two matrices is saved in the array *result*. The offset parameters are offsets into the arrays where data are read or written. The following is the code for the class *MyRenderer* of our example:

```
public class MyRenderer implements GLSurfaceView.Renderer
{
  private final float[] mvpMatrix = new float[16];
  private final float[] projectionMatrix = new float[16];
  private final float[] viewMatrix = new float[16];
  private Tetrahedron tetrahedron;
  private Context context;

  public MyRenderer( Context context0 ) {
```

```
      context = context0;
  }
  public void onSurfaceCreated(GL10 unused, EGLConfig config) {
    // Set the background frame color
    GLES20.glClearColor(0.9f, 0.9f, 0.9f, 1.0f);
    // construct a tetrahedron object
    tetrahedron = new Tetrahedron ( context );
  }
  public void onDrawFrame ( GL10 unused ) {
    // Redraw background color
    GLES20.glClear( GLES20.GL_COLOR_BUFFER_BIT );
    // Set the camera position (View matrix)
    Matrix.setLookAtM(viewMatrix,0,0.5f,0,4,0f,0f,0f,0f,1.0f,0.0f);

    // Calculate the product of projection and view transformation
    Matrix.multiplyMM(mvpMatrix,0,projectionMatrix,0,viewMatrix, 0);
    //Draw tetrahedron with resulted model-view projection matrix
    tetrahedron.draw( mvpMatrix );
  }

  public void onSurfaceChanged(GL10 unused, int width, int height) {
    GLES20.glViewport(0,  0, width,   width  );
    Matrix.frustumM( projectionMatrix, 0, -1, 1, -1, 1, 2, 10);
  }
}
```

In the code, the **setLookAtM**() method, has set the viewing point to $(0.5, 0, 4)$ and the view center to $(0, 0, 0)$. The up-vector is $(0, 1, 0)$. This means that the observer is at the x-z plane, looking at the origin mostly along the negative z direction. The y axis is pointing in the up direction. The final model-view projection matrix is held in the array variable *mvpMatrix*, which is passed to the **draw** method of the *Tetrahedron* class, which in turn passes it to the vertex shader.

Tetrahedron

In our project, the *Tetrahedron* class is similar to the *Square* class we discussed in previous sections. However, for simplicity and clarity, we draw the tetrahedron using line strips rather than triangles. The following is a portion of the code of *Tetrahedron* modified from *Square*:

```
public class Tetrahedron
{
  .....
  // vertices coordinates of tetrahedron
  static float tetraCoords[] = {
     1, 0, -0.707f,  -1, 0, -0.707f,
     0, 1,  0.707f,   0, -1, 0.707f
  };
  // Order of indices of drawing the tetrahedron
  private short drawOrder[] = { 0, 1, 2, 0, 3, 1, 2, 3 };
  float color[] = { 0.9f, 0.1f, 0.9f, 1.0f };

  // Constructor
  Tetrahedron( Context context0){
    context = context0;
    // get shader codes from res/raw/vshader and res/raw/fshader
```

```
    vsCode = getShaderCode( GLES20.GL_VERTEX_SHADER );
    fsCode = getShaderCode( GLES20.GL_FRAGMENT_SHADER );
    .....
    ByteBuffer bb = ByteBuffer.allocateDirect(tetraCoords.length * 4);
    bb.order(ByteOrder.nativeOrder());
    vertexBuffer = bb.asFloatBuffer();
    vertexBuffer.put(tetraCoords);
    vertexBuffer.position(0);
    // initialize byte buffer for the draw list
    //  with # of coordinate values * 2 bytes per short
    ByteBuffer bbDrawOrder=ByteBuffer.allocateDirect(drawOrder.length*2);
    bbDrawOrder.order(ByteOrder.nativeOrder());
    indexArray = bbDrawOrder.asShortBuffer();
    indexArray.put(drawOrder);
    indexArray.position(0);
  } // Tetrahedron Constructor

public void draw( float[] mvpMatrix ) {
    // Add program to OpenGL ES environment
    GLES20.glUseProgram(program);
    // get handle to shape's transformation matrix i shader
    int mvpMatrixHandle =
              GLES20.glGetUniformLocation( program, "mvpMatrix");
    // Pass model-view projection transformation matrix to the shader
    GLES20.glUniformMatrix4fv(mvpMatrixHandle,1,false,mvpMatrix,0);
    // get handle to vertex shader's vPosition member
    int positionHandle = GLES20.glGetAttribLocation(program,"vPosition");
    // Enable a handle to the triangle vertices
    GLES20.glEnableVertexAttribArray( positionHandle);

    // Prepare the triangles coordinate data
    int vertexStride = 0;
    GLES20.glVertexAttribPointer( positionHandle, COORDS_PER_VERTEX,
            GLES20.GL_FLOAT,false,vertexStride,vertexBuffer);

    // get handle to fragment shader's vColor member
    int colorHandle = GLES20.glGetUniformLocation(program, "vColor");
    // Set color for drawing the triangle
    GLES20.glUniform4fv(colorHandle, 1, color, 0);
    // Draw the tetrahedron using lines
    GLES20.glLineWidth(5);
    GLES20.glDrawElements( GLES20.GL_LINE_STRIP, drawOrder.length,
                          GLES20.GL_UNSIGNED_SHORT, indexArray );
     // Disable vertex array
     GLES20.glDisableVertexAttribArray(positionHandle);
  }
  .....
  }
```

Shaders

The fragment shader is the same as before. It simply set the fragment color to the vertex color pass from the application:

```
uniform vec4 vColor;
```

```
void main() {
    gl_FragColor = vColor;
}
```

The vertex shader is almost as simple except that now it has to multiply the vertex positions with the model-view projection matrix passed from the application:

```
// Source code of vertex shader
uniform mat4 mvpMatrix;
attribute vec4 vPosition;
void main() {
    gl_Position = mvpMatrix * vPosition;
}
```

Figure 6-13 shows the program's output, which is a tetrahedron drawn with line strips.

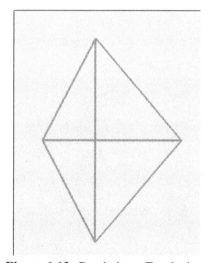

Figure 6-13   Rendering a Tetrahedron

6.4.3   Rotating a Color Tetrahedron

So far the tetrahedron we have drawn is a wireframe, without any actual face. Here, we discuss drawing a solid tetrahedron, each face having a different color. Moreover, we will rotate the tetrahedron by dragging the mouse.

Suppose we call this project and application *Tetrahedron1*. We use the same three java files, *MainActivity.java*, *MyRenderer.java* and *Tetrahedron.java* that we have used in the previous sections but with some modifications.

MyRenderer

To rotate a 3D object, one can use the **setRotateM** or **rotateM** method of the class *Matrix*, which rotates the object for a given angle around a specified axis. We use **rotateM** to rotate the tetrahedron, which is performed in the method **onDrawFrame** of the class *MyRenderer*:

```
Matrix.setLookAtM(viewMatrix,0,0.5f,0.5f,5,0f,0f,0f,0f,1f,0.0f);
Matrix.rotateM (rvMatrix, 0, viewMatrix, 0, angle, 1f, 0.2f, 0.2f);
```

Here, the **setLooAtM** method sets the viewing matrix *viewMatrix* as before with the observation point at $(0.5, 0.5, 5)$, looking towards the origin and the up direction is $(0, 1, 0)$, which is along the y-axis. The second and third parameters are offset indices of the result matrix (*rvMatrix*) and the source matrix (*viewMatrix*); both offsets are 0 in the example. The **rotateM** method calculates the matrix that rotates an object around the axis $(1, 0.2, 0.2)$ for an angle specified by the variable *angle*. (Note that the axis in the example has a dominant x component. The rotation is almost like one rotating around the x-axis.) This matrix is multiplied to *viewMatrix* and the result is saved in *rvMatrix*, which is our model-view matrix. This matrix is multiplied to the projection matrix to form the model-view projection matrix *mvpMatrix*, which is eventually used by the vertex shader to render the vertices of the object:

```
Matrix.multiplyMM(mvpMatrix, 0, projectionMatrix, 0, rvMatrix, 0);
tetrahedron.draw( mvpMatrix );
```

To draw a solid tetrahedron, we need to enable the depth-test and cull the back faces, which are facing the interior of the object. In our example, we set front facging to counter-clockwise. The following is the code for the modified *MyRenderer* that does the face culling and rotation:

```
public class MyRenderer implements GLSurfaceView.Renderer
{
.....
// view matrix with rotation
private final float[] rvMatrix = new float[16];
private float angle = 0;    // angle of rotation
.....
public void onSurfaceCreated(GL10 unused, EGLConfig config) {
   // Set the background frame color
   GLES20.glClearColor(0.9f, 0.9f, 0.9f, 1.0f);
   // Cull back faces
   GLES20.glEnable(GLES20.GL_CULL_FACE);
   GLES20.glCullFace(GLES20.GL_BACK);
   // Set front-facing to be counter-clockwise
   GLES20.glFrontFace(GLES20.GL_CCW);

   GLES20.glEnable ( GLES20.GL_DEPTH_TEST );
   //larger z values are nearer to viewpoint
   GLES20.glDepthFunc(GLES20.GL_GREATER);
   // Construct a Tetrahedron object
   tetrahedron = new Tetrahedron ( context );
}

public void onDrawFrame ( GL10 unused ) {
   // Redraw background color, clear depth buffer
   GLES20.glClear(GLES20.GL_COLOR_BUFFER_BIT|GLES20.GL_DEPTH_BUFFER_BIT);
   // Set the camera position (View matrix)
   Matrix.setLookAtM(viewMatrix,0,0.5f,0.5f,5,0f,0f,0f,0f,1f,0.0f);
   // Multiply view matrix by rotation matrix, result in rvMatrix
   Matrix.rotateM (rvMatrix,0,viewMatrix,0,angle,1f,0.2f,0.2f);
   // Calculate the projection and view transformation
   Matrix.multiplyMM(mvpMatrix,0,projectionMatrix, 0,rvMatrix,0);
   // Draw the object with the transformation matrix
   tetrahedron.draw( mvpMatrix );
}

// Get and set angle of rotation
public float getAngle() {
    return angle;
}
```

```
public void setAngle(float angle0) {
    angle = angle0;
}
}
```

Tetrahedron

The class *Tetrahedron* is similar to that described in the previous section. It is responsible for reading, compiling, loading and running the shaders. Like before, we just need one array to store the coordinates of the four vertices of a tetrahedron; the vertices are shared by the four faces (triangles) of the tetrahedron. We can use a set of draw order to specify one face. For example, the set of indices $(0, 2, 3)$ means to draw the triangle $v_0 v_2 v_3$; these vertices must be arranged in a counter-clockwise direction when we look at the face from the outside of the object. As there are four faces, we need a total of four draw order lists. Moreover, we need four different colors, one for each face, and we have chosen the colors to be red, green, blue and yellow. We draw the face one at a time, using a different color and draw-order list. Each time we draw a face, the specified color is passed to the fragment shader uniform variable *vColor*. The following is the modified portion of the code of *Tetrahedron*..

```
public class Tetrahedron
{
    . . . . .
    private FloatBuffer vertexBuffer;
    private FloatBuffer colorBuffer[];
    private ShortBuffer indexArray[];
    // number of faces in object
    static final int N_FACES = 4;
    // coordinates of tetrahedron vertices
    static float tetraCoords[] = {
        1, 0, -0.707f,   // vertex v0
       -1, 0, -0.707f,   // v1
        0, 1,  0.707f,   // v2
        0, -1, 0.707f    // v3
    };

    // draw order of  each face
    private short drawOrders[][] = {
        {0, 1, 2},  {0, 2, 3},  {0, 3, 1},  {3, 2, 1}
    };

    // color for each face
    static float colors[][] = {
        {1.0f, 0.0f, 0.0f, 1.0f},    // v0,v1,v2 red
        {0.0f, 1.0f, 0.0f, 1.0f},    // 0, 2, 3 green
        {0.0f, 0.0f, 1.0f, 1.0f},    // 0, 3, 1 blue
        {1.0f, 1.0f, 0.0f, 1.0f}     // 3, 2, 1 yellow
    };

    // Constructor
    Tetrahedron( Context context0){
        . . . . .
        // alloocate memory to store tetrahedron vertices
        ByteBuffer bb = ByteBuffer.allocateDirect(tetraCoords.length * 4);
        bb.order(ByteOrder.nativeOrder());
        vertexBuffer = bb.asFloatBuffer();
```

```
      vertexBuffer.put(tetraCoords);
      vertexBuffer.position(0);
      // do the same for colors
      colorBuffer = new FloatBuffer[N_FACES]; // a color for each face
      indexArray = new ShortBuffer[N_FACES];   // N_FACES triangles
      for ( int i = 0; i < N_FACES; i++) {
        ByteBuffer bbc = ByteBuffer.allocateDirect(colors[i].length*4);
        bbc.order(ByteOrder.nativeOrder());
        colorBuffer[i] = bbc.asFloatBuffer();
        colorBuffer[i].put( colors[i] );
        colorBuffer[i].position(0);

        // initialize byte buffer for each face, 2 bytes per short
        ByteBuffer bbDrawOrder =
               ByteBuffer.allocateDirect( drawOrders[i].length * 2);
        bbDrawOrder.order(ByteOrder.nativeOrder());
        indexArray[i] = bbDrawOrder.asShortBuffer();
        indexArray[i].put(drawOrders[i]);
        indexArray[i].position(0);
      }
  } // Tetrahedron Constructor

  public void draw( float[] mvpMatrix ) {
      // get handle to shape's transformation matrix
      int mvpMatrixHandle=GLES20.glGetUniformLocation(program,"mvpMatrix");
      // Pass the projection and view transformation to the shader
      GLES20.glUniformMatrix4fv(mvpMatrixHandle,1,false,mvpMatrix,0);
      // Draw one face at a time
      for ( int i = 0; i < N_FACES; i++){
        // get handles to shaders' vPosition and  vColor member
        int positionHandle=GLES20.glGetAttribLocation(program,"vPosition");
        int colorHandle = GLES20.glGetUniformLocation(program, "vColor");
        // Enable a handle to the triangle vertices
        GLES20.glEnableVertexAttribArray( positionHandle);
        //  GLES20.glEnableVertexAttribArray( colorHandle );

        // Prepare the triangle coordinate and color data
        int vertexStride = 0;
        GLES20.glUniform4fv(colorHandle, 1, colors[i], 0);
        GLES20.glVertexAttribPointer(positionHandle, COORDS_PER_VERTEX,
                   GLES20.GL_FLOAT, false, vertexStride, vertexBuffer);
        GLES20.glDrawElements(GLES20.GL_TRIANGLES,drawOrders[i].length,
                         GLES20.GL_UNSIGNED_SHORT, indexArray[i] );
        GLES20.glDisableVertexAttribArray(positionHandle);
      }
  }
  .....
}
```

MyGLSurfaceView

Like before, this class, *MyGLSurfaceView*, is part of the program file *MainActivity.java*. It is responsible for responding to touch events.

In order to make an OpenGL ES application respond to touch events, we have to implement the **onTouchEvent**() method in the *GLSurfaceView* class. We follow the example presented in the Android developers web site to do our implementation, which listens for **Motion-Event.ACTION_MOVE** events and translates them to an angle of rotation for an object. The following is the code of this class that handles touch events:

```
class MyGLSurfaceView extends GLSurfaceView
{
  private final MyRenderer renderer;

  public MyGLSurfaceView(Context context){
    super(context);
    // Create an OpenGL ES 2.0 context
    setEGLContextClientVersion ( 2 );

    // Set the Renderer for drawing on the GLSurfaceView
    renderer = new MyRenderer ( context );
    setRenderer( renderer );
    // Render the view only when there is a change in the drawing data
    setRenderMode(GLSurfaceView.RENDERMODE_WHEN_DIRTY);
  }

  private final float TOUCH_SCALE_FACTOR = 180.0f / 320;
  private float previousX, previousY;

  @Override
  public boolean onTouchEvent(MotionEvent e) {
    // MotionEvent reports input details from the touch screen
    // and other input controls. Here we are only interested
    // in events where the touch position has changed.
    float x = e.getX();
    float y = e.getY();
    switch (e.getAction()) {
      case MotionEvent.ACTION_MOVE:
        float dx = x - previousX;
        float dy = y - previousY;

        // reverse direction of rotation above the mid-line
        if (y > getHeight() / 2)
          dx = dx * -1 ;
        // reverse direction of rotation to left of the mid-line
        if (x < getWidth() / 2)
          dy = dy * -1 ;

        renderer.setAngle( renderer.getAngle() +
            ((dx + dy ) * TOUCH_SCALE_FACTOR));  // = 180.0f / 320
        requestRender();
    }
    previousX = x;
    previousY = y;
    return true;
  }
}
```

Note that in the code above, after calculating the rotation angle, it calls **requestRender**() to inform the renderer to render the frame. Such an approach is the most efficient in this example because we do not need to redraw a frame unless the rotation angle has been changed. However, this will take effect only if we also request that the renderer redraws only when the data changes. This can be done by setting the render mode to RENDERMODE_WHEN_DIRTY using the **setRenderMode()** method as this class does in its constructor.

Shaders

There is not much change in the shaders. They are just as simple as before:

```
// Source code of vertex shader
uniform mat4 mvpMatrix;
attribute vec4 vPosition;

void main() {
    gl_Position = mvpMatrix * vPosition;
}

// Source code of fragment shader
precision mediump float;
uniform vec4 vColor;
void main() {
    gl_FragColor = vColor;
}
```

When we run the program, we should see a solid color tetrahedron. We can rotate it by dragging the mouse on the screen. Figure 6-14 below shows some sample outputs of this example.

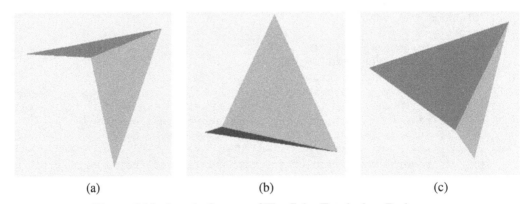

(a)   (b)   (c)

Figure 6-14   Sample Outputs of The Color Tetrahedron Project

6.5 Drawing Spheres

6.5.1 Spherical Coordinates

We can use a mesh of triangles to approximate a spherical surface. We have to define the vertices coordinates of each triangle and every vertex is on the surface of the sphere. In practice, it is easier to calculate the position of a point on a sphere using spherical coordinates, where a point is specified by three numbers: the radial distance r of that point from a fixed origin, its polar angle θ (also called inclination) measured from a fixed zenith direction, and the azimuth angle ϕ of its orthogonal projection on a reference plane that passes through the origin as shown in Figure 6-15.

So in spherical coordinates, a point is defined by (r, θ, ϕ) with some restrictions:

$$
\begin{aligned}
&r \geq 0 \\
&0^o \leq \theta \leq 180^o \\
&0^o \leq \phi < 360^o
\end{aligned}
\tag{6.6}
$$

Cartesian coordinates of a point (x, y, z) can be calculated from the spherical coordinates, (radius r, inclination θ, azimuth ϕ), where $r \in [0, \infty)$, $\theta \in [0, \pi]$, $\phi \in [0, 2\pi)$, by:

$$
\begin{aligned}
x &= r \sin \theta \cos \phi \\
y &= r \sin \theta \sin \phi \\
z &= r \cos \theta
\end{aligned}
\tag{6.7}
$$

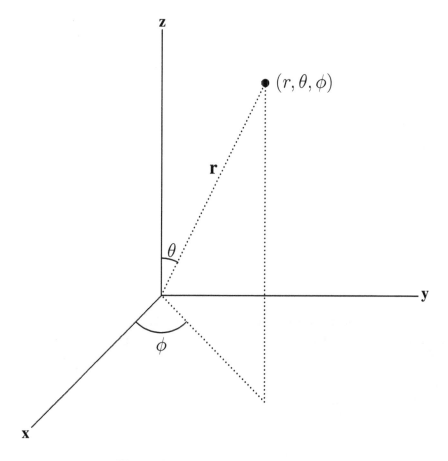

Figure 6-15 Spherical Coordinate System

Conversely, the spherical coordinates can be obtained from Cartesean coordinates by:

$$
\begin{aligned}
r &= \sqrt{x^2 + y^2 + z^2} \\
\theta &= \cos^{-1}\left(\frac{z}{r}\right) \\
\phi &= \tan^{-1}\left(\frac{y}{x}\right)
\end{aligned}
\tag{6.8}
$$

6.5.2   Rendering a Wireframe Sphere

To render a sphere centered at the origin, we can divide the sphere into slices around the z-axis (similar to lines of longitude), and stacks along the z-axis (similar to lines of latitude). We simply draw the slices and stacks independently, which will form a sphere. Each slice or stack is formed by line segments joining points together. Conversely, each point is an intersection of a slice and a stack.

Suppose we want to divide the sphere into m stacks and n slices. Since $0 \leq \theta \leq \pi$, the angle between two stacks is $\pi/(m-1)$. On the other hand, $0 \leq \phi < 2\pi$, the angle between two slices is $2\pi/n$ as the angle 2π is not included. That is,

$$\delta\theta = \frac{\pi}{m-1}$$
$$\delta\phi = \frac{2\pi}{n}$$

(6.9)

Figure 6-16 below shows a portion of two slices and two stacks, and their intersection points.

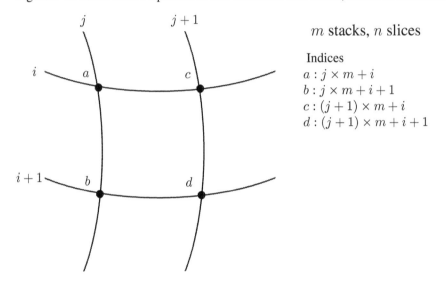

m stacks, n slices

Indices
$a : j \times m + i$
$b : j \times m + i + 1$
$c : (j+1) \times m + i$
$d : (j+1) \times m + i + 1$

Quad $abdc = \triangle abc + \triangle cbd$

Figure 6 - 16. Spherical Surface Formed by Stacks and Slices

Our task is to calculate the intersection points. Suppose we calculate the points along a slice starting from $\phi = 0$, spanning θ from 0 to 2π, and then incrementing ϕ to calculate the next slice. We apply equation (6.7) to calculate the x, y, and z coordinates of each point. For convenience, we define a class called *XYZ* that contains the x, y, z coordinates of a point, and save the points in an *ArrayList* called *vertices*. The following code shows an implementation of such a task, assuming that r is the radius of the sphere:

```
ArrayList<XYZ> vertices = new ArrayList<XYZ>();
final double PI = 3.1415926;
final double TWOPI = 2 * PI;
XYZ p = new XYZ();    // a point
double phi,  theta;

for ( int j = 0; j < n; j++ ) {   // n slices
  phi = j * TWOPI / n;
  for ( int i = 0; i < m; i++ ) { // m stacks
    theta = i * PI / (m-1);        //0 to pi
    p.x = r * (float) (Math.sin ( theta ) * Math.cos ( phi ));
    p.y = r * (float) (Math.sin ( theta ) * Math.sin ( phi ));
    p.z = r * (float) Math.cos ( theta );
    vertices.add ( new XYZ ( p ) );
```

```
   }
 }
```

We can save these coordinates in a **float** array and put them in a byte buffer like what we did in previous examples:

```
int nVertices = vertices.size();
float sphereCoords[] = new float[3*nVertices];
k = 0;
for ( int i = 0; i < nVertices; i++ ) {
  XYZ v = vertices.get ( i );
  sphereCoords[k++] = v.x;
  sphereCoords[k++] = v.y;
  sphereCoords[k++] = v.z;
}
ByteBuffer bb=ByteBuffer.allocateDirect(sphereCoords.length * 4);
bb.order(ByteOrder.nativeOrder());
vertexBuffer = bb.asFloatBuffer();
vertexBuffer.put(sphereCoords);
vertexBuffer.position(0);
```

Now we have obtained all the intersection points. The remaining task is to define a draw order list that tells us how to connect the points. We use a **short** array, named *drawOrderw* to hold the indices of the vertices in the order we want to connect them. Suppose we first draw the slices. The following code shows how to calculate the indices for the points of the slices:

```
int k = 0;
for ( int j = 0; j < n; j++ ) {
 for ( int i = 0; i < m-1; i++ ) {
   drawOrderw[k++] = (short) (j * m + i);
   drawOrderw[k++] = (short)( j* m + i + 1 );
 }
}
```

The two indices $(j * m + i)$ and $(j * m + i + 1)$ defines two points of a line segment of a slice. Each slice is composed of $m - 1$ line segments. The following code shows the calculations for the stacks:

```
for ( int i = 1; i < m - 1; i++) {
  for ( int j = 0; j < n; j++){
    drawOrderw[k++] = (short) (j * m + i);
    if ( j == n - 1)  //wrap around: j + 1 --> 0
      drawOrderw[k++] = (short) ( i);
    else
      drawOrderw[k++] = (short) ((j+1)*m + i);
  }
}
```

Each pair of indices define two end points of a line segment of a stack. When j equals $n - 1$, the next point wraps around so that the last point of the stack joins its first point to form a full circle. So each stack is composed of n segments. Also we do not need to draw the poles, and there are only $m - 2$ stacks. Therefore, the total number of indices in *drawOrderw* is

$$2 \times n \times (m - 1) + 2 \times (m - 2) \times n = 4 \times m \times n - 6 \times n$$

As before, We can put the indices in a byte array to draw slices and stacks, which will form a wireframe sphere:

```
ByteBuffer bbIndices = ByteBuffer.allocateDirect(
                        drawOrderw.length * 2);
bbIndices.order(ByteOrder.nativeOrder());
sphereIndices = bbIndices.asShortBuffer();
sphereIndices.put( drawOrderw );
sphereIndices.position(0);
GLES20.glDrawElements( GLES20.GL_LINES, drawOrderw.length,
               GLES20.GL_UNSIGNED_SHORT, sphereIndices );
```

Since the first index in *drawOrderw* references the point that is the north pole of the sphere, we can draw the pole using the statement:

```
GLES20.glDrawElements( GLES20.GL_POINTS, 1,
               GLES20.GL_UNSIGNED_SHORT, sphereIndices );
```

The shaders are similar to those described in previous examples except now we need to specify the point size using **gl_PointSize**:

```
// Source code of vertex shader
uniform mat4 mvpMatrix;
attribute vec4 vPosition;
void main() {
  gl_PointSize = 15;
  gl_Position = mvpMatrix * vPosition;
}
// Source code of fragment shader
precision mediump float;
uniform vec4 vColor;
void main() {
  gl_FragColor = vColor;
}
```

Suppose we set the number of slices to be 24 and the number of stacks to be 16. When we run the program, we will see a wireframe sphere like the one shown in Figure 6-17 below. The point near the bottom of the sphere is its north pole.

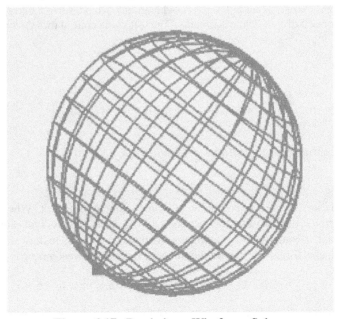

Figure 6-17   Rendering a Wireframe Sphere

6.5.3   Rendering a Color Solid Sphere

Rendering a color solid sphere is similar to rendering a color solid tetrahedron except that we have to calculate the vertices of the triangle mesh. We have already learned how to decompose a sphere into slices and stacks in the previous section. Suppose we have saved all the vertices in *vertexBuffer* as we did in the previous example. The shaders are also the same as those in the previous example, which are very simple.

As shown in Figure 6-16, the intersection points of two latitudes and two longitudes form a quadrilateral, which can be decomposed into two triangles. Since all the vertices coordinates have been calculated, we just need to find out the order of drawing them in the form of triangles.

As shown in the figure, to draw the quad abcd, we first draw the triangle abc and then draw the other triangle cbd, both in a counter-clockwise direction. That means the drawing order of the vertices is a, b, c, c, b, d. The following code shows the implementation of this procedure:

```
// n slices, m stacks
int nTriangles = 2 * n * (m - 1);    //number of triangles
short  drawOrders[][] = new short[nTriangles][3];
int k = 0;
for ( int j = 0; j < n; j++ ) {
  for ( int i = 0; i < m-1; i++ ) {
    short j1 = (short)(j + 1);
    if ( j == n - 1 ) j1 = 0;       //wrap around
    short ia = (short)( j * m + i ) ;
    short ib = (short)( j * m + i + 1);
    short ic = (short) (j1 * m + i );
    short id = (short)( j1 * m + i + 1 );
    drawOrders[k] = new short[3]; //first triangle
    drawOrders[k][0] = ia;
    drawOrders[k][1] = ib;
    drawOrders[k][2] = ic;
    k++;
    drawOrders[k] = new short[3]; //second triangle
    drawOrders[k][0] = ic;
    drawOrders[k][1] = ib;
    drawOrders[k][2] = id;
    k++;
  }
}
```

Suppose we just use the four colors, red, green, blue, and yellow to draw the whole sphere, alternating the colors between adjacent triangles. We can define a **float** array to hold the four colors:

```
static float colors[][] = {
  {1.0f, 0.0f, 0.0f, 1.0f},   // red
  {0.0f, 1.0f, 0.0f, 1.0f},   // green
  {0.0f, 0.0f, 1.0f, 1.0f},   // blue
  {1.0f, 1.0f, 0.0f, 1.0f}    // yellow
};
```

We need a **float** buffer to hold the color and a **short** buffer to hold the vertices of each triangle of the mesh. This can be implemented as follows:

```
// a color for each face
FloatBuffer colorBuffer[] = new FloatBuffer[nTriangles];
ShortBuffer sphereIndices[] = new ShortBuffer[nTriangles];
```

```
for ( int i = 0; i < nTriangles; i++) {
  int j = i % 4;
  ByteBuffer bbc=ByteBuffer.allocateDirect(colors[j].length*4);
  bbc.order(ByteOrder.nativeOrder());
  colorBuffer[i] = bbc.asFloatBuffer();
  colorBuffer[i].put( colors[j] );
  colorBuffer[i].position(0);
  ByteBuffer bbIndices = ByteBuffer.allocateDirect(
                                    drawOrders[i].length * 2);
  bbIndices.order(ByteOrder.nativeOrder());
  sphereIndices[i] = bbIndices.asShortBuffer();
  sphereIndices[i].put( drawOrders[i] );
  sphereIndices[i].position(0);
}
```

To draw the sphere, we simply draw all the triangles, each of which is defined by three vertices and three colors:

```
for ( int i = 0; i < nTriangles; i++){
  int positionHandle=GLES20.glGetAttribLocation(program, "vPosition");
  int colorHandle = GLES20.glGetUniformLocation(program, "vColor");
  // Enable a handle to the triangle vertices
  GLES20.glEnableVertexAttribArray( positionHandle);
  int j = i % 4;    // only 4 colors
  GLES20.glUniform4fv(colorHandle, 1, colors[j], 0);
  GLES20.glVertexAttribPointer( positionHandle, COORDS_PER_VERTEX,
              GLES20.GL_FLOAT, false, vertexStride, vertexBuffer);
  GLES20.glDrawElements(GLES20.GL_TRIANGLES, drawOrders[i].length,
                  GLES20.GL_UNSIGNED_SHORT, sphereIndices[i]);
  // Disable vertex array
  GLES20.glDisableVertexAttribArray(positionHandle);
}
```

When we run the program, we will see an output similar to the one shown in Figure 16-17 below.

6.5.4 Lighting a Sphere

Lighting is an important feature in graphics for making a scene appear more realistic and more understandable. It provides crucial visual cues about the curvature and orientation of surfaces, and helps viewers perceive a graphics scene having three-dimensionality. Using the sphere we have constructed in previous sections, we discuss briefly here how to add lighting effect to it.

To create lighting effect that looks realistic, we need to first design a lighting model. In graphics, however, such a lighting model does not need to follow physical laws though the laws can be used as guidelines. The model is usually designed empirically. In our discussion, we more or less follow a simple and popular model called Phong lighting model to create lighting effect. In the model we only consider the effects of a light source shining directly on a surface and then being reflected directly to the viewpoint; second bounces are ignored. Such a model is referred to as a local lighting model, which only considers the light property and direction, the viewer's position, and the object material properties. It considers only the first bounce of the light ray but ignores any secondary reflections, which are light rays that are reflected for more than once by surfaces before reaching the viewpoint. Nor does a basic local model consider shadows created by light.

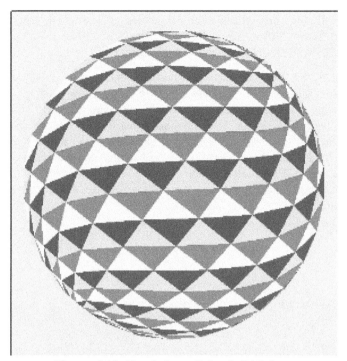

Figure 6-18   Rendering a Color Solid Sphere

In the model, we consider the following features:

1. All light sources are modeled as point light sources.
2. Light is composed of red (R), green (G), and blue (B) colors.
3. Light reflection intensities can be calculated independently using the principle of superposition for each light source and for each of the 3 color components (R, G, B). Therefore, we describe a source through a three-component intensity or illumination vector

$$\mathbf{I} = \begin{pmatrix} R \\ G \\ B \end{pmatrix} \tag{6.10}$$

Each of the components of $\mathbf{I}$ in (6.10) is the intensity of the independent red, green, and blue components.

4. There are three distinct kinds of light or illumination that contribute to the computation of the final illumination of an object:

   - **Ambient Light**: light that arrives equally from all directions. We use this to model the kind of light that has been scattered so much by its environment that we cannot tell its original source direction. Therefore, ambient light shines uniformly on a surface regardless of its orientation. The position of an ambient light source is meaningless.
   - **Diffuse Light**: light from a point source that will be reflected diffusely. We use this to model the kind of light that is reflected evenly in all directions away from the surface. (Of course, in reality this depends on the surface, not the light itself. As we mentioned earlier, this model is not based on real physics but on graphical experience.)
   - **Specular Light**: light from a point source that will be reflected specularly. We use this to model the kind of light that is reflected in a mirror-like fashion, the way that a light ray reflected from a shinny surface.

5. The model also assigns each surface material properties, which can be one of the four kinds:

- Materials with **ambient reflection properties** reflect ambient light.
- Materials with **diffuse reflection properties** reflect diffuse light.
- Materials with **specular reflection properties** reflect specular light.

In the model, ambient light only interacts with materials that possess ambient property; specular and diffuse light only interact with specular and diffuse materials respectively.

Figure 6-19 below shows the vectors that are needed to calculate the illumination at a point. In the figure, the labels *vPosition*, *lightPosition*, and *eyePosition* denote points at the vertex, the light source, and the viewing position respectively. The labels **L**, **N**, **R**, and **V** are vectors derived from these points (recall that the difference between two points is a vector), representing the light vector, the normal, the reflection vector, and the viewing vector respectively. The reflection vector **R** is the direction along which a light from **L** will be reflected if the the surface at the point is mirror-like. Assuming that the center of the sphere is at the origin $O = (0,0,0)$, some of them can be expressed as

$$
\begin{aligned}
\text{light vector } \mathbf{L} &= lightPosition - vPosition \\
\text{normal } \mathbf{N} &= vPosition - O \\
\text{view vector } \mathbf{V} &= eyePosition - vPosition
\end{aligned}
\tag{6.11}
$$

We can normalize a vector by dividing it by its magnitude:

$$
\mathbf{l} = \frac{\mathbf{L}}{|\mathbf{L}|}, \quad \mathbf{n} = \frac{\mathbf{N}}{|\mathbf{N}|}, \quad \mathbf{v} = \frac{\mathbf{V}}{|\mathbf{V}|}, \quad \mathbf{r} = \frac{\mathbf{R}}{|\mathbf{R}|}
\tag{6.12}
$$

One can easily show that the normalized reflection vector **r** can be calculated from **l** and **n** by the formula,

$$
\mathbf{r} = 2(\mathbf{n} \cdot \mathbf{l})\mathbf{n} - \mathbf{l}
\tag{6.13}
$$

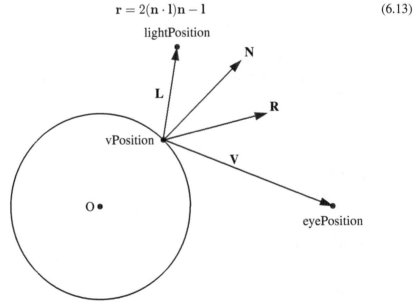

Figure 6-19 Lighting Vectors

Suppose I^{in} denotes the incident illumination from the light source in the direction l. The ambient, diffuse, and specular illumination on the point *vPosition* can be calculated according to the following formulas.

The ambient illumination is given by

$$
I_a = c_a I_a^{in}
\tag{6.14}
$$

where I_a^{in} is the incident ambient light intensity and c_a is a constant called the *ambient reflectivity coefficient*.

The diffuse illumination is

$$I_d = c_d I_d^{in} \mathbf{1} \cdot \mathbf{n} \tag{6.15}$$

where $\mathbf{1} \cdot \mathbf{n} = \mathbf{r} \cdot \mathbf{n}$, I_d^{in} is the incident diffuse light intensity and c_d is a constant called the *diffuse reflectivity coefficient*.

The specular illumination can be calculated by

$$I_s = c_s I_s^{in} (\mathbf{r} \cdot \mathbf{v})^f \tag{6.16}$$

where c_s is a constant called the *specular reflectivity coefficient* and the exponent f is a value that can be adjusted empirically on an ad hoc basis to achieve desired lighting effect. The exponent f is ≥ 0, and values in the range 50 to 100 are typically used for shinny surfaces. The larger the exponent factor f, the narrower the beam of specularly reflected light becomes.

The total illumination is the sum of all the above components:

$$\begin{aligned} I &= I_a + I_d + I_s \\ &= c_a I_a^{in} + c_d I_d^{in} (\mathbf{1} \cdot \mathbf{n}) + c_s I_s^{in} (\mathbf{r} \cdot \mathbf{v})^f \end{aligned} \tag{6.17}$$

This model can be easily implemented in the glsl shader language. In our example, where the illuminated object is a sphere, the shader code is further simplified. The positions of the light source, the vertex, and the eye (viewing point) are passed from the the application to the vertex shader as **uniform** variables. The vertex shader calculates the vectors **L**, **N**, and **V** from the positions and pass them to the fragment shader as **varying** variables:

```
// Source code of vertex shader
uniform mat4 mvpMatrix;
attribute vec4 vPosition;
uniform vec4 eyePosition;
uniform vec4 lightPosition;
varying vec3 N; //normal direction
varying vec3 L; //light source direction
varying vec3 V; //view vector
void main() {
    gl_Position = mvpMatrix * vPosition;
    N = vPosition.xyz;    //normal of  a point on sphere
    L = lightPosition.xyz - vPosition.xyz;
    V = eyePosition.xyz - vPosition.xyz;
}
```

The fragment shader obtains the vectors **L**, **N**, and **V** from the vertex shader, normalizes them, and calculates the reflection vector **r**. It then uses formulas (6.14) to (6.17) to calculate the illumination at the vertex:

```
// Source code of fragment shader
  precision mediump float;
  varying vec3 N;
  varying vec3 L;
  varying vec3 V;
  uniform vec4 lightAmbient;
  uniform vec4 lightDiffuse;
  uniform vec4 lightSpecular;
  //in this example, material color same for ambient, diffuse, specular
  uniform vec4 materialColor;
  uniform float shininess;
```

```
void main() {
  vec3 norm = normalize(N);
  vec3 lightv = normalize(L);
  vec3 viewv = normalize(V);
  // diffuse coefficient
  float Kd = max(0.0, dot(lightv, norm));

  // calculating specular coefficient
  // consider only specular light in same direction as normal
  float cs;
  if(dot(lightv, norm)>= 0.0) cs =1.0;
  else cs = 0.0;
  //reflection vector
  vec3 r = 2.0 *  dot (norm, lightv) * norm  - lightv;
  float Ks = pow(max(0.0, dot(r, viewv)), shininess);
  vec4 ambient = materialColor * lightAmbient;
  vec4 specular = cs * Ks * materialColor *lightSpecular;
  vec4 diffuse = Kd * materialColor *  lightDiffuse;

  gl_FragColor = ambient + diffuse + specular;
}
```

One can modify the code or juggle with it to obtain various lighting effects empirically.

Similar to previous examples, the OpenGL application has to provide the actual values of the **uniform** and **attribute** parameters. The sphere is constructed in the same way that we did in the previous example. However, we do not need to pass in the colors for each triangle as the appearance of the sphere is now determined by its material color and the light colors, and the color at each pixel is calculated by the fragment shader using the lighting model. The following code shows how the application supplies the lighting parameters:

```
public class Sphere
{
.....
float eyePos[] = {5f, 5f, 10f, 1f};          //viewing position
float lightPos[] = {5f, 10f, 5f, 1f};        //light source position
float lightAmbi[] = {0.1f, 0.1f, 0.1f, 1f};//ambient light
float lightDiff[] = {1f, 0.8f, 0.6f, 1f};  //diffuse light
float lightSpec[] = {0.3f, 0.2f, 0.1f,1f} ;//specular light
//material same for ambient, diffuse, and specular
float materialColor[] = {1f, 1f, 1f, 1f};
float shininess = 50f;

public void draw( float[] mvpMatrix ) {
 // Add program to OpenGL ES environment
 GLES20.glUseProgram(program);
 // get handle to shape's transformation matrix
 int mvpMatrixHandle=GLES20.glGetUniformLocation(program,"mvpMatrix");
 // Pass the projection and view transformation to the shader
 GLES20.glUniformMatrix4fv(mvpMatrixHandle, 1, false, mvpMatrix, 0);
 // Pass lighting parameters
 int eyePosHandle=GLES20.glGetUniformLocation(program, "eyePosition");
 int lightPosHandle=GLES20.glGetUniformLocation(program,"lightPosition");
 int lightAmbiHandle=GLES20.glGetUniformLocation(program,"lightAmbient");
 int lightDiffHandle=GLES20.glGetUniformLocation(program,"lightDiffuse");
 int lightSpecHandle=GLES20.glGetUniformLocation(program,"lightSpecular");
```

```
    int materialColorHandle=GLES20.glGetUniformLocation(program,
                                                    "materialColor");
    int shininessHandle=GLES20.glGetUniformLocation(program, "shininess");
    GLES20.glUniform4fv(eyePosHandle, 1, eyePos, 0);
    GLES20.glUniform4fv(lightPosHandle, 1, lightPos, 0);
    GLES20.glUniform4fv(lightAmbiHandle, 1, lightAmbi, 0);
    GLES20.glUniform4fv(lightDiffHandle, 1, lightDiff, 0);
    GLES20.glUniform4fv(lightSpecHandle, 1, lightSpec, 0);
    GLES20.glUniform1f(shininessHandle, shininess);
    GLES20.glUniform4fv(materialColorHandle, 1, materialColor, 0);
    int vertexStride = 0;
    // Draw the sphere
    GLES20.glLineWidth(3);
    for ( int i = 0; i < nTriangles; i++){
      int positionHandle=GLES20.glGetAttribLocation(program,"vPosition");
      // Enable a handle to the triangle vertices
      GLES20.glEnableVertexAttribArray( positionHandle);
      GLES20.glVertexAttribPointer( positionHandle, COORDS_PER_VERTEX,
                      GLES20.GL_FLOAT, false, vertexStride, vertexBuffer);
      GLES20.glDrawElements(GLES20.GL_TRIANGLES, drawOrders[i].length,
                            GLES20.GL_UNSIGNED_SHORT, sphereIndices[i]);
      // Disable vertex array
      GLES20.glDisableVertexAttribArray(positionHandle);
    }
  }
  .....
}
```

Figure 6-20 below shows an output of this application, where the same sphere of Figure 6-18 has been used.

Figure 6-20 Example Rendered Lit Sphere

Chapter 7   Thread Programming

7.1   Processes and Threads

Processes are fundamental in any computing system. A **process** is a program in execution, plus the data, the stack, registers, and all the resources required to run the program. We can create several processes from the same program and each of them is considered as an independent execution unit. A **multitasking** system allows several processes coexist in the system's memory at the same time. A process has different states, which can be one of the following as shown in Figure 7-1:

1. **New**: when the process is created.
2. **Running**: when instructions are executed, consuming CPU time.
3. **Blocked**: when the process is waiting for some event such as receiving a signal or completing an I/O task to happen.
4. **Ready**: when the process is temporarily stopped, letting another process run and waiting to be assigned to a processor.
5. **Terminated**: when the process has finished execution.

The names are not unique and may be called differently in different systems but the states they represent exist in every system. A system maintains a process table to keep track of the states of the system's processes.

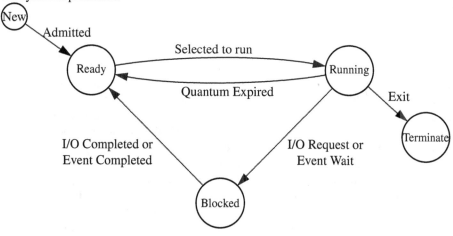

Figure 7-1. States of a Process or a Thread

A process could be bulky, consuming a lot of resources and has its own address space. It performs its own **thread** of operation. Most modern operating system, including Android, extends the process concept discussed to let a process to have multiple threads of operations, allowing it to perform multiple tasks concurrently.

A **thread**, sometimes referred to as a **lightweight process** (LWP), is a basic unit of CPU utilization. It has a thread ID to identify itself, a program counter (PC) to keep track of the next instruction to be executed, a register set to hold its current working variables, and a stack to store the execution history. A thread must execute in a process and shares with its peers the resources allocated to the process. Threads make a system run much more effectively. For example, a web browser might have one thread displaying text and images while another retrieving data from a remote database. A word processor may have one thread accepting text inputs while another performing spelling check in the background. A modern computing system can run thousands of threads at the same time easily but running thousands of processes concurrently will consume so much resources that it might make the system come to a halt. Figure 7-2 below compares a traditional single-threaded process with a multi-threaded process.

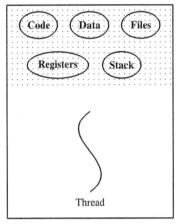

Single-threaded Process

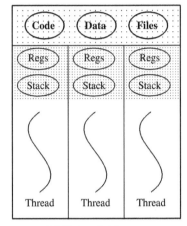

Multi-threaded Process

Figure 7-2. Single-threaded and Multi-threaded Processes

The Android official site provides a discussion of Android processes and threads at

http://developer.android.com/guide/components/processes-and-threads.html

7.2   Java Threads

Since Android applications are developed using Java, Android threads inherit the properties of the Java language, which includes direct support for threads at the language level for thread creation and management. However, by design, Java does not support asynchronous behavior. For example, if a Java program tries to connect to a server, the client is blocked, suspending its activities and waiting for the establishment of a connection or the occurrence of a timeout. Typically, the Java app creates a communication thread which attempts to make a connection to the server and a timer thread which will sleep for the timeout duration. When the timer thread wakes up, it checks to see whether the communication thread has finished establishing the connection. If not, the timer thread generates a signal to stop the communication thread from continuing to try.

All Java programs comprise at least one single thread of control, consisting of a **main**() method, running in the Java Virtual Machine (JVM). Correspondingly, a single-thread process (activity) of Android contains the **onCreate**() method.

7.2.1 Thread Creation by Extending *Thread* Class

One way to create a thread is to extend the *Thread* class and to override its **run**() method as shown in the following code:

```
public class CreateThread extends Activity
{
  @Override
  public void onCreate(Bundle savedInstanceState)
```

```
    {
      super.onCreate(savedInstanceState);
      Athread t1 = new Athread();

      t1.start();
      System.out.println ( "I am the main thread!" );
    }
}

class Athread extends Thread
{
  public void run()
  {
    System.out.println ("I am a thread!");
  }
}
```

If we create and run this program in the Eclipse IDE, we shall see outputs in the **LogCat** that are similar to the following:

TID	Application	Tag	Text
1650	example.createthread	System.out	I am a thread!
1650	example.createthread	System.out	I am the main thread!

7.2.2 Thread Creation by Implementing *Runnable* Interface

Another way to create a thread is to implement the *Runnable* interface directly, which is defined as follows:

```
public interface Runnable
{
  public abstract void run();
}
```

The *Thread* class that our program in the last section extends also implements the *Runnable* interface.

This is why a class that extends *Thread* also needs to provide a **run**() method.

The following code shows a complete example of using this technique to create thread:

```
public class CreateThread1 extends Activity
{
    @Override
    public void onCreate(Bundle savedInstanceState)
    {
      super.onCreate(savedInstanceState);
      Athread1 t1 = new Athread1();

      t1.run();
      System.out.println ( "I am the main thread!" );
    }
}

class Athread1 implements Runnable
{
  public void run()
  {
```

```
    System.out.println ("I am a thread!");
  }
}
```

Again, if we run the code in the Eclipse IDE, we shall obtain outputs similar to those of the previous section.

Each of the two techniques of creating threads has drawbacks and advantages and both are equally popular. The advantage of the first technique, extending the *Thread* class, is that it can use all the methods of the *Thread* class. However, since Java does not support multiple inheritance, if a class has already extended another class, it will not be allowed to extend *Thread*, and we need to use the second technique to create a thread. Of course, if a class implements the *Runnable* interface and does not extend the *Thread* class, none of the the methods provided by *Thread* can be used in the new class. In the above code, we cannot even use the **start**() method to start running the thread!

The *Thread* class provides a few methods to manage threads, including:

1. **stop**(): Terminates the thread. Once a thread has been terminated, it cannot be resumed or restarted.
2. **suspend**(): Suspends execution of the running thread. A suspended thread can be resumed to run.
3. **sleep**(): Puts the running thread to sleep for a specified amount of time.
4. **resume**(): Resumes execution of the suspended thread.

If we construct directly an instance of a class that implements *Runnable* like what we did above, we cannot use any of these methods; a better way to construct a thread with this technique is to pass the object variable of the class as an input parameter to the *Thread* class constructor as follows:

```
public class CreateThread1 extends Activity
{
  @Override
  public void onCreate(Bundle savedInstanceState)
  {
    super.onCreate(savedInstanceState);

    Runnable runner = new Athread1 ();
    Thread t1 = new Thread ( runner );
    t1.start();
    System.out.println ( "I am the main thread!" );
  }
}
```

Besides the threads created by users, a Java environment has a few threads running asynchronously on behalf of the Java Virtual Machine (JVM). These system threads carry out housekeeping tasks such as memory management and memory controls. In particular, the garbage-collector (GC) thread examines objects in the system to check whether they are alive. Anything that is not alive is designated as garbage and is returned to the memory heap. This garbage collection mechanism allows developers to create objects without worrying about allocation and deallocation of memory. This would eliminate memory-leak problems and help developers create more robust programs in a shorter time. Other interesting system threads include the timer thread, which can be used to schedule tasks and handle time events, and the graphics control threads, which can be used to update the screen and control user interface events such as clicking a button.

7.2.3 Wait for a Thread

Very often after a parent has created a thread, the parent would like to wait for the child thread to complete before its own exit. This can be done using the **join**() method of the *Thread* class. The method forces one thread to wait for the completion of another. Suppose t is a Thread object. The statement

    t.join();

causes the currently executing thread to pause execution until Thread t terminates. A programmer may specify a waiting period by overloading the **join**() method. Like **sleep**, **join** depends on the OS for timing. So we should not assume that **join** will wait for the exact amount of time that we have specified.

Like **sleep**, when **join** is interrupted, it exits with an *InterruptedException*.

We present below an example of multi-threaded programming and the usage of **join**. In this example, we use a number of threads to multiply two matrices. The multiplication of an $M \times L$ matrix A and an $L \times N$ matrix B gives an $M \times N$ matrix C, and is given by the formula,

$$C_{ij} = \sum_{k=0}^{L-1} A_{ik} B_{kj} \quad 0 \le i < M,\, 0 \le j < N \qquad (7.1)$$

Basically, each element C_{ij} is the dot product of the i-th row vector of A with the j-th column vector of B. We use one thread to calculate a dot product. Therefore, we totally need $M \times N$ threads to calculate all the elements of matrix C. The calculating threads are created by the main thread, which must wait for all of them to complete. The following is the complete code for the program.

Program Listing 7-1   Multithreaded Matrix Multiplication

```
public class MatMulActivity extends Activity
{
  /** Called when the activity is first created. */
  @Override
  public void onCreate(Bundle savedInstanceState)
  {
    super.onCreate(savedInstanceState);
    double a[][] = {{1, 2, 3}, {4, 5, 6}};
    double b[][] = { {1, -1}, {-1, 1}, {1, 1} };
    final   int numRows = a.length;
    final   int numCols = b[0].length;
    final   int nThreads = numRows * numCols;
    double c[][] = new double[numRows][numCols];
    int k = 0;

    System.out.println ("Matrix a: ");
    printMat ( a );
    System.out.println ("Matrix b: ");
    printMat ( b );

    Thread threads[] = new Thread[nThreads];
    System.out.println ( "I am the main thread!" );

    for ( int i = 0; i < numRows; i++ )        //row
```

```
          for ( int j = 0; j < numCols; j++ ) {  //column
            threads[k] = new MatMul ( i, j, a, b, c );
            threads[k].start();
            k++;
          }
        try {
          for ( int i = 0; i < k; i++ )
            threads[i].join();      //wait for threads[i] to complete
        } catch ( InterruptedException e ) {}

        System.out.println ("Matrix c = a x b: ");
        printMat ( c );
      }

    //print a matrix
    public static void printMat ( double a[][] )
    {
      int numRows = a.length;
      int numCols = a[0].length;

      for ( int i = 0; i < numRows; i++ ) {
        for ( int j = 0; j < numCols; j++ ) {
          System.out.printf ( "%6.2f, ", a[i][j] );
        }
        System.out.printf("\n");
      }
    }
  }

//Thread calculates dot product of a row-vector and a column-vector
class MatMul extends Thread
{
  private int row, col;
  private double a[][];
  private double b[][];
  private double c[][];

  //Calculate dot product of row-vector a0[row0] and column vector
  //  b0[][col0]. Save result in c0[row0][col0].
  public MatMul(int row0, int col0, double a0[][], double b0[][],
                                                  double c0[][])
  {
    row = row0;
    col = col0;
    a = a0;
    b = b0;
    c = c0;
  }

  public void run()
  {
    System.out.println ("I am a MatMul  thread!");
    double sum = 0.0;
    int n = a[0].length;      //number of columns
```

```
      for ( int i = 0; i < n; i++ )
        sum += a[row][i] * b[i][col];

      c[row][col] = sum;
    }
}
```

When we run the program in Eclipse IDE, we will see in the **LogCat** some outputs similar to the following:

```
System.out: Matrix a:
System.out:    1.00,    2.00,    3.00,
System.out:    4.00,    5.00,    6.00,
System.out: Matrix b:
System.out:    1.00,   -1.00,
System.out:   -1.00,    1.00,
System.out:    1.00,    1.00,
System.out: I am the main thread!
System.out: I am a MatMul  thread!
System.out: I am a MatMul  thread!
System.out: I am a MatMul  thread!
System.out: I am a MatMul  thread!
System.out: Matrix c = a x b:
System.out:    2.00,    4.00,
System.out:    5.00,    7.00,
```

7.3 Synchronization

In a multitasking system, several threads may be running at the same time (concurrently). There are situations that the activities of the threads need to be **synchronized** so that the activity of one thread will not interfere or disturb the activity of another. For example, we certainly do not want two threads to print something simultaneously using the same printer. Figure 7-3 shows a World War I Fighter Aircraft, which can be used to illustrate the concept of synchronization. In the days of World War I, the engineering of fighter aircrats was relatively primitive. A machine gun was mounted in front of the pilot but behind whirling propeller. At the beginning of the war, a pilot would not shoot enemy aircrafts which were at the same altitude as the bullets might damage the propeller of his own fighter. Later, the Germans could fly their more advanced aircrafts higher; a German pilot would turn off the engine at higher altitude, diving at the enemy fighter and firing without hitting the propeller. This is an example of **mutual exclusion** where only one event can occur at a time, either running the propeller or firing the machine gun. This would be called **coarse-grained synchronization**. The Germans later developed even more advanced technologies that automatically synchronized the propeller whirling and gun firing, so that bullets were shot only when their blades were not in the way. This would be called **fine-grained synchronization**.

7.3.1 Mutual Exclusion

In a computing system, very often resources are shared among threads. Some resource such as a printer, a memory segment or a file may allow only one thread to access it at a time. The requirement to ensure that only one thread or process is accessing such a shared resource is referred to as **mutual exclusion**. Of course, a thread is a running program and it executes a certain code segment to access the resources. To deny a thread to access a resource means to deny the thread to execute the corresponding piece of code segment that access the resource. A code segment in a process in which a shared resource is access is referred to as a **critical section**. When the program is about to execute the code segment, we literally say that it is entering the critical section, and when it is finishing its execution, we say that it is leaving the critical section. Situations where two or more threads are competing to enter a critical section is referred to as **race conditions**. Mutual exclusion is often abbreviated to **mutex**.

Figure 7-3 World War I Fighter Aircraft

Achieving mutual exclusion usually involves some locking mechanisms. It is in analogy of the situation when we access a small public restroom that allows only one a person to use it at one time such as one in a small Starbuck or fast food restaurant. When a lady wants to use the restroom, she first examines whether it is *vacant* (unlocked) or *occupied* (locked). If it is locked, she will wait until it is unlocked. If it is unlocked, she will lock it and use it; when she has finished using it, she unlocks the restroom and leaves it. In general, mutual exclusion for accessing a critical section is achieved by following the steps:

1. Create a lock to protect the shared resource.
2. Acquire the lock.
3. Enter the critical section (accessing the shared resource).
4. Release the lock.

In practice, all threads should be able to enter a critical section in finite time. That is, no thread will be in a **starvation** state, waiting infinitely for the desired resource. Another important requirement to achieve mutual exclusion is that the locking and unlocking process must be **atomic**, which means that the action is indivisible. Once it is started, it will not be interrupted by any other thread. In our restroom analogy, when a lady is locking the restroom halfway, no other customer is allowed to enter the restroom to do the same thing. In a computing system, the mechanism is usually achieved with the help of special hardware instructions.

Java uses a concept called **monitor** to achieve synchronization. Every Java object is associated with a lock. Any attempt to lock a monitor that has been locked causes the thread to wait until the lock is released (unless the owner of the lock itself is trying to acquire the lock again). However, Java synchronization is **block-based**. That is, instead of locking the whole object, a thread is able to lock a block of code. This implies that normally the lock is ignored when the object is being accessed; any method or block of code can be accessed as usual unless it is declared as **synchronized**.

A Java thread can always put a lock on a synchronized block of code whenever it needs and releases the lock as it desires. But if a synchronized block has been locked by a thread, no other thread can access any synchronized method of the object. This mechanism is achieved by using the keyword **synchronized** in the declaration of a method or a block of code in the class. The JVM ensures that only one thread is allowed to lock a method or a block of statements at any instance while other threads remain active, being able to access other availble methods and objects.

A thread calling a synchronized method must first own the lock before it can access the method. If the lock has been acquired by another thread, the calling thread blocks itself and is put in a waiting set, waiting to be waken up to acquire the lock. The following is an example of using the keyword **synchronized**:

```
public class Score
{
  private double score;
  private double total;

  public synchronized void setScore ( double s )
  {
    score = s;
  }

  public synchronized void addScore ( double s )
  {
    total += s;
  }

  public double getScore ()
  {
    return score;
  }
  .....
}
```

In the example, at any instance only one thread is allowed to access the method **setScore()** or **addScore)()**. When a thread is accessing **setScore()**, another thread cannot access the other synchronized method **addScore()** but it can access **getScore()**. Here the method **getScore()** is not synchronized, so multiple threads can access it at the same time without acquiring the lock. This is in analogy of clients accessing the rooms of a building, where some rooms have a lock and others do not. Only one key exists, held by a receptionist at the entrance of the building, and the key can open all lock-rooms. A client can always enter any room that does not have a lock. However, if she wants to enter any room that has a lock, she must first acquire the key. If the key has been checked out, she must wait. When she is done using the lock-room, she would return the key to the receptionist. In this analogy, the same key is used to access all the rooms that has a lock corresponding to the situation that only one synchronized method can be accessed within an object. In other words, only one thread is active inside a monitor. This defeats the purpose of concurrency and could be a drawback of of using a monitor to achieve synchronization in some applications; this shortcoming may be remedied using a tool called *serializer*, which is similar to a monitor except that it contains a special code section called *hollow region*, where threads can be concurrently active. The discussion of serializer is beyond the scope of this book.

As an example of using **synchronized** methods, we use the **synchronized** keyword to write a *Lock* class that can lock any statement or a block of statements:

```
public class Lock
{
  private boolean locked = false;
```

```
public synchronized void lock () throws InterruptedException
{
  while ( locked )
    wait ();
  locked = true;
}

public synchronized void unlock ()
{
  locked = false;
  notify ();
}
}
```

The **wait** method is to wait for a signal to wake up the thread. When a thread calls **wait**(),
the state of the thread is set to **Blocked** (see Figure 7-1), and the thread is put in a waiting set
for the synchronized block. The **notify** method is to send a signal to wake up a thread chosen
randomly from the waiting set and the awaken thread is placed in the ready queue shown in Figure
7-1. Using this *Lock* class, we can implement the *Score* class like the following without using the
synchronized keyword explicitly:

```
public class Score
{
  private double score;
  private Lock lock = new Lock ();

  public void setScore ( double s )
  {
    try {
      lock.lock ();
    } catch ( InterruptedException e ) {
      e.printStackTrace ();
    }
    score = s;
    lock.unlock ();
  }
  . . . . .
}
```

Starting from Java 5, Java provides a lock package that implements a number of locking mechanisms. So you may not need to implement your own locks. To use the package, you just need to
add the import statement:

import java.util.concurrent.locks.*;

7.3.2 Semaphore

Mutual exclusion ensures that only one thread is accessing a shared resource at one time. It is
a very common form of synchronization. However, in many applications we may want to allow
more than one thread to access a resource simultaneously but will block further threads from
accessing when the current number of threads using the resource has reached a certain number.
For example, we want to limit the number of clients reading a web site simultaneously but would
let more than one client to read it at the same time. Problems like this and many others cannot
be handled by mutual exclusion. They can be solved using the *semaphore*, a synchronization
operation introduced by the renown Computer Scientist *E.W. Dijkstra* in the 1960s.

A semaphore S is an integer variable, which, apart from initialization, is accessed through two standard atomic operations called **down** and **up**. Many people also call the two operations **wait** and **signal** or **P** and **V** respectively. Less often, some people refer to the two operations as **lock** and **unlock**. The names **P** and **V** were given by Dijkstra who was Dutch and in Dutch, they may be the initials of two words meaning *decrement* and *increment*:

> **down**(S):   an atomic operation that waits for semaphore S to become positive, then
>   decrements it by 1; also referred to as **wait**(S) or **P**(S).
> **up**(S) :   an atomic operation that increments semaphore S by 1;
>   also referred to as **signal**(S) or **V**(S).

We use the following notations to describe the atomic operations **down** and **up**. The **down**(S) operation is given by:

> **when** ($S > 0$) [
> $S = S - 1$;
>]

In the above code, the statements enclosed by the square brackets are referred to as the *command sequence*, and the expression following **when** is referred to as the *guard*. The *command sequence* is executed only when the *guard* is true. The entire code segment is known as a *guarded command*, which is always executed atomically. That is, no other operations could interfere with it while it is executing.

The **up**(S) operation is simpler, simply incrementing S by 1:

> $[S = S + 1;]$

Apart from initialization, there is no other way for manipulating the value of a semaphore besides these two operations. Therefore, if S is initially 1 and two threads concurrently operate on it, one executing *down*, the other *up*, then the resulting value of S is always 1. If its initial value is 0 and the two concurrent threads are executing *down* and *up*, the thread executing *down* must wait until the other thread finishes the *up* operation that makes the semaphore's value positive. Then the waiting thread will finish its *down* operation, decrementing the semaphore's value to 0.

If a semaphore's value is restricted to 0, and 1, it is referred to as a *binary semaphore*. Regular semaphores with no such restriction are usually called *counting semaphores*. Binary semaphores are implemented in the same way as regular semaphores except multiple **up** operations will not increase the semaphore value to anything greater than 1.

When a thread executes the **down** operation and finds that the semaphore value is not positive, it must wait. However, rather than busy waiting, the thread can block itself, placing itself in a waiting queue associated with the semaphore, and the state of the thread is switched to the sleeping state (blocked state). The sleeping thread is restarted by a signal (wakeup) associated with the **up** operation.

In Java, a semaphore can be implemented by making use of the **synchronized** keyword. Listing 7-2 below shows an example of implementing semaphore.

Program Listing 7-2   Sample Semaphore Implementation

```
public final class Semaphore
{
  private int S;

  // default initial value is 0
  public Semaphore() {
```

```
    S = 0;
  }

  // initialization of semaphore value
  public Semaphore(int v) {
    S = v;
  }

  // keyword synchronized makes the method 'atomic' and
  //  mutual-exclusive; only one object can access it at one time
  public synchronized void down() {
    while (S == 0) {
      try {
        wait(); // Causes current thread to wait until another
                //  thread invokes the notify() method or the
                //  notifyAll() method for this object.
      }
      catch (InterruptedException e) { }
    }
    S--;              // decrement semaphore value
  }

  public synchronized void up() {
    S++;       // increment semaphore value
    notify();      // wakes up a single thread that is waiting on
                   //  this object's monitor.
  }
}
```

In the code, the keyword **final** means the class cannot be further extended. The keyword **synchronize** guarantees mutual exclusion and that when a thread executes the **up** or **down** operation, no other thread can interfere.

Listing 7-3 presents a demo program showing how to use a semaphore to access a simulated critical section.

Program Listing 7-3   Simulating Usage of Semaphore

```
public class SemaphoreTest extends Activity
{
  @Override
  protected void onCreate(Bundle savedInstanceState)
  {
    super.onCreate(savedInstanceState);
    setContentView(R.layout.activity_semaphore_test);
    //initialize semaphore with value 1
    Semaphore semaphore = new Semaphore ( 1 );

    final int nThreads =  10;

    Athread[] threads = new Athread[nThreads];
    /*
      Semaphore semamphore is shared among the Athread objects.
      Because of the synchronized keyword, only one Athread
```

```
      can 'access' it at a time.
    */
    for (int i = 0; i < nThreads; i++)
       threads[i] = new Athread ( semaphore, "Athread " +
                                  (new Integer(i)).toString() );

    for (int i = 0; i < nThreads; i++)
       threads[i].start();
  }
}

class Tasks
{
   // simulate a critical section
   public static void criticalSection() {
     try {
       Thread.sleep( (int) (Math.random() * 3000) );
     }
     catch (InterruptedException e) { }
   }

   // simulate a noncritical section
   public static void nonCriticalSection() {
     try {
       Thread.sleep( (int) (Math.random() * 3000) );
     }
     catch (InterruptedException e) { }
   }
}

class Athread extends Thread
{
  private Semaphore s;
  private String tname;

  public Athread ( Semaphore s0, String name ) {
    tname = name;
    s = s0;
  }

  public void run()
  {
    while (true) {
      System.out.println ( tname + " trying to enter CS" );
      s.down();
      System.out.println ( tname + " entering CS" );
      Tasks.criticalSection();
      System.out.println ( tname + " exited CS" );
      s.up();

      Tasks.nonCriticalSection();
    }
  }
}
```

When we run the program in the Eclipse IDE, we will see in the **LogCat** outputs similar to the following:

```
Athread 0 trying to enter CS
Athread 0 entering CS
Athread 1 trying to enter CS
Athread 2 trying to enter CS
.....
Athread 0 exited CS
Athread 1 entering CS
Athread 1 exited CS
.....
```

7.3.3 Producer-Consumer Problem

The producer-consumer problem is a common paradigm for thread synchronization and we use it as an example to illustrate the usage of semaphores in synchronization. This problem also will be used to solve practical problems in later chapters.

In the problem, a *producer* thread produces information which is consumed by a *consumer* thread. This is in analogy with whats happening in a fast-food restaurant. The chef produces food items and put them on a shelf; the customers consume the food items from the shelf. If the chef makes food too fast and the shelf is full, she must wait. On the other hand, if the customers consume food too fast and the shelf is empty, the customers must wait.

To allow producer and consumer threads to run concurrently (simultaneously), we must make available a buffer (like the shelf in our fast-food analogy) that can hold a number of items and be **shared** by the two threads; the producer fills the buffer with items while the consumer empties it. A producer can produce an item while the consumer is consuming another item. Trouble arises when the producer wants to put a new item in the buffer, which is already full. The solution is for the producer to go to sleep, to be awakened when the consumer has removed one or more items. Similarly, if the consumer wants to remove an item from the buffer and finds it empty, it goes to sleep until the producer puts something in the buffer and wakes the consumer up. The **unbounded-buffer** producer-consumer problem places no practical limit on the size of the buffer. The consumer may have to wait for new items, but the producer can always produce new items without waiting. The **bounded-buffer** producer-consumer problem puts a limit on the buffer size; the consumer must wait when the buffer is empty, and the producer must wait when the buffer is full.

The approach sounds simple enough, but if not properly handled, the two threads may **race** to access the buffer and the final outcome depends on who runs first.

In many practical applications, we may use a circular queue to hold more than one item at a time. The producer inserts an item at the tail of the queue and the consumer removes an item at the head of it. We advance the tail and head pointers after an insert and a remove operation respectively. The pointers wrap around when they reach the "end" of the queue. If the tail reaches the head, the queue is full and the producer has to sleep. If the head catches up with the tail, the queue is empty and the consumer has to sleep. Actually, such a queue may handle the situation of multiple producers and multiple consumers. This concept is illustrated in Figure 7-4 below.

Physically, a bounded-buffer is a circular queue. However, logically, we can consider it as a linear queue extending to infinity as shown in Figure 7-5; using this model, when $head = tail$, the bounded-buffer is empty, and when $tail - head = buffer\ size$ (which is 8 in this example), the buffer is full. We increment $tail$ when an item is inserted and increment $head$ when an item is removed from the buffer. The increment operations should be done mutual-exclusively. Therefore, we can define two synchronized methods in the same class to perform the operations.

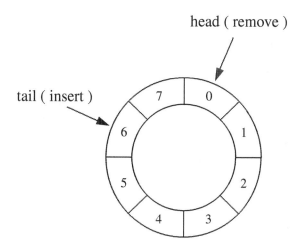

Figure 7-4. Circular Queue with Eight Slots

To simplify things, we make all operations on the tail and the head of the circular buffer **synchronized**. That is, only one thread is allowed to perform an operation at one time. We also assume that the variables *head* and *tail* have large enough bit fields that they never overflow in the applications.

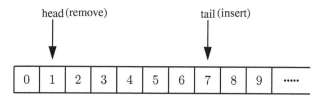

Figure 7-5. Infinite Linear Queue

Listing 7-4 below presents a simple solution to the problem. Certainly this is not the best solution as it only allows one thread to operate on a slot of the buffer at a time. A better solution would allow multiple threads to access the buffer and operate on the slots simultaneously as long as they work on different slots. An object of the *BoundedBuffer* class is to be shared by a number of producer and consumer threads.

Program Listing 7-4   Shared *BoundedBuffer* in the Producer-Consumer Problem

```
// Buffer shared by threads
public class BoundedBuffer
{
    public double buffer[];
    private int head;
    private int tail;
    public int length;   //number of slots in buffer

    //default constructor
    BoundedBuffer ()
    {
        head = tail = 0;
        length = 1;
```

```
      buffer = new double[length];
  }

  BoundedBuffer ( int len )
  {
    head = tail = 0;
    if ( len > 0 )
      length = len;
    else
      length = 1;
    buffer = new double[length];
  }

  public synchronized int insert ( double item )
  {
    // insert only if the buffer is not full
    while ( tail >= head + length ){
      try {
        System.out.println( "Buffer full, producer waits." );
        wait();
      } catch ( InterruptedException e ) {
       e.printStackTrace();
      }
    }
    int t = tail % length;
    buffer[t] = item;       //insert item at tail of queue
    tail++;                 //advance tail
    notifyAll();            //wake up all waiting threads

    return t;       //returns slot position of insertion
  }

  //remove only if buffer not empty,returns value in item0[0]
  public synchronized  int remove ( double item0[] )
  {
    while ( tail <= head ){    //Buffer empty
      try {
        System.out.println( "Buffer empty, consumer waits." );
        wait();
      } catch ( InterruptedException e ) {
        e.printStackTrace();
      }
    }
    int h = head % length;
    item0[0] = buffer[h];  //delete at head
    head++;
    notifyAll();                //wakeup all waiting threads

    return h;       //returns slot position of removal
  }
}
```

Listing 7-5 below shows a typical usage of the shared *BoundedBuffer* in a producer-consumer case. In the example, the buffer has five slots, and a *Producer* class and a *Consumer* class are presented. Four *Consumer* threads and three *Producer* threads are created to simulate the production and consumption operations.

Program Listing 7-5   An Example of Producer-Consumer Problem using *BoundedBuffer*

```
public class ProducerConsumerMain extends Activity
{
  @Override
  protected void onCreate(Bundle savedInstanceState) {
    super.onCreate(savedInstanceState);
    final int n1 =   4, n2 = 3;
    final int length = 5;
    //shared buffer
    BoundedBuffer buffer = new BoundedBuffer ( length );

    //Create n1 Consumer threads and n2 Producer threads
    Consumer [] cons = new Consumer[n1];
    Producer [] prods = new Producer[n2];
    for (int i = 0; i < n1; i++)
      cons[i] = new Consumer(buffer,"Consumer " +
                          (new Integer(i)).toString());
    for (int i = 0; i < n2; i++)
      prods[i] = new Producer(buffer,"Producer " +
                          (new Integer(i)).toString());

  //start the threads
  for (int i = 0; i < n1; i++)
    cons[i].start();
  for (int i = 0; i < n2; i++)
    prods[i].start();
  }

class Producer extends Thread
{
  private BoundedBuffer buffer;
  private String tname;

  public Producer (BoundedBuffer b,  String name)
  {
    buffer = b;
    tname = name;
  }

  double produceItem()
  {
    double x = Math.random();
    return x;
  }

  public void run()
  {
    int p;
    while (true) {
```

```
        double item = produceItem();

        int t = buffer.insert ( item );
        System.out.printf("%s inserted into slot %d value:\t%1.3f\n",
                                                    tname, t, item);
         try {
           Thread.sleep( (int) (Math.random() * 2000) );
         } catch (InterruptedException e) { }
    }
  }
}

class Consumer extends Thread
{
  private BoundedBuffer buffer;
  private String tname;

  public Consumer ( BoundedBuffer b,  String name ) {
    buffer = b;
    tname = name;
  }

  public void run()
  {
    double [] item = new double[1]; //holds one item
    int h;
    while (true) {
      h = buffer.remove( item );
      System.out.printf("%s got from slot %d value:\t%1.3f\n",
                                          tname,h,item[0]);
      try {
        Thread.sleep( (int) (Math.random() * 3000) );
      } catch (InterruptedException e) { }
    }
  }
}
```

When we run the program using Eclipse IDE, we will see in the **LogCat** console messages similar to the following:

```
Buffer empty, consumer waits.
Buffer empty, consumer waits.
Buffer empty, consumer waits.
Buffer empty, consumer waits.
Producer 0 inserted into slot 0 value:  0.024
Buffer empty, consumer waits.
Consumer 3 got from slot 0 value:       0.024
Buffer empty, consumer waits.
Buffer empty, consumer waits.
Producer 2 inserted into slot 1 value:  0.550
Producer 1 inserted into slot 2 value:  0.883
Consumer 0 got from slot 1 value:       0.550
Consumer 1 got from slot 2 value:       0.883
Buffer empty, consumer waits.
```

```
Producer 2 inserted into slot 3 value:   0.779
Consumer 2 got from slot 3 value:        0.779
Producer 0 inserted into slot 4 value:   0.224
Producer 1 inserted into slot 0 value:   0.540
Producer 1 inserted into slot 1 value:   0.078
......
```

7.3.4 Condition Variable

We have seen that semaphores are elegant tools, which can be conveniently used to solve many synchronization problems. However, for many other problems, it is cumbersome to use semaphores and their solutions expressed in semaphores could be complex. Therefore, many computing systems, including Android, provide an additional construct called *condition variable* for concurrent programming. A *condition variable* is a queue of threads (or processes) waiting for some sort of notifications. This construct has been supported by POSIX , SDL (Simple DirectMedia Layer), and Win-32 events in C/C++ programming environments. The Java utility library and the Android platform both provide support of this construct.

A condition variable queue can only be accessed with two methods associated with its queue. These methods are typically called **wait** and **signal**. The **signal** method is also referred to as **notify** in Java. This tool provides programmers a convenient way to implement guarded commands. Threads waiting for a guard to become true enter the queue. Threads that change the guard from false to true could wake up the waiting threads in the queue.

The following code segments show the general approach presented in guarded commands and an outline of implementation using Android Java with exception code omitted.

Guarded Command

```
When ( guard ) [
    statement 1
    .....



    statement n
]
```

Android Implementation

```
class SharedResource
{
    final Lock mutex = new ReentrantLock();
    final Condition condVar = mutex.newCondition();
    boolean condition = false;
    .....
    public void methodA() throws InterruptedException
    {
        mutex.lock();
        while ( !condition )
            condVar.await();
        statement 1
        .....
        statement n
        mutex.unlock();
    }
    .....
}
```

The above code shows that the execution of statements is protected by a guard. In the Android implementation, to evaluate a guard safely, a thread must mutually exclude all other threads evaluating it. This is accomplished by declaring a condition variable, (*condVar* in the example), which always associate with a lock (*mutex* in the example). The thread first locks the lock *mutex* to achieve mutual exclusion. If the guard is true, the thread can execute the command sequence, still locking *mutex*. It unlocks *mutex* only when all statements of the command sequence have been executed.

An interesting situation arises when the guard is false, which makes the thread execute the **await**() method of the condition variable *condVar*; the operation puts the thread in the queue of the condition variable and the thread is suspended. It seems that the thread would wait forever in the queue as the guard is locked by *mutex* and no other thread can access it. But what we want is that the thread waits until the guard becomes true. Here is what the condition variable comes into play. Right before the thread enters the queue and gets suspended, it unlocks *mutex* temporarily so that another thread can change the value of the guard. The thread that changes the guard from false to true is also responsible for waking up the waiting thread.

So the **await**() method of a condition variable works in the following way.

1. It causes the current thread to wait until it is signaled or interrupted.
2. The lock associated with the condition variable is atomically released and the current thread is suspended until one of four events happens:

    (a) Some other thread executes the **signal**() method of this condition variable and the current thread happens to be selected from the queue as the thread to be awakened.
    (b) Some other thread executes the **signalAll**() method of this condition variable, which wakes up all waiting threads in the queue.
    (c) The current thread is interrupted by some other thread, and interruption of thread suspension is supported.
    (d) An event of *spurious wakeup* occurs.

In any of the four cases when the current thread wakes up, before the method returns, the thread must re-acquire the lock associated with the condition variable. This guarantees that the thread works in the same way when the guard is true at the beginning.

The following code segment shows the situation that the guard is modified by a thread.

Guarded Command	**Android Implementation**
| ```
//code modifying guard
.....



]
``` | ```
class SharedResource
{
  .....
  public void methodB() throws InterruptedException
  {
    mutex.lock();
    condition = true; //or code modifying guard
    .....
    condVar.signal();
    mutex.unlock();
  }
}
``` |

Android provides two classes, *Condition* and *ConditionVariable*, to create condition variable objects. The *Condition* class is provided by the Java utility library. It uses the method **signal**() to wake up one waiting thread, and **signalAll**() to wake up all waiting threads.

The class *ConditionVariable*, which implements the condition variable paradigm, is unique to Android, not supported by traditional Java. Its methods **open, close,** and **block** are sticky, its exact function depending on the state of the thread. The method **open** corresponds to the traditional **signalAll** method that releases all threads that are blocked (waiting). The method **block** corresponds to the traditional **wait** method, which blocks the current thread until the condition becomes true (or opened in the Android's documentation). If **open** is called before **block**, the method **block** will not block but instead returns spontaneously.

As a condition variable always associates with a lock, to use the *Condition* class, we need to include in our program the import statments:

> import java.util.concurrent.locks.Condition;
> import java.util.concurrent.locks.Lock;
> import java.util.concurrent.locks.ReentrantLock;

To use *ConditionVariable*, we need to include:

> import android.os.ConditionVariable;

Now we can present a solution to the producer-consumer problem using condition variables. We rewrite the *BoudedBuffer* class discussed above with use of condition variables. Here, for simplicity and clarity of presentation, we hard-code the buffer size, omit the print statements and do not return the current head and tail positions of the queue. We use two condition variables *notFull* and *notEmpty* for the producer threads to wait until the buffer is not full and the consumer threads to wait until the buffer is not empty. The lock *mutex* is to ensure that only one thread is examining the status buffer; the thread releases *mutex* if it has to wait for the condition to become true and re-acquire it when it is awakened. The complete code of the class is shown in Listing 7-6 below.

Program Listing 7-6   Implementation of *BoundedBuffer* with Condition Variables

```
class BoundedBuffer
{
  final Lock mutex = new ReentrantLock();
  final Condition notFull  = mutex.newCondition();
  final Condition notEmpty = mutex.newCondition();
  final int length = 100;
  final Object[] items = new Object[length];
  int tail, head;

  public void insert ( Object x ) throws InterruptedException
  {
    mutex.lock();          //Exclude others while examining guard
    try {
      while ( tail >= head + length )   //buffer full
      notFull.await();     //wait until buffer not full
      int t = tail % length;
      items[t] = x;        //insert item at tail
      tail++;              //advance tail
      notEmpty.signal();
    } finally {
      mutex.unlock();
    }
  }
}

  public Object remove() throws InterruptedException
  {
    mutex.lock();
    try {
      while ( tail == head )  //buffer empty
        notEmpty.await();     //wait until buffer not empty
```

```
            int h = head % length;
            Object x = items[h];
            head++;              //Advance head
            notFull.signal();
            return x;
        } finally {
            mutex.unlock();
        }
    }
}
```

7.3.5 Readers-Writers Problem

The readers-writers problem concerns the access of a shared file or database, where some threads, known as *readers*, may want to read the shared resource, whereas others, *known as writers*, may want to write to it. The problem allows concurrent reads but mutual exclusion must be maintained when a writer modifies the data. This is a good example of a synchronization problem that lacks an elegant solution using semaphores only, but can be solved conveniently using condition variables. The following code presents a solution expressed using guarded commands:

void reader() {
    when (nWriters == 0) [
        nReaders++;
    ]
 	
    // read
 	
    [nReaders–;]
}
	void writer() {
	    when(nReaders==0 && nWriters==0)[
	        nWriters++;
	    ]
	
	    // write
	
	    [nWriters–]
	}

In the code, *nReaders* is the number of readers, the number of threads that are currently reading, and *nWriters* is the number of writers that are currently writing. Listing 7-7 below shows an Android implementation of this solution.

Program Listing 7-7   Readers-Writers Problem with Condition Variables

```
class ReaderWriter
{
  final Lock mutex = new ReentrantLock();
  final Condition readerQueue=mutex.newCondition();//cond variable
  final Condition writerQueue=mutex.newCondition();//cond variable

  int nReaders = 0;  //number of reader threads
  int nWriters = 0;  //number of writer threads (0 or 1)

  void reader() throws InterruptedException
  {
    mutex.lock();    //mutual exclusion
    while ( !(nWriters == 0) )
```

```
      readerQueue.await();//wait in readerQueue till no more writers
    nReaders++;     //one more reader
    mutex.unlock();
    //read
    //........
    //finished reading
    mutex.lock();    //need mutual exclusion
    if ( --nReaders == 0 )
      writerQueue.signal(); //wake up a waiting writer
    mutex.unlock();
  }

  void writer() throws InterruptedException
  {
    mutex.lock();
    while ( !((nReaders == 0) && (nWriters == 0)) )
      writerQueue.await();   //wait in writerQueue
                             //  until no more writer & readers
    nWriters++;              //one writer
    mutex.unlock();
    //write
    //........
    //finished writing
    mutex.lock();                //need mutual exclusion
    nWriters--;                  //only one writer at a time
    writerQueue.signal();        //wake up a waiting writer
    readerQueue.signalAll();     //wake up all waiting readers
    mutex.unlock();
  }
}
```

Here *readers* wait on the condition variable *readerQueue* when the number of *writers* is not 0, indicating a thread is modifying the data. The *writers* wait on the condition variable *writerQueue* when either *nReaders* or *nWriters* is not zero, indicating the presence of some threads that are reading or a thread that is writing. When a reader thread has finished reading and finds that no more thread is reading, it wakes up all the first waiting *writers* and all the waiting *readers*. The awakened threads will all try to acquire the *mutex* lock. If one of the *readers* gets the lock first, reading occurs with the awakened writer thread waiting, otherwise writing takes palce and all *readers* have to wait.

Some readers might have noticed that if *readers* arrive frequently, the writer thread may be in **starvation**, never getting a chance to write. This problem is actually referred to as the readers-writers problem with readers priority. This is in analogy of the situation that a female janitor tries to clean a gentlemen restroom. She has to wait until all users have left. If the restroom is heavily used and gentlemen arrive continuously, she will never have a chance to clean it. In practice, to resolve the issue, she would put up a sign to block new entries and enter the men's room after the last current user has left.

In the same way, the starvation issue in the readers-writers problem can be solved by giving *writers* higher priorities, and the problem is now referred to as readers-writers problem with writers priority. The writers-priority solution is to let the writer just wait for current *readers* to finish and block newly arrived *readers*. The following code presents a solution in guarded commands:

```
void reader() {
    when ( nWriters == 0 ) [
        nReaders++;
    ]

    // read

    [nReaders--;]
}
```

```
void writer() {
    nWriters++;
    when(nReaders==0 && nActiveWriters==0)[
        nActiveWriters++;
    ]

    // write

    [nWriters--; nActiveWriters;]
}
```

In this code, *nWriters* represents the number of *writers* that have arrived, either currently writing or waiting to write. The new variable *nActiveWriters*, which can either be 0 or 1, represents the number of *writers* that are currently writing. *Readers* must now wait until no more *writers*, either writing or waiting to write, has arrived. *Writers* wait as before, until no other threads are reading or writing.

The Android implementation of this solution is presented in Listing 7-8 below:

Program Listing 7-8   Solution of Readers-Writers Problem with Writers-Priority

```
class ReaderWriterPriority
{
  final Lock mutex = new ReentrantLock();
  final Condition readerQueue = mutex.newCondition(); //cond variable
  final Condition writerQueue = mutex.newCondition(); //cond variable

  int nReaders = 0;   //number of reader threads
  int nWriters = 0;   //number of writer threads (0 or 1)
  int nActiveWriters = 0;   //number of threads currently writing

  void reader() throws InterruptedException
  {
    mutex.lock();      //mutual exclusion
    while ( !(nWriters == 0) )
      readerQueue.await();//wait in readerQueue until no more writers
    nReaders++;        //one more reader
    mutex.unlock();
    //read
    //........
    //finished reading
    mutex.lock();      //need mutual exclusion
    if ( --nReaders == 0 )
      writerQueue.signal();    //wake up a waiting writer
    mutex.unlock();
  }

  void writer() throws InterruptedException
  {
    mutex.lock();
    nWriters++;                    //a writer has arrived
    while ( !((nReaders == 0) && (nActiveWriters == 0)) )
      writerQueue.await();       //wait in writerQueue
```

```
                                    //   until no more writer & readers
      nActiveWriters++;             //one active writer
      mutex.unlock();
      //write
      //........
      //finished writing
      mutex.lock();                 //need mutual exclusion
      nActiveWriters--;             //only one active writer at a time
      if ( --nWriters == 0 )        //no more waiting writers, so wake
        readerQueue.signalAll();    // up all waiting readers
      else                          //has waiting writer
        writerQueue.signal();       //wake up one waiting writer
      mutex.unlock();
    }
  }
```

7.4 Deadlocks

Suppose you have a turkey dinner with your siblings and cousins and all of you are highly civilized like what is shown in Figure 7-6. There is a cooked whole turkey on the table. Also on the table are a public knife and a public fork, which will be shared by all of you. If you want to eat turkey meat you must first acquire the public knife and the public fork to cut a piece and put it on your own private plate. After returning the knife and the fork to the table, you can begin to enjoy eating your turkey meat using your own private utensils. If each of you acquires the tools (knife and fork) one by one, you may run into a situation in which you have acquired the knife and your little brother has acquired the fork. If no one wants to share the usage of the public tools, then you have to wait for him to release the fork and he he has to wait for you to release the knife. If none wants to yield, no one can proceed to get any turkey. Both of you have to wait forever and this situation is called **deadlock**.

Figure 7-6 Resource Sharing (Image downloaded from *http://disney-clipart.com/Thanksgiving/*)

In this simple example, *is there any way to prevent deadlock by setting some rules of using the tools*? Actually, there a simple way to prevent deadlock by ordering the acquiring of tools.

For example, you can set a simple rule of using the tools: *if you need to use both the knife and the fork, you must first hold (have acquired) the knife before you are allowed to pick up the fork.* Under this rule, deadlock will not occur as only one of you can hold the knife at any instance. Of course, while you are holding the knife, if your little brother has acquired the fork, he is certainly allowed to use it to get some other food such as mashed potato and beans that do not need a knife to fetch. After he has finished fetching those food, he has to put the fork back on the table before he is allowed to get the knife to get any turkey meat and now you can pick it up to fetch the turkey meat. In computer systems, ordering shared resources and enforcing the rule of acquiring them in order is a simple way to prevent deadlock. The following two examples demonstrate this method. In the examples, two threads will acquire two *Mutex* variables to access a critical section. In the first example, the two threads do not acquire the *Mutex* objects in the same order, and deadlock occurs, while in the second example, they acquire *Mutex* objects in the same order and the system is deadlock free.

The following program creates two threads that result in a deadlock state:

Program Listing 7-9 Deadlocked Threads

```
// A demo of the existence of deadlock
package thread.deadlock;
import android.app.Activity;
import android.os.Bundle;
import android.util.Log;
import android.view.Menu;

public class MainActivity extends Activity
{
  @Override
  public void onCreate(Bundle savedInstanceState) {
    super.onCreate(savedInstanceState);
    Mutex mutexX = new Mutex( "mutexX" );
    Mutex mutexY = new Mutex( "mutexY" );

    // Thread A tries to acquire mutexX, then mutexY
    Athread A = new Athread( mutexX, mutexY, "A");
    // Thread B tries to acquire mutexY, then mutexX
    Athread B = new Athread( mutexY, mutexX, "B");

    A.start();
    B.start();
  }
}

class Mutex
{
  public String mname;
  public Mutex( String name )
  {
    mname = name;
  }
}

class Athread extends Thread
{
```

```
private Mutex first, second;
private String tname;

public Athread(Mutex f, Mutex s, String name ) {
   first = f;
   second = s;
   tname = name;
}

public void run() {
  synchronized (first) {
     // do something
  try {
      Thread.sleep( ((int)(Math.random()+1))*1000);
  } catch (InterruptedException e) {}
    Log.v ("Thread Info", tname + " thread got " + first.mname);
    synchronized (second) {
      // do something
      Log.v("Thread Info", tname + " thread got " + second.mname );
    }
  }
 }
}
```

In the example, each of the threads tries to acquire both of the mutex objects, *mutexX* and *mutexY* but they try to acquire them in different orders. Consequently, each can only obtain one mutex and wait for the other one, resulting in a deadlock state. When we run the program, we will see in the log output the following statements:

```
Thread Info: A thread got mutexX
Thread Info: B thread got mutexY
```

This indicates that neither thread has acquired both mutex objects and they have to wait forever.

By modifying the code so that both threads acquire the mutex objects in the same order, we can ensure that the two threads are deadlock free. The following code listing shows this situation:

Program Listing 7-10   Deadlock-Free Threads

```
// Deadlock free code
package thread.deadlockfree;

public class MainActivity extends Activity
{
  @Override
  public void onCreate(Bundle savedInstanceState)
  {
    super.onCreate(savedInstanceState);
    Mutex mutexX = new Mutex( "mutexX" );
    Mutex mutexY = new Mutex( "mutexY" );

    // Both Thread A and  try to acquire mutexX, then mutexY
    Athread A = new Athread( mutexX, mutexY, "A");
    Athread B = new Athread( mutexX, mutexY, "B");
```

```
    A.start();
    B.start();
  }
}
// Rest of code same as Listing 7-9
```

When we run the code, we obtain the following log outputs; both threads have acquired both *Mutex* objects successfully.

```
Thread Info: A thread got mutexX
Thread Info: A thread got mutexY
Thread Info: B thread got mutexX
Thread Info: B thread got mutexY
```

This means that no deadlock has occurred. In developing muti-threaded applications, one has to be careful to avoid deadlock situations.

Chapter 8   Network Communication

8.1   Introduction

Devices connected to the Internet use networking protocol TCP/IP to communicate. The protocol is divided into layers as shown in Figure 8-1 below. At the top of the model is the application layer, which can be any Internet applications such as creating graphics, streaming videos, and searching information. At the bottom is the physical layer, which deals with the actual transfer of the data bits. Below *application* is the transport layer that controls network traffic and the TCP/IP model provides the *Transmission Control Protocol (TCP)* and the *User Datagram Protocol (UDP)* for applications to communicate. The *network* layer is responsible for the routing of a packet, which consists of the source and the destination addresses. The *data link* layer is responsible for handling errors when transferring the data. In the model, a layer is only allowed to communicate with its adjacent layers directly. For example, the *network* layer is only allowed to 'talk' to the *transport* layer and the *data link* layer.

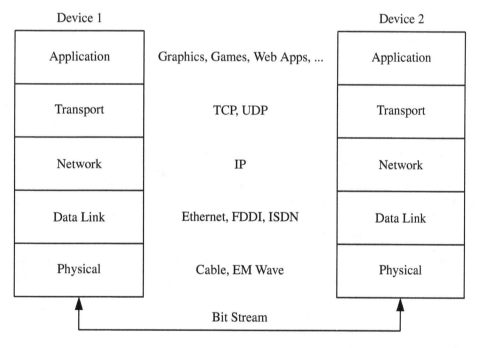

Figure 8-1 TCP/IP Layering Model

Normally we program at the application level and do not need to know the details of the low level layers. Traditionally, people write Internet communication programs in C/C++, calling several *socket* functions to establish a communication channel, which is fairly complicated to program. However, Java has largely simplified the coding of such applications. Developing a simple client-server application may just involve a few lines of codes. We explain a few terms commonly used in TCP/IP data communication below.

TCP

TCP (Transmission Control Protocol) is a connection-oriented protocol, where data packets are transmitted along a fixed established route between the sender and the receiver. It provides a reliable flow of data between two computers by requiring the receiver to send an acknowledgment to the sender, after it has received a data packet.

The protocol is at the *Transport Layer* as shown in Figure 8-1. When two applications communicate to each other reliably, they first establish a connection route and send data back and forth over that route. This is analogous to making a telephone call to a friend, in which a connection is frist established by your dialing a phone number and your friend picking up her phone. Data are sent back and forth over the connection when both of you speak to one another over the phone lines. TCP guarantees that data received are in the same order as they were sent.

The Hypertext Transfer Protocol (HTTP), File Transfer Protocol (FTP), and Telnet are all examples of applications that are built on top of TCP, which provides a point-to-point reliable communication channel. In many applications, the order in which the data are sent and received over the network is critical, otherwise the information received will be invalid.

UDP

UDP (User Datagram Protocol) is a connectionless-oriented protocol that transmits independent blocks of data, called **datagrams**, from one computer to another with no guarantees about arrival. No fixed route is established during the transmission. It is possible that different data blocks take different routes to get to the receiver from the sender. This is in analogous to sending letters through the postal service, in which the order of delivery is not important and first-come-first-served is not guaranteed, and each letter is independent of any other. The protocol is also at the *Transport Layer*.

For the applications that do not require strict standards of reliability and order of delivery, the UDP can provide faster service as it does not need the extra overhead to meet the strict requirements. For example, a clock server that sends the current time to a client that requests it does not really need to resend a packet that the client misses as the client can make another request later. If the client makes two requests and receives the packets out of order, it does not matter much because the client will find the packets out of order and could make another request. By neglecting reliability requirements of TCP, the server can improve its performance. Another example of a service that does not need reliable communication channel is the *ping* command, which is to test the connection between two machines over the network. Actually *ping* needs to know about out-of-order or dropped packets to determine how good a connection is. A reliable protocol would invalidate this service altogether. Also, in a Local Area Network (LAN) the communication medium is very reliable. Packets rarely lose. So it is desirable to use an unreliable protocol such as UDP in many LAN applications. On the other hand, the physical communication links in the Internet are not very reliable as they extend over very large areas. So it makes sense to use a reliable protocol such as TCP in many Internet applications.

Sockets

When we write Android network applications, we program at the application level, often utilizing the *socket* API to send and receive data. A **socket** is a software endpoint that establishes bidirectional communication between a server program and one or more client programs. The socket associates the server program with a specific hardware port on the machine where it sends and receives data. A client socket has to associate with the same port if it wants to communicate with the server. The socket API was first developed by UC Berkeley in the 1980s for UNIX systems and is open-source. Later it was adopted by other organizations and platforms. The original Berkeley sockets are referred to as BSD sockets.a As the API has evolved with little modification from a de facto standard into part of the POSIX specification, POSIX sockets are basically BSD sockets.

A server program typically provides services or resources to a number of client programs. A client sends requests to the server, which responds to them. To handle multiple requests from multiple clients, the server can create one thread dedicated to servicing each client. A multi-threaded server program can accept a connection from a client, create and start a thread for that communication, and continue to listen for requests from other clients.

Ports

Physically, a computer connects to a network through a single medium. How can a process (a running program) communicate with several different processes at the same time? The trick is to use ports, which are virtualised endpoints. The virtualisation makes multiple concurrent connections on a single network interface possible. Each process that communicates with another process identifies itself to the TCP/IP protocol suite by one or more ports. A port is specified by a 16-bit number. The purpose of specifying ports is to differentiate multiple endpoints on a given network address. Strictly speaking, an endpoint (socket) is identified by an IP address and a port number. The TCP and UDP protocols use ports to associate incoming data to a particular process running on a computer as shown in Figure 8-2 below.

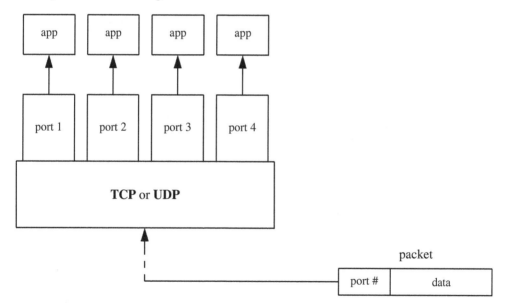

Figure 8-2   TCP/IP Ports

In the following sections, we will present a few examples to illustrate how Android devices communicate in a network.

8.2   Connecting to a Server

The first example that we will discuss is about connecting an Android device to a server program running in a desktop machine and transmitting a message using a socket. Such a server program is very simple if written in Java. It can be run in any common platform such as Linux, MS Windows, or Mac OS/X, though we run it in a 64-bit Linux machine. The following is the complete code for this program.

Program Listing 8-1   *DemoServer.java*

```java
// A simple TCP server for Demo

import java.io.InputStreamReader;
import java.io.BufferedReader;
import java.io.IOException;
import java.net.ServerSocket;
import java.net.Socket;

public class DemoServer {
  public static void main(String[] args) throws IOException {

    if (args.length != 1) {
      System.err.println("Usage: java Server <port number>");
      System.exit(1);
    }

    int portNumber = Integer.parseInt(args[0]);
    try {
      ServerSocket serverSocket = new ServerSocket(portNumber);
      Socket clientSocket = serverSocket.accept();
      BufferedReader input = new BufferedReader (
        new InputStreamReader(clientSocket.getInputStream()));

      String inputLine = null;
      while ( ( inputLine = input.readLine() ) != null ) {
        System.out.println ( inputLine );
      }
    } catch (IOException e) {
        System.out.println("Exception caught on listening on port "
              + portNumber );
        System.out.println(e.getMessage());
    }
  }
}
```

In the code, the statement

ServerSocket serverSocket = new ServerSocket(portNumber);

creates an endpoint at the specified port number, which is provided by the user as an input argument
to the program. *ServerSocket* is a *java.net* class that provides a system-independent implementation of the server side of a client/server socket connection. If the server successfully binds to the
specified port, the *ServerSocket* object (*serverSocket*) is successfully created.

The next statement,

Socket clientSocket = serverSocket.accept();

tells the server process to listen to the port for any request from a client and accepts the connection
if everything has been done properly. If no request has been detected, it just continues to listen.
TCP is used but Java has hidden all the handshaking and house keeping details from the user,

and has simplified the coding of using sockets. When a connection is successfully established, the **accept** method returns a new *Socket* object (*clientSocket*), which is bound to the same local port and has its remote address and remote port set to that of the client. The server process can communicate with the client process over this new *clientSocket* and continue to listen for client connection requests on the original *serverSocket*. However, this simple program can only handle one client at a time. If we want to handle multiple clients, we need to modify the program.

The subsequent few lines of code simply tell the server read in data from the client and print them out on the console.

We can compile the program with the command *javac DemoServer.java*, which generates the class *DemoServer.class*. Suppose we choose the port number to be 1989. We can execute the program using the following command:

    $ java DemoServer 1989

The process then waits and listens for requests at port 1989.

To communicate with the server, the client also needs to know the IP address of the server, which can be found out by executing the command *ifconfig* in the console of a Linux machine or *ipconfig* in MS Windows. The IP of the machine we used in this example is *192.168.1.69*.

The Android client program that sends messages to the server is also simple. The following are the steps of developing this client program in the Eclipse IDE. Suppose we call the project and application *Client*.

1. As usual, in Eclipse IDE, create the project and application *Client* with package name *comm.client*.
2. Grant Internet access permissions to the application by adding a couple of *uses-permission* tags in the file *AndroidManifest.xml* like the following:

```
<?xml version="1.0" encoding="utf-8"?>
<manifest xmlns:android="http://schemas.android.com/apk/res/android"
.....
<uses-permission android:name="android.permission.INTERNET" >
</uses-permission>

<uses-permission android:name="android.permission.ACCESS_NETWORK_STATE">
</uses-permission>
.....
</manifest>
```

3. Modify the file *res/layout/activity_main.xml* to the following, which defines the UI layout to display a button and to accept text input.

```
<LinearLayout xmlns:android="http://schemas.android.com/apk/res/android"
    android:layout_width="fill_parent"
    android:layout_height="fill_parent"
    android:orientation="vertical" >
  <EditText
        android:id="@+id/EditText1"
        android:layout_width="fill_parent"
        android:layout_height="wrap_content"
        android:text="Hello, Friend." >
  </EditText>
  <Button
        android:id="@+id/myButton"
        android:layout_width="wrap_content"
        android:layout_height="wrap_content"
```

```
        android:onClick="onClick"
        android:text="Send" >
    </Button>
</LinearLayout>
```

4. Modify the program *MainActivity.java* to the following.

```
------------------------------------------------------------------------
package comm.client;

import android.app.Activity;
import android.os.Build;
import android.os.Bundle;
import android.view.View;
import android.widget.EditText;
import java.io.IOException;
import java.io.PrintWriter;
import java.io.BufferedWriter;
import java.io.OutputStreamWriter;
import java.net.Socket;
import java.net.InetAddress;
import java.net.UnknownHostException;

public class MainActivity extends Activity {
  private Socket socket;
  private static final int PORT_NO = 1989;
  // Need to change IP address to the IP of your server
  private static final String SERVER_IP = "192.168.1.69";
  @Override
  public void onCreate(Bundle savedInstanceState) {
    super.onCreate(savedInstanceState);
    setContentView(R.layout.activity_main);
    new Thread(new ClientThread()).start();
  }

  public void onClick(View view) {
    try {
      EditText editText = (EditText) findViewById(R.id.EditText1);
      String str = editText.getText().toString();
      PrintWriter out = new PrintWriter(new BufferedWriter(
      new OutputStreamWriter(socket.getOutputStream())), true);
      out.println(str);
    } catch (UnknownHostException e) {
      e.printStackTrace();
    } catch (IOException e) {
      e.printStackTrace();
    } catch (Exception e) {
      e.printStackTrace();
    }
  }

  // inner class
  class ClientThread implements Runnable {
    @Override
    public void run() {
      try {
```

```
            InetAddress serverAddr=InetAddress.getByName(SERVER_IP);
            socket = new Socket(serverAddr, PORT_NO );
        } catch (UnknownHostException e) {
            e.printStackTrace();
        } catch (IOException e) {
            e.printStackTrace();
        }
    }
  }
} //class MainActivity
```

In the code, the port number and the IP address of the server are hard-coded. The main class *MainActivity* defines a *Socket* class variable called *socket* as a data member:

    private Socket socket;

The actual creation of a *Socket* object to communicate with the server is done by the thread *ClientThread*. The **onCreate**() method of *MainActivity* creates and starts this thread by the statement:

    new Thread(new ClientThread()).start();

The thread class *ClientThread* is implemented as an inner class of *MainActivity*. Inner classes have full access to the class in which they are nested, and in our case, the inner class *ClientThread* can access all the data members, *socket, PORT_NO*, and *SERVER_IP* defined in *MainActivity*. It creates the communication channel to the server with the statements:

    InetAddress serverAddr=InetAddress.getByName(SERVER_IP);

    socket = new Socket(serverAddr, PORT_NO);

The method **onClick**() of *MainActivity* defines an editable text field and a button. When the button is clicked, the text in the text field is sent to the server through the communication channel, which is achieved by the statements:

    EditText editText = (EditText) findViewById(R.id.EditText1);

    String str = editText.getText().toString();

    PrintWriter out = new PrintWriter(new BufferedWriter(

    new OutputStreamWriter(socket.getOutputStream())), true);

    out.println(str);

When we run the program, the Android UI shows a *Send* button and an editable text field as shown in Figure 8-3 below.

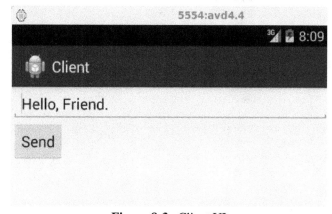

Figure 8-3   Client UI

We can type in any text message in the text area. Upon clicking the *Send* button, the message is sent to the server, which then reads in the text and prints it to the console. The following shows the operation on the server side and sample text received from the Android client.

```
$ java DemoServer 1989
Hello, Friend.
Android the Beautiful!
```

8.3 Communication Between Android Devices

We have discussed how to send a message from an Android device to a server running on a PC in the previous section. Suppose now we want to send messages from an Android client to an Android server and we want to do the test in AVD emulators. In this case, the client program is the same as the one presented above except that the hard-coded IP address needs to be changed to the one that an AVD emulator runs, which is 10.0.2.2. That is, in the program *MainActivity*.java of the *Client* project discussed above, we need to modify the statement specifying the IP address to:

```
private static final String SERVER_IP = "10.0.2.2";
```

We will still use the port number 1989 for the client.

The Android server program is different from the server program running on a PC as it is run as an Android application. Suppose we develop this program in the Eclipse IDE and name the project and application *Server* and the package *comm.server*. Like what we did to the *Client* application described above, we have to grant Internet access permission to the *Server* application; this is done by adding <uses-permission> statements in the file *AndroidManifest.xml* (see the *Client* project description in the previous section). The listing below shows the complete Java code of *MainActivity.java* of the server program.

Program Listing 8-2   *MainActivity.java* of Server

```java
package comm.server;
import android.os.Build;
import android.app.Activity;
import android.os.Bundle;
import android.os.Handler;
import android.widget.TextView;
import java.io.InputStreamReader;
import java.io.BufferedReader;
import java.io.IOException;
import java.net.ServerSocket;
import java.net.Socket;

public class MainActivity extends Activity {

    private ServerSocket serverSocket;
    private String str;
    Handler textHandler;
    Thread serverThread = null;
    private TextView textView;
    public static final int portNumber = 2014;

    @Override
    public void onCreate(Bundle savedInstanceState) {
        super.onCreate(savedInstanceState);
```

```
      setContentView(R.layout.activity_main);
      textView = (TextView) findViewById(R.id.text1);
      textHandler = new Handler();
      new Thread(new ServerThread()).start();
   }

   @Override
   protected void onStop() {
      super.onStop();
      try {
         serverSocket.close();
      } catch (IOException e) {
         e.printStackTrace();
      }
   }

   //Inner class
   class ServerThread implements Runnable {
      public void run() {
         Socket commSocket = null;
         try {
            serverSocket = new ServerSocket(portNumber);
         } catch (IOException e) {
            e.printStackTrace();
         }
         while (!Thread.currentThread().isInterrupted()) {
            try {
               commSocket = serverSocket.accept();
               BufferedReader input = new BufferedReader (
                  new InputStreamReader( commSocket.getInputStream() ));
               while ( ( str = input.readLine() )  != null )
                  textHandler.post(new ShowText ());
            } catch (IOException e) {
               e.printStackTrace();
            }
         }
      }
   } //ServerThread

   // Inner class
   class ShowText implements Runnable {
      @Override
      public void run() {
         textView.setText(textView.getText().toString() +
            "Client said: " + str + "\n");
      }
   } //ShowText
} //MainActivity
```

In the code, the server port number is hard-coded to be 2014. We created a *Handler* object, which is referred to by the variable *textHandler*, to process any incoming message. A *Handler* allows us to send and process *Message* and *Runnable* objects associated with the *MessageQueue* of a thread. Normally, the main thread of a process is dedicated to running a message queue that manages the top-level application objects such as activities, and broadcast receivers, and any windows they create. The application can create other threads, and communicate back with the main thread through a *Handler*. A newly created *Handler* is bound to the thread/message queue of the creating thread, delivering messages and runnables to the message queue and executing them as they come out of the message queue. Its method **post**() takes a thread as an argument and adds the thread to the message queue. In our code, *ShowText* is an inner class that displays text on the defined text area, and an object of it is passed as an argument to **post**().

ServerThread is another inner class that creates a socket with the specified port number, listening to incoming messages. When it reads a line, it uses *textHandler* to pass the information to the main thread. The statement

```
textHandler.post(new ShowText ());
```

creates a *ShowText* thread and adds it to the message queue. This thread then displays the message on the screen while *ServerThread* continues to listen to other messages.

To test the application, we first use **Eclipse** to run with one AVD the *Server* program, which uses port 2014. The client program will use port 1989. The AVD emulator running the server would use port 5554. We want to access this emulator and redirect client messages to its port. This can be done using **telnet** and its **redir** command. So the next step is to issue the telnet command in the machine that runs the AVD emulator like the following:

```
$ telnet localhost 5554
Trying ::1...
telnet: connect to address ::1: Connection refused
Trying 127.0.0.1...
Connected to localhost.
Escape character is '^]'.
Android Console: type 'help' for a list of commands
OK
redir add tcp:1989:2014
OK
```

The command *redir add tcp:1989:2014* redirects messages from port 1989 to port 2014. Also an AVD emulator runs on the alias IP 10.0.2.2.

Lastly, we run the client program using another AVD emulator (different from the one used to run the server program). When these are done, we see two emulators running on our PC, one for *Client* and one for *Sever*. When we enter text in the client and click the button, the text is sent to the server for display. Figure 8-3 below shows two emulators that run the client and server programs.

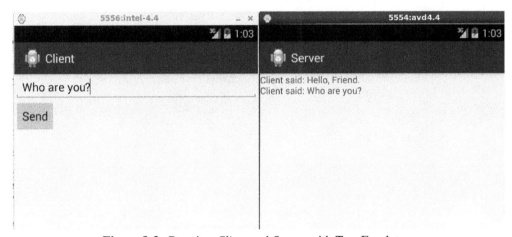

Figure 8-3 Running *Client* and *Server* with Two Emulators

8.4   A Remote Calculator

In the example of this section, we present a simple remote calculator, which works like a typical client-server application. The client is an Android program, managing the UI and interacting with the user. The server is a Java program running in a PC, performing the actual arithmetic calculations. The client accepts inputs from the user and sends them to the remote server, which carries out the calculations and returns the result to the client. Obviously, there are many ways to write such an application.

To introduce more programming techniques, we define a client thread using an independent external class instead of using an inner class like what we did did before.

8.4.1   JSON

We also introduce here the usage of **JSON**, which stands for *JavaScript Object Notation*, to pass data between the client and the server. JSON is a lightweight data-interchange format, easy for humans to read and write, and easy for machines to parse and generate. It is a languate independent text format based on a subset of the JavaScript Programming Language, Standard ECMA-262 3rd Edition deployed in 1989, using conventions that are familiar to programmers of common languages such as C/C++, Java and Python. JSON is open-source, making it an ideal data-interchange language. It is built on two structures:

1. **A collection of name/value pairs**, which can be realized as an *object, record, struct, dictionary, hash table, keyed list*, or *associative array*.
2. **An ordered list of values**, which can be realized as an *array, vector, list*, or *sequence*.

As these are universal data structures, supported by virtually all modern programming languages, it makes sense to have a data format, which is interchangeable with programming languages, to be based on these structures.

In JASON, they take on one of the forms: *object, array, value*, and *string*. For details, please refer to its official web site at:

http://www.json.org/

In our application, we will only use the *object* form. An object is an unordered set of *name/value* pairs, starting with { (left brace) and ends with } (right brace). Each name is followed by : (colon) and the *name/value* pairs are separated by , (comma) as shown in Figure 8-4 below.

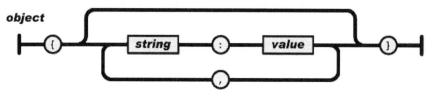

Figure 8-4   Object Form of JSON

We will use this form to pass data structures between the client and the server. For example, we can express the calculation of the sum of two numbers, $2 + 1$, by the text,

$$\{\,\text{``}calcOp\text{''} : \text{``} + \text{''}, \text{``}op1\text{''} : \text{``}2\text{''}, \text{``}op2\text{''} : \text{``}1\text{''}\,\}$$

where the string *calcOp* indicates the calculation operator; the string *op1* indicates the first operand, and *op2*, the second operand. The JSON package that we have used, *json-simple-1.1.1.jar*, is a simple version, which was downloaded from the site,

http://code.google.com/p/json-simple/

8.4.2   Server Running on PC

The application's server, which runs on a PC, carries out the calculations. The code of reading in a message from a socket is similar to the server code *DemoServer.java* presented in Listing 8-1 of Section 8.2. However, here the code has to parse the input line to a JSON object, extract the operator and the operands, perform the calculation and send the result back to the client. Suppose we call our server program *CalcServer.java*, and we assume that we will use port 1989 to communicate. The following lists the complete server code:

Program Listing 8-3   *CalcServer.java*

```java
// Remote Calculator Server running on PC
import java.io.*;
import java.net.*;
import java.util.Arrays;
import org.json.simple.*;
import static java.lang.System.in;

public class CalcServer
{
  public static void main(String[] args) throws IOException
  {
    if (args.length != 1) {
      System.err.println("Usage: java CalcServer <port number>");
      System.exit(1);
    }
    int portNumber = Integer.parseInt(args[0]);
    JSONObject   jsonObject;
    try {
      ServerSocket serverSocket =  new ServerSocket ( portNumber );
      while ( true ) {
        System.out.println( "Waiting for Client!" );
        Socket socket = serverSocket.accept();
        String inputLine = null;
        // get input from socket
        BufferedReader input = new BufferedReader (
           new InputStreamReader(socket.getInputStream()));
        double result = 0.0;

        while  ( (inputLine = input.readLine() )  != null ) {
          System.out.print( "  Received request: " );
          System.out.println ( inputLine );
          jsonObject = (JSONObject) JSONValue.parse ( inputLine );
          result = calculate ( jsonObject );
          PrintWriter ow=new PrintWriter(socket.getOutputStream(),true);
          ow.println ( result );
          System.out.println( "  Result sent to client!");
        }
        socket.close();
      } // while ( true )
    } catch (IOException e) {
        System.out.println("Exception caught on listening on port "
                 + portNumber );
        System.out.println(e.getMessage());
```

```
                System.exit ( 1 );
      }
  }


  public static double calculate ( JSONObject jsonObject )
  {
    double result = 0;
    // Extract operator and operands.
    String calcOp = (String) jsonObject.get("calcOp");
    double op1=Double.parseDouble((String)jsonObject.get("op1"));
    double op2=Double.parseDouble((String)jsonObject.get("op2"));

    // Do the actual calculation
    if (calcOp.equals( "+" ))
      result = op1 + op2;
    else if (calcOp.equals( "-"))
      result = op1 - op2;
    else if (calcOp.equals( "*" ))
      result = op1 * op2;
    else if (calcOp.equals( "/" ))
    if ( op2 != 0 )
      result = op1 / op2;
    System.out.printf( "  %f %s %f = %f : ",op1,calcOp,op2,result);

    return result;
  }
}
```

In the code, the **main** method creates a *ServerSocket* object with the specified port and listens to the port by creating a *Socket* object and using its **accept**() method to accept any incoming message as a string, and form a JSON object from the string by the statement,

           jsonObject = (JSONObject) JSONValue.parse (inputLine);

It then calls the method **calculate**(), which takes a JSON object as the input parameter, to do the calculation. The **calculate** method parses the JSON object using the **get**() method of the JSON simple package to extract the operator and the two operands. It then does the arithmetic calculation and returns the result as a **double** to **main**, which sends the result to the client through the socket by the two statements:

        PrintWriter ow = new PrintWriter (socket.getOutputStream(), true);
        ow.println (result);

After the result has been sent, it closes the current *Socket* object using the statement

        socket.close();

and goes back to the beginning of the while-loop to create another socket for listening and accepting another message.

Suppose we put the simple JSON package *json-simple-1.1.1* in the same directory as the server program, *CalcServer.java*. We can compile the server program in a PC with the following command,

        $ javac -cp .:./json-simple-1.1.1.jar CalcServer.java

and run it with the command,

        $ java -cp .:./json-simple-1.1.1.jar CalcServer 1989

where the input parameter 1989 is the port number that will be used by the server. The running program will respond with the message:

```
Waiting for Client!
```

while waiting for any request from a client.

8.4.3 Client Running on Android

The application's client program runs on Android. Suppose we call the project *CalcClient* and the package *comm.calcclient*. We divide the application into two classes. The main class *MainActivity* is for UI, accepting inputs and displaying results. The other class, named *Client* is for communicating with the server, sending the operation strings to and accepting results from the server. The following lists the code of the class *MainActivity*, omitting the import and package statements.

> **Program Listing 8-4**   *MainActivity.java* of CalcClient Project

```
public class MainActivity extends Activity
                          implements View.OnClickListener
{
  public static double result = 0;
  public static String oper = "";
  public static String nums1;
  public static String nums2;

  private String str = "";
  private int displayCount = 0;
  EditText t1, t2;
  ImageButton plusButton, minusButton, multiplyButton, didvideButton;
  TextView displayResult;

  /** Called when the activity is first created. */
  @Override
  public void onCreate(Bundle savedInstanceState) {
    super.onCreate(savedInstanceState);
    setContentView(R.layout.activity_main);

    // find elements defined in res/layout/activity_main.xml
    t1 = (EditText) findViewById(R.id.t1);
    t2 = (EditText) findViewById(R.id.t2);
    plusButton = (ImageButton) findViewById(R.id.plusButton);
    minusButton = (ImageButton) findViewById(R.id.minusButton);
    multiplyButton = (ImageButton) findViewById(R.id.multiplyButton);
    didvideButton = (ImageButton) findViewById(R.id.divideButton);
    displayResult = (TextView) findViewById(R.id.displayResult);

    // set listeners
    plusButton.setOnClickListener(this);
    minusButton.setOnClickListener(this);
    multiplyButton.setOnClickListener(this);
    didvideButton.setOnClickListener(this);
  }

  // @Override
```

```
public void onClick(View view) {
   // check if the fields are empty
   if (TextUtils.isEmpty(t1.getText().toString())
         || TextUtils.isEmpty(t2.getText().toString()))
     return;

   // read numbers from EditText
   nums1 = t1.getText().toString();
   nums2 = t2.getText().toString();

   // determine which image button has been clicked
   switch (view.getId()) {
     case R.id.plusButton:
       oper = "+";
       break;
     case R.id.minusButton:
       oper = "-";
       break;
     case R.id.multiplyButton:
       oper = "*";
       break;
     case R.id.divideButton:
       oper = "/";
       break;
     default:
       break;
   }
   // Create thread to send request
   Client client = new Client ( nums1, nums2, oper );
   Thread sendThread = new Thread ( client );
   sendThread.start();
   try {
     result = client.getResult();
   } catch (InterruptedException e) {
     e.printStackTrace();
   }
   // form the output line, display at most 4 lines on screen
   if ( displayCount < 4 ){
     str += nums1 + " " + oper + " " + nums2 + " = " + result + "\n";
     displayCount++;
   } else {
     displayCount = 1;
     str = nums1 + " " + oper + " " + nums2 + " = " + result + "\n";
   }
   displayResult.setText( str );
  }
}
```

The UI part of the code is straight forward and easy to understand. The UI is defined in the layout file of *res/layout/activity_main.xml*, which is not presented here as it is similar to some of the layout files we have explained in previous chapters. (The complete code of this book can be downloaded from the site *hppt://www.forejune.com*.) In the UI, the user enters two numbers in the two *EditText* fields. Upon clicking an image button, the method **onClick**() is called; the method reads in the two numbers and chooses the corresponding operator of the image button. It then creates a *Client* thread to send the operation string to the server, which returns the result of operation to the *Client* object. The **onClick** method calls the **getResult**() method of *Client* to get the operation result. It then displays the operation string and the result on the screen using the **setText**() method of *TextView*. (See Figure 8-5 below.)

The code of the *Client* class is fairly simple and is presented in Listing 8-5 below. Its method **remoteCalculation**() is responsible for sending the operation string in the JSON object form to the server, which returns the result of operation; the method saves the result in the **double** variable *result*.

The only task of the method **getResult**() is supposed to return the value of *result* as a double to whatever calls it. However, we cannot simply return *result* without checking the situation. This is because the method may be called before the result is available. That is, it is called before **remoteCaculation** has obtained the result from the server, and thus returning an invalid value. To prevent this from happening, we can use the **guard** concept we discussed in Chapter 7 to force the method to wait until the result is available. We define a *Condition* variable, *resultReady*, to enforce the waiting with the statement

resultReady.await();

It suspends the execution of the method until **resultReady.signal**() is executed by the method **remoteCalculation** or some other routines, after the result has been obtained from the server. Consequently, **getResult** always returns a valid result. However, we need to address one more issue – there could be situations that the **signal**() command is executed before **await**(), leaving it waiting forever. To guard against this situation, we define an integer variable, *count*. The method waits only if the value of *count* is 0, which is incremented by **remoteCalculation** when the result is available. This is illustrated in Figure 8-5 below:

int count = 0;

```
double getResult()                   void remoteCalculation()
{                                    {
    while ( count == 0 )                 . . . . .
        resultReady.await();             count++;
    count = 0;                           resultReady.signal();
                                         . . . . .
    return result;                   }
}
```

Figure 8-5   Enforcing Valid Result with Condition Variable

In our actual code, the *count* increment and the execution of **signal** are done in the **run**() method. The complete code of the *Client* class is listed below with import and package statements omitted.

Program Listing 8-5   *Client.java* of CalcClient Project

```
public class Client implements Runnable {
  private static Socket socket;
  private static String nums1;
  private static String nums2;
  private static String calcOp;
  private static double result = 0;
  final Lock mutex = new ReentrantLock();
  final Condition resultReady = mutex.newCondition();
  private int count = 0;
```

```java
public Client ( String n1, String n2, String op )
{
  nums1 = n1;
  nums2 = n2;
  calcOp = op;
}
@Override
public void run() {
  // TODO Auto-generated method stub

  String serverAddr = "192.168.1.69";
  int portNumber = 1989;

  mutex.lock();
  try {
    //socket = initiateContact(serverAddr, portNumber);

    remoteCalculation( serverAddr, portNumber );
    count++;
    resultReady.signal();
  } catch (UnknownHostException e1) {
      e1.printStackTrace();
  } catch (IOException e1) {
      e1.printStackTrace();
  } finally{
    mutex.unlock();
  }
}


public void remoteCalculation(String serverAddr, int portNumbe)
 throws IOException
{
  Socket socket = null;
  socket = new Socket(serverAddr, portNumber);

  BufferedReader stdIn = new BufferedReader(new
                            InputStreamReader( System.in));
  // Form JSON object string
  String jsonString = "{" + "\"calcOp\":\""
      + calcOp + "\"," + "\"op1\":\""
      + nums1 + "\"," + "\"op2\":\""
      + nums2 + "\"}";

  System.out.println( jsonString );
    sendMessage( socket, jsonString);
  String serverReply = receiveMessage( socket );
  System.out.println("Result: " + serverReply);
  result = Double.parseDouble((String) serverReply);
  stdIn.close();
  socket.close();
}

public double getResult()  throws InterruptedException
{
  mutex.lock();
```

```
      System.out.println("getResult wait");
      // The count is to ensure the function won't wait forever
      //   if signal has been issued before  await.
      while ( count == 0 )
        resultReady.await();     // Condition wait
      count = 0;
      mutex.unlock();

      return result;
    }

    // Receive message from a socket
    public static String receiveMessage(Socket socket)
                          throws IOException {
      String inputLine = null;
      BufferedReader inputBuffer = null;
      inputBuffer = new BufferedReader( new InputStreamReader
                                  ( socket.getInputStream()));
      inputLine = inputBuffer.readLine();

      return inputLine;
    }

    // send message to socket
    public static void sendMessage(Socket socket, String outputLine)
         throws IOException {
      PrintWriter outputWriter = null;
      outputWriter = new PrintWriter(socket.getOutputStream(), true);
      outputWriter.println(outputLine);
    }
}
```

When we run the code in Android, we will see an UI like the one shown in Figure 8-6. The text below the image buttons are the calculation expressions we have entered and the results returned by the server.

Also, correspondingly, the server will print out some messages. While the client is running in Android, the server running in a PC will display output messages similar to the following, which tells the user it receives requests from the client, does the calculations, and returns the results.

```
Waiting for Client!
  Received request: {"calcOp":"+","op1":"1989","op2":"64"}
  1989.000000 + 64.000000 = 2053.000000 :   Result sent to client!
Waiting for Client!
  Received request: {"calcOp":"-","op1":"1989","op2":"64"}
  1989.000000 - 64.000000 = 1925.000000 :   Result sent to client!
Waiting for Client!
  Received request: {"calcOp":"*","op1":"1989","op2":"64"}
  1989.000000 * 64.000000 = 127296.000000 :   Result sent to client!
Waiting for Client!
  Received request: {"calcOp":"/","op1":"1989","op2":"64"}
  1989.000000 / 64.000000 = 31.078125 :   Result sent to client!
Waiting for Client!
```

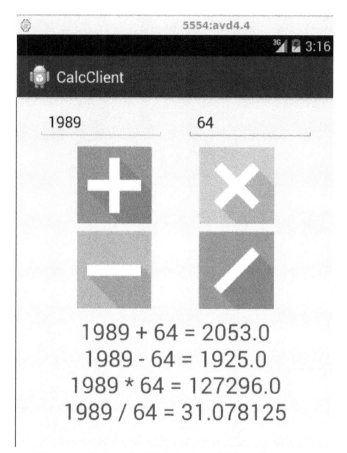

Figure 8-6   Sample I/O Display of Client Calculator

8.5 Broadcast Receiver

A broadcast receiver (or receiver for short) is an Android component for detecting system or application events, responding to system-wide broadcast announcements, such as low battery level or file downloading done. A broadcast receiver is implemented as a subclass of *BroadcastReceiver* and each broadcast is delivered as an *Intent* object. *BroadcastReceivers* are one of Androids four standard app component types (activities, services, content providers, and broadcast receivers), each of which serves a distinct purpose and has a distinct life cycle that defines how the component is created and destroyed. Details of the *BroadcastReceiver* class can be found at

   http://developer.android.com/reference/android/content/BroadcastReceiver.html

A broadcast receiver must first be registered before it will receive any announcement. All registered receivers for an event are notified by the Android runtime once the event occurs. For example, an application can register for the ACTION_BOOT_COMPLETED system event, which occurs when the Android system has completed the boot process.

We can register a receiver statically via the *AndroidManifest.xml* file or dynamically via the *Context*.**registerReceiver**() method.

Implementation of a broadcast receiver consists of two steps:

1. declaring a subclass of *BroadcastReceiver*, and
2. implementing the **onReceive**() method.

The following sample code shows the form of the implementation:

```
import android.content.Context;
import android.content.Intent;
import android.content.BroadcastReceiver;

public class MyReceiver extends BroadcastReceiver
{
  @Override
  public void onReceive(Context context, Intent intent) {
    // Response to an  event
  }
}
```

The Android runtime calls the **onReceive**() method on all registered receivers whenever the event occurs. This method takes two parameters:

Parameter

context The *Context* object on which the receiver is running. We can use it to access additional information or to start services or activities.

intent The *Intent* object being received. It contains additional information that we can use in our implementation.

System-wide Events

A lot of system events are defined as final static fields of the *Intent* class. Furthermore throughout the API there are many more classes that offer specific broadcast events themselves. Some examples are BluetoothDevice or TextToSpeech.Engine and nearly all the Manager classes like UsbManager or AudioManager. Android really offers plenty of events that we can make use of in our apps.

The following list is only a small sample of all available events.

Table 8-1 System-Wide Events Samples

Event	Broadcast Action
Intent.ACTION_BATTERY_LOW	The battery level is low.
Intent.ACTION_BATTERY_OKAY	The battery level is good again.
Intent.ACTION_BOOT_COMPLETED	System has finished booting. Requires android. permission.RECEIVE_BOOT_COMPLETED.
Intent.ACTION_DEVICE_STORAGE_LOW	Storage space on the device is low.
Intent.ACTION_DEVICE_STORAGE_OK	Storage space on the device is good again.
Intent.ACTION_HEADSET_PLUG	A headset has been plugged in or removed.
Intent.ACTION_INPUT_METHOD_CHANGED	An input method has been changed.
Intent.ACTION_LOCALE_CHANGED	The language of the device has been changed.
Intent.ACTION_MY_PACKAGE_REPLACED	The app has been updated.
Intent.ACTION_PACKAGE_ADDED	A new app has been added to the system.
Intent.ACTION_POWER_CONNECTED	Has connected to external power.
Intent.ACTION_POWER_DISCONNECTED	The device has been upplugged from power.
KeyChain.ACTION_STORAGE_CHANGED	The keystore has been changed.
BluetoothDevice.ACTION_ACL_CONNECTED	Has established a Bluetooth ACL connection.
AudioManager. ACTION_AUDIO_BECOMING_NOISY	The internal audio speaker will be used, not other output means like a headset.

Registration in Manifest File

We can statically register and configure a broadcast receiver in the manifest file, *AndroidMani-fest.xml* using the <receiver> element and we can specify what event the receiver should react to using the nested element <intent-filter>.

Registration in Java Program

Alternatively, we can register a *BroadcastReceiver* object dynamically in our Java program by calling the **registerReceiver**() method on the corresponding *Context* object.

The following sample code shows the form of the implementation, using the system event *ConnectivityManager*.CONNECTIVITY_ACTION, which responds to a change in network connectivity, as an example:

```
import android.content.BroadcastReceiver;
import android.content.IntentFilter;
import android.net.ConnectivityManager;

public class MainActivity extends Activity
{
  BroadcastReceiver receiver;
  IntentFilter intentFilter;

  @Override
  protected void onCreate(Bundle savedInstanceState) {
    super.onCreate(savedInstanceState);
    setContentView(R.layout.activity_main);
    receiver = new MyReceiver();
    intentFilter =
      new IntentFilter(ConnectivityManager.CONNECTIVITY_ACTION);
    ....
  }
  @Override
  protected void onPause() {
    unregisterReceiver(receiver);
    super.onPause();
  }

  @Override
  protected void onResume() {
    registerReceiver( receiver, intentFilter );
    super.onResume();
  }
}
```

The method **registerReceiver**() takes two parameters:

> **Parameter**
> *receiver*   The *BroadcastRegister* we want to register.
> *intentFilter*   The *IntentFilter* object specifying the event that the *receiver* should listen to.

If in our example we just simply print a message to the *Log* in response to a network change, our receiver would like like the following:

```
public class MyReceiver extends BroadcastReceiver
{
  @Override
  public void onReceive(Context context, Intent intent) {
    Log.v("MyReceiver", "Network connectivity changed!");
  }
}
```

8.6   Fetch Data From a Web Site

We have discussed *services* and the usage of services for process communications in Chapter 3. In this section, we present an example that demonstrates the usage of a service to fetch data from the Internet. We call the project and application *FetchData* and the package *comm.fetchdata*.

An *Activity* of the application displays a button for the user to click on to download a file from a Web site. When it is done, the *Service* notifies the *Activity* through a broadcast receiver. Upon receiving the notification, the receiver flashes a *Toast* message on the screen.

In the example, the file name and the URL of the Web site are hard-coded. The data downloaded are saved in an external storage using a method discussed in Chapter 5. After we have used the Eclipse IDE to create the project and default files, we need to modify the manifest file *Android-Manifest.xml*, the layout file *res/layout/activity_main.xml* and the main Java program *MainActivity.java*. In addition, we will create two class files, *FetchData.java*, which is an *Activity* responsible for downloading and saving the data in the background, and *DataReceiver.java*, which is a receiver that flashes a finishing message on the screen using the *Toast* class.

8.6.1   Using a Broadcast Receiver

We will use a broadcast receiver as we have explained in Section 8.5 to communicate with the main activity. The *MainActivity* creates a broadcast receiver, *DataReceiver* and dynamically register it for the event of finishing download. The service *FetchData* generates a signal when the event occurs, and broadcast the signal to all the registered receivers using the method **sendBroadcast**(). The following figure shows this communication scheme.

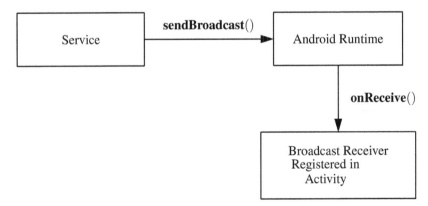

Figure 8-7 Communication Using Broadcast Receiver

The listing below shows the implementation of *DataReceiver* of the project.

Program Listing 8-6   *DataReceiver.java* of *FetchData* Project

---

```java
package comm.fetchdata;

import android.app.Activity;
import android.content.*;
import android.os.Bundle;
import android.widget.Toast;

public class DataReceiver extends BroadcastReceiver
{
  @Override
  public void onReceive(Context context, Intent intent) {
    Bundle bundle = intent.getExtras();
    if (bundle != null) {
      String string = bundle.getString(FetchData.FPATH);
      int resultCode = bundle.getInt(FetchData.RESULT);
      if (resultCode == Activity.RESULT_OK) {
        Toast.makeText(context, "Fetch complete. Store URI: "
                  + string, Toast.LENGTH_LONG).show();
      } else {
        Toast.makeText(context, "Fetch failed",
              Toast.LENGTH_LONG).show();
      }
    }
  }
}
```

The method **onReceive**(*Context, Intent*) of this class is invoked when *FetchData* calls **send-Broadcast**(*Intent*). *FetchData* also creates an *Intent* to pass data to *DataReciever* through the *Intent* parameter of **sendBroadcast** to **onReceive**, which extracts the data using the method **getExtras**() of the *Bundle* class. The other parameter, *Context* of **onReceive** is the *Context* of the class (*MainActivity* in this example) that registers *DataReceiver*. Through this *Context* parameter, the receiver can exchange data with *MainActivity*.

8.6.2   Connecting to and Accessing a URL

In this example, the *FetchData* project, we make use of Java's *URL* class of the *java.net* package to connect the Android device to an Internet site. In general, URL is the acronym for *Uniform Resource Locator*, an address that references a resource on the Internet. We provide URLs to a Web browser to locate files on the Internet. The term URL may be ambiguous. It may refer to an Internet address or a URL object in a Java program. To avoid this ambiguity, we follow the convention used by the Java official site. When the meaning of URL needs to be specific, we use "URL address" to refer to an Internet address and "URL object" to an instance of the URL class in a program. Moreover, if we use italics, a *URL* is referring to a URL object or URL class.

Creating a URL

A URL object can be created with a URL constructor, which may take one argument as a string that specifies a URL address. Or it may take two arguments, one of which is a URL object referring to the base URL address of a web site; the other is a string specifying an address relative to the base address. The general forms of the constructors are:

1. URL (String *url_address*);
2. URL (URL *baseURL*, String *relative_url*);

The following are some examples:

1. URL myURL = new URL ("http://www.forejune.com/index.html");

2. ULR baseURL = new URL ("http://www.forejune.com/");
   URL url1 = new URL (baseURL, "index1.html");
   URL url2 = new URL (baseURL, "index2.html");

The class *URL* provides a few methods to parse a URL. For example, methods **getHost**(), **getPort**(), and **getPath**() return the hostname, the port number, and the path components of the URL respectively.

Connecting to and Accessing a URL

We can connect to a URL by first using method **openConnection**() of the class *URL* to open and start a connection. The method returns an object of the class *URLConnection*, which has several method for establishing and initializing a communication link between our Java program and the URL address over the network. We will use the method **connect**() of the class *URLConnection* to establish a connection. If the connection is established successfully, we can treat it as a data stream and use one of the many Java I/O streaming methods to process the data of the remote Web site. The following simple code is a typical example of establishing a link to and reading data from a URL address; actually, it is a complete Java program that saves the downloaded data in the file *downloaded.txt*.

```java
// ReadURL.java: Compile: javac ReadURL.java
// Execute: java ReadURL
import java.io.*;
import java.net.URL;

public class ReadURL {
  public static void main ( String args[] )
  {
    String urlAddress = "http://www.forejune.com/";

    InputStream is = null;
    FileOutputStream fos = null;
    try {
      URL url = new URL( urlAddress );
      is = url.openConnection().getInputStream();
      InputStreamReader isr = new InputStreamReader ( is );
      fos = new FileOutputStream( "downdloaded.txt" );
      int next = -1;
      while ((next = isr.read()) != -1)
        fos.write(next);
    } catch (Exception e) {
      e.printStackTrace();
    }
  }
}
```

The class file *FetchData.java* of our *FetchData* project uses the same technique to connect to a hard-coded URL, and read the data, saving them in an external storage with a specified filename.

Program Listing 8-7 below shows the code of *FetchData.java*.

Program Listing 8-7   *FetchData.java* of *FetchData* Project

```
package comm.fetchdata;

import java.io.*;
import java.net.URL;
import android.os.*;
import android.net.Uri;
import android.util.Log;
import android.widget.Toast;
import android.app.Activity;
import android.content.Intent;
import android.app.IntentService;

public class FetchData extends IntentService
{
  private int result = Activity.RESULT_CANCELED;
  public static String URL_ADDRESS = "http://www.forejune.com";
  public static String FNAME = "downloaded.html";
  public static String FPATH = "./";
  public static String RESULT = "result";
  public static  String NOTIFICATION = "comm.fetchdata.receiver";

  public FetchData() {
    super("FetchData");
  }

  // will be called asynchronously by Android
  @Override
  protected void onHandleIntent(Intent intent) {
    String urlUsed = intent.getStringExtra( URL_ADDRESS );
    String fileName = intent.getStringExtra(FNAME);

    File output = new File(Environment.getExternalStorageDirectory(),
        fileName);
    if (output.exists()) {
      output.delete();
    }

    InputStream is = null;
    FileOutputStream fos = null;
    Toast.makeText(FetchData.this, "Testing FetchData",
                      Toast.LENGTH_LONG).show();
    try {
     URL url = new URL ( urlUsed );
     is = url.openConnection().getInputStream();
     InputStreamReader isr = new InputStreamReader( is );
     fos = new FileOutputStream(output.getPath());
     int next = -1;
     while ((next = isr.read()) != -1)
       fos.write(next);
     result = Activity.RESULT_OK;
```

```
    } catch (Exception e) {
      e.printStackTrace();
    } finally {
      if ( is != null) {
        try {
          is.close();
        } catch (IOException e) {
          e.printStackTrace();
        }
      }
      if (fos != null) {
        try {
          fos.close();
        } catch (IOException e) {
          e.printStackTrace();
        }
      }
    }
    notifying(output.getAbsolutePath(), result);
  }

  private void notifying( String outputPath, int result ) {
    Intent intent = new Intent(NOTIFICATION);
    intent.putExtra(FPATH, outputPath);
    intent.putExtra(RESULT, result);
    sendBroadcast(intent);
  }
}
```

This class, *FetchData*, extends *IntentService* so that it can receive data from or send data to the main class that starts it. *IntentService* is a base class for *Service* objects that handle asynchronous requests, which are expressed as *Intents*, on demand. Typically, clients send requests with **start-Service**(*Intent*) calls to start the service when needed. The method handles each *Intent* object in turn using a worker thread, and stops itself when it runs out of work. These usually work in the background. When the work is done, it signals the *DataReceiver* using the **sendBroadcast**() method, which is called inside the **notifying**() method of *FetchData*, where another *Intent* object is created to pass some relevant information to the receiver, *DataReceiver*.

In the code, the *String* variables *URL_ADDRESS*, and *FNAME* are initialized when they are declared as data members in the class *FetchData*. However, their values are not used and the actual values are supplied by the main class, *MainActivity* in the **onHandleIntent**() method through the statements,

```
    String urlUsed = intent.getStringExtra( URL_ADDRESS );
    String fileName = intent.getStringExtra ( FNAME );
```

To supply the values, the *MainActivity* class should have corresponding statements of **putStringExtra**() like the following:

```
    intent.putExtra( FetchData.FNAME, "downloaded.txt");
    intent.putExtra( FetchData.URL_ADDRESS,
        "http://www.forejune.com/index.html");
```

The class *FetchData* implements the **onHandleIntent** (*Intent*) method of *IntentService*. The method is invoked on the worker thread with a request to process. Only one *Intent* object is processed at one time, but each worker thread runs independently, not relying on other requests. When all requests have been handled, the *IntentService* stops itself. The parameter of **onHandleIntent**() is the *Intent* object passed to the method **startService**(*Intent*), which is a method of the class *Context*, and is used for starting services. In our example, this method is called in method **onClick**() of the *MainActivity* class, and the *Intent* parameter is a *FetchData* object. In other words, *FetchData* will work in the background to fetch data from a URL address and save the data in an external storage.

8.6.3   UI Handled by *MainActivity*

In this project, *MainActivity* handles the UI and let *FetchData* do the downloading and storing. It also creates a *DataReceiver* object and registers it as we have discussed before. It starts the *FetcData* activity in background by calling the method **startService**(*Intent*) and passes data to *FetchData* through the *Intent* parameter. The following lists the complete code of this class:

> **Program Listing 8-8**   *MainActivity.java* of *FetchData* Project

```
package comm.fetchdata;

import android.app.*;
import android.os.*;
import android.view.*;
import android.widget.*;
import android.content.*;

public class MainActivity extends Activity
{
  public TextView textView;
  DataReceiver receiver;
  @Override
  protected void onCreate(Bundle savedInstanceState) {
  super.onCreate(savedInstanceState);
  setContentView(R.layout.activity_main);
  receiver = new DataReceiver ();
  textView = (TextView) findViewById(R.id.status);
}

@Override
protected void onResume() {
  super.onResume();
  registerReceiver(receiver,new IntentFilter(FetchData.NOTIFICATION));
}

@Override
protected void onPause() {
  super.onPause();
  unregisterReceiver(receiver);
}

public void onClick(View view) {
  Intent intent = new Intent(this, FetchData.class);
```

```
    // add info for the service of fetching file
    intent.putExtra(FetchData.FNAME, "downloaded.txt");
    intent.putExtra(FetchData.URL_ADDRESS,
        "http://www.forejune.com/index.html");
    // Start FetchData to run as background
    startService(intent);
    textView.setText("Service started");
}
```

After we have written these three Java programs, *MainActivity.java*, *FetchData.java* and *DataReceiver.java*, we have to modify the manifest file, *AndroidManifest.xml* to grant access permissions to the Internet and the external storage to the application. We also need to declare the *FetchData* service in the file as shown in the Listing below.

Listing 8-9   *AndroidManifest.xml* of *FetchData* Project

```
<?xml version="1.0" encoding="utf-8"?>
 <manifest xmlns:android="http://schemas.android.com/apk/res/android"
    .....
    <uses-permission android:name="android.permission.INTERNET"/>
    <uses-permission
        android:name="android.permission.WRITE_EXTERNAL_STORAGE"/>

    <application
        .....
        <activity
        .....
        </activity>
        <service android:name="comm.fetchdata.FetchData" >
        </service>
    </application>
</manifest>
```

To incorporate the UI features of our project, we also need to modify the layout file, *activity_main.xml* to Listing 8-10. reflect the UI

Listing 8-10   *activity_main.xml* of *FetchData* Project

```
<?xml version="1.0" encoding="utf-8"?>
<LinearLayout xmlns:android="http://schemas.android.com/apk/res/android"
    android:layout_width="match_parent"
    android:layout_height="match_parent"
    android:orientation="vertical" >

    <Button
        android:id="@+id/button1"
        android:layout_width="wrap_content"
        android:layout_height="wrap_content"
        android:onClick="onClick"
        android:text="Get File" />

    <LinearLayout
```

```
        android:layout_width="wrap_content"
        android:layout_height="wrap_content" >

    <TextView
        android:layout_width="wrap_content"
        android:layout_height="wrap_content"
        android:text="Status: " />

    <TextView
        android:id="@+id/status"
        android:layout_width="wrap_content"
        android:layout_height="wrap_content"
        android:text="Not started" />
 </LinearLayout>
</LinearLayout>
```

After we have done all these, we can compile and run the application. Figure 8-8 below shows portions of the output display. Figure 8-8 (a) shows the screen when the application has started but the service *FetchData* has not been started. One can start the service in the background by clicking on the *Get File* button. When the *FetchData* service has finished its task, it broadcasts a signal to *DataReceiver*, which displays a *Toast* message as shown in Figure 8-8 (b).

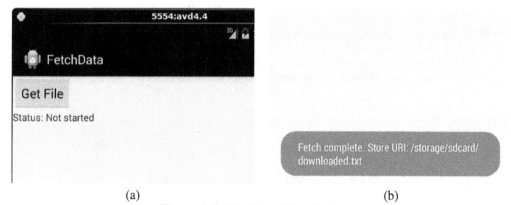

(a)   (b)

Figure 8-8 UI of *FetchData* Project

8.7   AIDL (Android Interface Definition Language)

8.7.1   AIDL Interface

As we mentioned in Chapter 3, Android provides AIDL (Android Interface Definition Language) to ease interprocess communication (IPC). It is similar to the traditional interface definition language (IDL) that describes the interface between components in remote procedure calls (RPC) for C/C++ applications. The language allows a user to define a common programming interface for a client to communicate with a server, which runs a service. Normally, a process is not allowed to access the memory of another process and the objects created by one process may not be understood by the other. For two processes to communicate seamlessly, the exchanging objects must be decomposed into primitives and marshalled. Android provides AIDL tools to do the marshalling.

An AIDL interface is defined in a file ending with *.aidl* using the Java programming language syntax. The file should be saved in the source code directories (*src/*) of both the application hosting the service and any other application that binds to the service.

When we build an application that contains the *.aidl* file, the AIDL tools generate a corresponding *IBinder* interface, which is saved in the project's *gen/* directory. The service program has to implement an appropriate *IBinder* interface so that client applications can bind to the service and call the *IBinder* methods to communicate with it.

In general, three steps are involved in building an AIDL service:

1. **Create a file with** *.aidl* **extension** to define the interface to be used by client processes.
2. **Implement the interface** based on the Java program generated from the *.aidl* file by the Android SDK tools.
3. **Expose the interface** to clients by implementing a *Service*, where we override the **onBind**() method.

8.7.2 The .aidl File

We have to create a *.aidl* file inside the project's *src/* directory. If Eclipse IDE is used in the development, it automatically generates an *IBinder* interface file in the *gen* directory when we save the *.aidl* file that has no syntax error. The Eclipse IDE also indicates any syntax error with a red dot.

The syntax of a *.aidl* file is simple. We can declare an interface with one or more methods that can take parameters and return values. Each *.aidl* can only define a single interface. If we need to define more than one interface, we have to create multiple *.aidl* files inside the *src* directory. AIDL supports all primitive types such as **int, long, char**, and **boolean** of the Java programming language. It also suppots built-in Java classes including *String, CharSequence, List*, and *Map*. The following shows an example of a simple *.aidl* file, named *IRemoteService.aidl*; the method **multiply** is supposed to multiply two numbers and to return the product.

```
// IRemoteService.aidl
package comm.aidlcalc;

// Declare any non-default types here with import statements

/** Example service interface */
interface IRemoteService {
  // You can pass values in, out, or inout.
  // Primitive datatypes (e.g. int, char) can only be passed in.
  float multiply (in float num1, in float num2);
}
```

A corresponding Java program, *IRemoteService.java* is generated inside the *gen* directory, which looks like the following

```
package comm.aidlcalc;
// Declare any non-default types here with import statements
/** Example service interface */
public interface IRemoteService extends android.os.IInterface
{
  /** Local-side IPC implementation stub class. */
  public static abstract class Stub extends android.os.Binder
                  implements comm.aidlcalc.IRemoteService
  {
    private static final java.lang.String DESCRIPTOR =
```

```
                                      "comm.aidlcalc.IRemoteService";
    /** Construct the stub at attach it to the interface. */
    public Stub()
    {
      this.attachInterface(this, DESCRIPTOR);
    }
    . . . . .
  }
  . . . . .
  public float multiply(float num1, float num2)
                      throws android.os.RemoteException;
}
```

8.7.3 Implement AIDL Interface

The AIDL tools generate a Java interface from a *.aidl* file. The interface includes a subclass named *Stub*, which is an abstract implementation of its parent interface and declares all the methods as shown in the above example. To implement the interface, we have to extend the generated *Binder* interface, *Stub* and the methods defined in the *.aidl* file.

Here is an example implementation of the *IRemoteService* of the above example, using an anonymous instance:

```
@Override
public IBinder onBind(Intent intent) {

  return new IRemoteService.Stub() {
     // Implement  multiply()
    public float multiply (float a, float b)
    throws RemoteException {
      return a * b;
    }
  };
}
```

Note that by default, RPC calls are synchronous, meaning the the client waits for the server's result before executing the next instruction. Therefore, if the service takes a relatively long time to finish the task of a request, we should not call the service from the main thread of the client's activity, which might lead to the Android system displaying a dialog of *Application is Not Responding*. To avoid this, we should typically call the service from a separate thread in the client.

8.7.4 Expose AIDL Interface to Clients

After implementing the remote service interface, we need to expose it to the clients, which will bind to it. This is done by extending the *Service* class, and implement its **onBind**() method, which will return an object of the class that implements *Stub*. The following is an example service that exposes the *IRemoteService* interface discussed above to clients:

```
public class RemoteService extends Service
{
  @Override
  public void onCreate() {
    super.onCreate();
  }
```

```
@Override
public IBinder onBind(Intent intent) {

  return new IRemoteService.Stub() {
    public float multiply (float a, float b)
     throws RemoteException {
       return a * b;
     }
  };
 }
}
```

When a client activity calls **bindService**() to connect to this service, the client's **onService-Connected**() callback receives the *IBinder* object returned by the service's **onBind**() method. The client also needs to access the interface class. Therefore if the client is not in the same application of the service, the client application must also have a copy of the *.aidl* file inside its *src/* directory, which will be used to generate the same Java program inside its *gen/* directory.

When the client receives the *IBinder* object in the **onServiceConnected**() callback, it must call the interface's *Stub*.**asInterface**() to cast the returned parameter to the same interface type as the service. The following is an example of such a callback:

```
class RemoteServiceConnection implements ServiceConnection
{
  IRemoteService remoteService;

  // Called when the connection with the service is established
  public void onServiceConnected (ComponentName name,
                                       IBinder boundService) {
    remoteService =
      IRemoteService.Stub.asInterface((IBinder) boundService);
      Toast.makeText(MainActivity.this, "Service connected",
           Toast.LENGTH_LONG).show();
  }

  // Called when connection with service disconnects unexpecteldy
  public void onServiceDisconnected(ComponentName name) {
    remoteService = null;
  }
}
```

8.7.5 A Remote Multiplier

The Android developer site presents a couple of detailed and complex examples on remote service communication. Here, to give readers a quick start of writing remote service applications, we present a very simple example, in which the remote service simply accepts two numbers from a client, multiplies them, and returns the product, and the client is responsible for the UI, accepting two numbers from the user, and displaying the result on the screen. A remote service here means a service that runs in a different process from that of the client. Actually, part of the code has already been presented in the examples of the previous two sections.

Again, we use Eclipse IDE to create the project of this example. We call the project *AidlCalc*, the application *AidlCalcServer*, and the package, *comm.aidlcalc*. The followig are the steps of creating and implementing this project.

1. As usual, we click on **File** and subsequent menus to create the project *AidlCalc* with package name *comm.aidlcalc*, along with default files, including *MainActivity.java*.

2. Create the file *IRemoteService.aidl*: click **File** > **New** > **File**. Enter *AidlCalc/src/comm/aidlcalc* for parent folder, and *IRemoteService.aidl* for **File name**. Click **Finish** to create the file. Edit the file to the following:

```
// IRemoteService.aidl
package comm.aidlcalc;
interface IRemoteService {
    float multiply (in float num1, in float num2); }
```

3. Implement the service class *RemoteService.java*: Click **File** > **New** > **Class**, and enter the apropriate names. Edit the file to the following:

```
//RemoteService.java
package comm.aidlcalc;

import android.app.Service;
import android.content.Intent;
import android.os.IBinder;
import android.os.RemoteException;
import android.util.Log;

public class RemoteService extends Service
{
  @Override
  public void onCreate() {
    super.onCreate();
  }
  @Override
  public IBinder onBind(Intent intent) {
    return new IRemoteService.Stub() {
      // Implement  multiply()
      public float multiply (float a,  float b)
            throws RemoteException {
        return a * b;
      }
    };
  }
  @Override
  public void onDestroy() {
    super.onDestroy();
  }
}
```

This class implements our remote service, which returns an *IBinder* object from the **on-Bind**() method. The AIDL-defined method **multiply**() is implemented as a method in the inner class. This code exposes the remote service.

4. Modify the file *MainActivity.java* to the following:

```java
// MainActivity.java
package comm.aidlcalc;

import android.app.Activity;
import android.content.*;
import android.os.Bundle;
import android.os.IBinder;
import android.os.RemoteException;
import android.text.TextUtils;
import android.util.Log;
import android.view.View;
import android.view.View.OnClickListener;
import android.widget.*;

public class MainActivity extends
            Activity implements View.OnClickListener
{
  IRemoteService remoteService;
  RemoteServiceConnection remoteConnection;
  EditText t1;
  EditText t2;
  Button multiply;
  TextView displayResult;

  @Override
  public void onCreate(Bundle savedInstanceState) {
    super.onCreate(savedInstanceState);
    setContentView(R.layout.activity_main);

    bindActivityToService();  // starts the service

    // Setup the UI
    t1 = (EditText) findViewById(R.id.t1);
    t2 = (EditText) findViewById(R.id.t2);
    multiply = (Button) findViewById(R.id.multiply);
    displayResult = (TextView) findViewById(R.id.displayResult);
    multiply.setOnClickListener( this);
  }

  public void onClick ( View view ) {
    float num1 = 0, num2 = 0, product = 0;
    // check if the fields are empty
    if (TextUtils.isEmpty(t1.getText().toString())
        || TextUtils.isEmpty(t2.getText().toString())) {
      return;
    }

    // read EditText and fill variables with numbers
    num1 = Float.parseFloat(t1.getText().toString());
    num2 = Float.parseFloat(t2.getText().toString());
```

```
   try {
      product = remoteService.multiply(num1, num2);
   } catch (RemoteException e) {
         e.printStackTrace();
   }
   // form the output line
   displayResult.setText( num1 + " * " + num2 + " = " + product );
}

/**
 * This class implements the actual service connection, casting
 * bound stub implementation of the service to AIDL interface.
 */
class RemoteServiceConnection implements ServiceConnection
{
  //Called when the connection with the service is established
  public void onServiceConnected(ComponentName name,
                                        IBinder boundService){
    remoteService =
       IRemoteService.Stub.asInterface((IBinder) boundService);
    Toast.makeText(MainActivity.this, "Service connected",
                                Toast.LENGTH_LONG).show();
  }

  //Called when connection with service disconnects unexpected
  public void onServiceDisconnected(ComponentName name) {
    remoteService = null;
    Toast.makeText(MainActivity.this, "Service disconnected",
                                Toast.LENGTH_LONG).show();
  }
}

/** Binds this activity to the service. */
private void bindActivityToService() {
  remoteConnection = new RemoteServiceConnection();
  Intent intent = new Intent();
  intent.setClassName("comm.aidlcalc",
                  comm.aidlcalc.RemoteService.class.getName());
  bindService(intent,remoteConnection,Context.BIND_AUTO_CREATE);
}

// Unbinds this activity from the service.
private void releaseService() {
  unbindService(remoteConnection);
  remoteConnection = null;
}

// Called when the activity is about to terminate
@Override
protected void onDestroy() {
```

```
        releaseService();
    }
```

As we have implemented the **onBind**() method in *RemoteService*, we need to establish a connection between the service and our client (*MainActivity*). This is done by implementing the *ServiceConnection* class in *RemoteServiceConnection*, where **onServiceConnected**() and **onServiceDiconnected**() methods are implemented. These callbacks will get the stub implementation of the remote service upon connection or disconnection.

Besides binding the activity to the remote service, the method **bindActivityToService**() also starts the service.

The UI of the application is very simple. There are two *EditText* fields and a *Button*, which represents multiplication. The *MainActivity* class has implemented the *OnClickListener* class. When the *Button* is clicked, the **multiply**() method is invoked on the service as if it were a local call.

5. Modify the file *res/layout/activity_main.xml* for our UI as follows:

```xml
<?xml version="1.0" encoding="utf-8"?>
<LinearLayout xmlns:android=
        "http://schemas.android.com/apk/res/android"
 android:orientation="vertical" android:layout_width="fill_parent"
 android:layout_height="fill_parent">
 <TextView android:layout_width="fill_parent"
   android:layout_height="wrap_content" android:text="AidlCalc"
   android:textSize="22sp" />
 <LinearLayout
   android:layout_width="match_parent"
   android:layout_height="wrap_content"
   android:id="@+id/linearLayout1"
   android:layout_marginLeft="12pt"
   android:layout_marginRight="12pt"
   android:layout_marginTop="4pt">

   <EditText
     android:layout_weight="1"
     android:layout_height="wrap_content"
     android:layout_marginRight="6pt"
     android:id="@+id/t1"
     android:layout_width="match_parent"
     android:text="1989"
     android:inputType="numberDecimal">
   </EditText>
   <Button
     android:layout_width="wrap_content"
     android:layout_height="wrap_content"
     android:text="*"
     android:textSize="10pt"
     android:id="@+id/multiply">
   </Button>
   <EditText
```

```
            android:layout_height="wrap_content"
            android:layout_weight="1"
            android:layout_marginLeft="6pt"
            android:id="@+id/t2"
            android:layout_width="match_parent"
            android:text="64"
            android:inputType="numberDecimal">
        </EditText>
    </LinearLayout>
    <TextView
            android:layout_height="wrap_content"
            android:layout_width="match_parent"
            android:layout_marginLeft="6pt"
            android:layout_marginRight="6pt"
            android:textSize="12pt"
            android:layout_marginTop="4pt"
            android:id="@+id/displayResult"
            android:gravity="center_horizontal">
    </TextView>
</LinearLayout>
```

6. Add the service to the file *res/AndroidManifest.xml* as follows:

```
<?xml version="1.0" encoding="utf-8"?>
<manifest xmlns:android="http://schemas.android.com/apk/res/android"
    package="comm.aidlcalc"
    .....
    <application
        .....
        <activity
            .....
        </activity>
        <service android:name=".RemoteService" />
    </application>
</manifest>
```

7. Run the application. When we run the application, the multiplier service is started in the background and the client activity presents us a UI like the one shown in Figure 8-9 below. When the activity has successfully connected to the service, it displays a *Toast* message, saying *Service connected* as shown in the lower part of the figure. We can enter two numbers and click the multiplication button, which calls the remote service to do the multiplication. When the client receives the result, it displays the multiplication operation and the result as shown in the upper half of the figure.

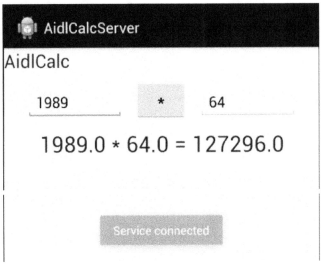

Figure 8-9   UI of *AidlCalc* Project

Chapter 9   Text To Speech (TTS) and Audio

9.1   Introduction

Android provides the text-to-Speech (TTS) feature for applications to synthesize speech from text in different languages.

Typically, a text-to-speech system, or referred to as an *engine*, is composed of two parts, a front-end and a back-end. The front-end performs some preprocessing of a raw text, converting symbols such as numbers and abbreviations to spelled-out words. It then performs text-to-phoneme conversion, assigning phonetic transcriptions to each word, and dividing the text into prosodic units, such as phrases, clauses, and sentences. The front-end output consists of the symbolic linguistic representation of prosody information and phonetic transcriptions. The back-end is the synthesizer that converts phonemes into sound waves. Figure 9-1 below shows such a system.

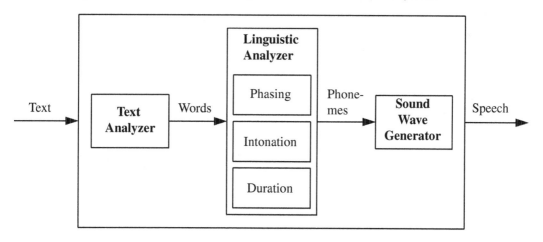

Figure 9-1 A Typical Text-to-Speech System

Researchers created the first generation computer-based speech synthesizers in the late 1950s. Noriko Umeda et al. developed the first general English text-to-speech system in 1968 at the Electrotechnical Laboratory of Japan. Since then significant advancement has been made in developing TTS systems in various languages. Sun Electronic first incorporated speech synthesis features in a video game in 1980. Milton Bradly Company first debuted a multi-player electronic game that has voice synthesis features in 1980.

Nowadays, a number of open-source TTS systems, usually written in C/C++ or Java are available and free for download. In particular, *FreeTTS* is a speech synthesizer written entirely in Java and is based upon *Flite*, which is a small run-time speech synthesis engine developed at Carnegie Mellon University (CMU). Flite is written completely in C, not using any C++ or scheme features for the reasons of portability, size and speed. It is derived from the Festival Speech Synthesis System from the University of Edinburgh and the Festvox project from CMU. FreeTTS supports a subset of the JSAPI 1.0 java speech synthesis specification.

Android provides a default text-to-speech (TTS) engine (Pico) with limited APIs. Other third party TTS engines are also available in the market. For instance, Samsung and LG preload their text-to-speech sets in their Android products.   Google TTS that comes with some devices, and Ivona TTS HQ that has high-quality sounding voices are well-known free engines. Popular low cost engines include *Classic TTS Engine* (which covers 40+ languages), CereProc, and Loquendo TTS Susan.

9.2 The *TextToSpeech* Class

Android provides the class *TextToSpeech* for synthesizing speech from text for immediate playback or creating a sound file. Using the class, an application can incoporate rich speech features such as speaking different languages, setting the pitch level and the speaking speed.

To utilize a *TextToSpeech* object to synthesize speech from a text, the application must first complete an initialization stage of the object. To know when the initialization is complete, we have to implement the **OnInitListner** of *TextToSpeech* to obtain a notification of completing the initialization. If the object is no longer in use, the application should call the **shutdown**() method to release any resources used by the speech engine. One can refer to Android's developer site for the detailed usage and all the methods of this class. Here we discuss a few simple features and present an example to illustrate its basic usage.

To use the class *TextToSpeech*, we need to implement its interface *OnInitListener*, which defines a callback to be invoked to indicate the completion of the *TextToSpeech* engine initialization; we have to override the abstract method **onInit**, which is called to signal the completion. The following is an example implementation:

```
public class MainActivity extends Activity
                    implements View.OnClickListener, OnInitListener
{
  ImageButton ttsButton;
  EditText editText1;
  TextToSpeech tts;
  .....
  protected void onCreate(Bundle savedInstanceState) {
    super.onCreate(savedInstanceState);
    .....
    ttsButton.setOnClickListener ( this );
    tts = new TextToSpeech(this, this);
  }

  public void onInit(int state) {
    if (state == TextToSpeech.SUCCESS) {
      int result = tts.setLanguage(Locale.US);

      if (result == TextToSpeech.LANG_MISSING_DATA
          || result == TextToSpeech.LANG_NOT_SUPPORTED) {
        .....
      } else {
        ttsButton.setEnabled(true);
        speak();
      }
    }
  }
}
```

In this example, we have used the constructor

TextToSpeech (Context *context*, TextToSpeech.OnInitListener *listener*)

of the *TextToSpeech* class, which uses the default TTS engine. It will also initialize the associated *TextToSpeech* engine if it is not already running. The variable *context* is the context that the instance is running in. The *listener* is the *TextToSpeech.OnInitListener* that will be called when the

TTS engine has initialized. The listener may be called immediately, in the case of a failure, before the *TextToSpeech* instance is fully constructed.

The method **setLanguage**() takes a *Locale* object as parameter, and sets the engine to speak the specified language. The class *Locale* represents a **language/country/variant** combination. Locale objects can be used to alter the presentation of information such as numbers or dates to suit the conventions in the region an application describes. The following table shows some available locales.

No.	Locale
1	US
2	CANADA_FRENCH
3	GERMANY
4	ITALY
5	JAPAN
6	CHINA

After we have specified the language, we can call the **speak** method of the class to produce speech from the text like the following code:

```
private void speak() {
  String text1 = editText1.getText().toString();
  tts.speak(text1, TextToSpeech.QUEUE_FLUSH, null);
}
```

The TTS engine manages a global queue of all the entries, also known as *utterances*, to synthesize speech. The **speak**() method of *TextToSpeech* produces speech from the text string using the specified queuing strategy and speech parameters. The method, which is asynchronous, adds the request to the TTS request queue and then returns. Note that at the time this method returns, the synthesis might not have finished or even started! Users are recommended to set an utterance progress listener and use the KEY_PARAM_UTTERANCE_ID parameter to reliably detect errors during synthesis.

The constant QUEUE_FLUSH represents the queue mode where all entries in the playback queue are dropped and replaced by the new entry. Thus in the example, *text1* is spoken immediately. Note that queues are flushed with respect to a given calling app but entries in the queue from other callees are not discarded.

If we want the engine to finish the utterances in the queue before playing the current one, we can use set the queue mode QUEUE_ADD, which adds the new entry at the end of the queue. For example, the statements

```
tts.speak(text1, TextToSpeech.QUEUE_FLUSH, null);
tts.speak(text2, TextToSpeech.QUEUE_ADD, null);
```

will first finish playing *text1* before playing *text2*.

Besides the **speak** method, the following table lists some available useful methods of the class.

Method	Description
addSpeech(String *text*, String *file*)	Adds a mapping between a text and a sound file.
getLanguage()	Returns a *Locale* object that describes the language.
isSpeaking()	Checks if *TextToSpeech* engine is busy speaking.
setPitch(float *pitch*)	Sets the speech pitch for the *TextToSpeech* engine.
setSpeechRate(float *speechRate*)	Sets the speech speed.
shutdown	Releases resources used by the *TextToSpeech* engine.
stop()	Stops speaking.

9.3   A Simple TTS Example

We present in this section a very simple example of using the class *TextToSpeech* to generate speech from the text entered in an *EditText* field. Suppose we call the project and the application *TtsDemo*, and the package *tts.ttsdemo*. As usual, we first use Eclipse IDE to create the default files. We modify the file *MainActivity.java* to implement *OnInitListener* as discussed above. We also declare a *TextView* for displaying related messages, an *EditText* for the user to enter text, and an *ImageButton* for the user to click on to convert the text to speech. The following Listing shows the modified code.

Program Listing 9-1   *MainActivity.java of TtsDemo*

```
package tts.ttsdemo;

import java.util.Locale;
import android.app.Activity;
import android.os.*;
import android.view.*;
import android.widget.*;
import android.speech.tts.TextToSpeech;
import android.speech.tts.TextToSpeech.OnInitListener;

public class MainActivity extends Activity
            implements View.OnClickListener, OnInitListener
{
    ImageButton ttsButton;
    TextView msg;
    EditText editText1;
    TextToSpeech tts;
    @Override
    protected void onCreate(Bundle savedInstanceState) {
        super.onCreate(savedInstanceState);
        setContentView(R.layout.activity_main);
        ttsButton = (ImageButton) findViewById(R.id.ttsButton);
        editText1 = (EditText) findViewById(R.id.editText1);
        msg = (TextView) findViewById(R.id.msg);
        ttsButton.setOnClickListener ( this );
        tts = new TextToSpeech(this, this);
    }

    public void onClick(View view) {
     speak();
    }
    @Override
    public void onInit(int state) {
      if (state == TextToSpeech.SUCCESS) {
        msg.setText("TTS initialized successfully!\n " +
            "Enter a sentence and click TTS.");
        int result = tts.setLanguage(Locale.US);
        if (result == TextToSpeech.LANG_MISSING_DATA
                || result == TextToSpeech.LANG_NOT_SUPPORTED) {
          msg.setText("TTS: Language not supported!");
        } else {
```

```
          ttsButton.setEnabled(true);
          speak();
        }
     } else {
        msg.setText("TTS: Initilization Failed!");
      }
    }
  }

  private void speak() {
    String text = editText1.getText().toString();
    tts.speak(text, TextToSpeech.QUEUE_FLUSH, null);
  }
  @Override
  public void onDestroy() {
      //  Shut down tts to release resources!
      if (tts != null) {
          tts.stop();
          tts.shutdown();
      }
      super.onDestroy();
  }
}
```

The code is very simple and most of its features have been explained in the previous section.

We also need to modify the layout file, *res/layout/activity_main.xml* that defines the UI of our project. The modified file is listed in Listing 9-2 below.

Program Listing 9-2 *activity_main.xml* of Project *TtsDemo*

```xml
<?xml version="1.0" encoding="utf-8"?>
<LinearLayout xmlns:android="http://schemas.android.com/apk/res/android"
    android:layout_width="fill_parent"
    android:layout_height="fill_parent"
    android:orientation="vertical" >
    <LinearLayout
        android:id="@+id/linearLayout1"
        android:layout_width="match_parent"
        android:layout_height="wrap_content"
        android:layout_marginLeft="12pt"
        android:layout_marginRight="12pt"
        android:layout_marginTop="4pt" >
        <EditText
            android:id="@+id/editText1"
            android:layout_width="match_parent"
            android:layout_height="wrap_content"
            android:layout_marginRight="6pt"
            android:layout_weight="1"
            android:inputType="text" >
        </EditText>
    </LinearLayout>
    <RelativeLayout
        android:id="@+id/linearLayout2"
        android:layout_width="match_parent"
```

```
            android:layout_height="wrap_content"
            android:layout_marginLeft="6pt"
            android:layout_marginRight="6pt"
            android:layout_marginTop="4pt" >
            <ImageButton
                android:id="@+id/ttsButton"
                android:layout_width="90dp"
                android:layout_height="90dp"
                android:layout_alignParentRight="true"
                android:layout_alignParentTop="true"
                android:layout_marginRight="60dp"
                android:adjustViewBounds="true"
                android:background="@drawable/tts"
                android:scaleType="centerCrop"
                android:src="@drawable/tts" />
    </RelativeLayout>
    <TextView
            android:id="@+id/msg"
            android:layout_width="match_parent"
            android:layout_height="wrap_content"
            android:layout_marginLeft="4pt"
            android:layout_marginRight="4pt"
            android:layout_marginTop="2pt"
            android:gravity="center_horizontal"
            android:textSize="10pt" >
    </TextView>
 </LinearLayout>
```

We also need to put a PNG image file in a drawable directory (we put it in *res/drawable-xhdpi*) to represent the TTS button that we click on to speak the entered text.

When we run the application, we will have a UI similar to the one shown in Figure 9-2. Clicking on the TTS image button, the text entered in the *EditText* field will be converted to audible speech.

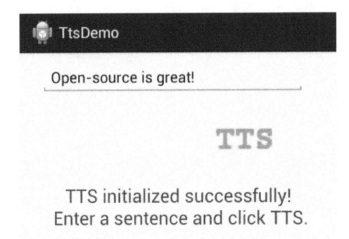

Figure 9-2 UI of *TtsDemo* Project

If we want to change the **language of the speech**, we can set the new language using the method **setLanguage** like tts.setLanguage(Locale.CHINESE);

which sets the speaking language to Chinese.

To set the **pitch rate** to another value other than the default value of 1, we can use the method **setPitch** like

tts.setPitch (0.8);

which sets the pitch level to 0.8.

The **speech speed** can be also changed from its default value of 1.0. For example,

tts.setSpeechRate (1.5);

increases the speech speed by 50%.

9.4   Writing Speech to a File

9.4.1   Playback Options

We can always associate an audio stream that is played with a stream type, defined in *android.media.AudioManager*. The **speak**() method actually takes three parameters:

speak(String text, int queueMode, HashMap<String, String> params)

The class *HashMap<String, String>*, the data type of the last parameter of **speak**, is a hash table based implementation of the *Map* interface, which associates a value with a key. The first parameter type (*String* here) inside the angular brackets represents the type of keys maintained by the map and the second parameter type (also *String* here) represents the type of mapped values. This parameter of **speak** allows us to pass to the TTS engine an optional *HashMap* parameter, specified as a key/value pair. (If no such pair is needed in our application, we can pass in **null** for the parameter.)

We can make use of this parameter to customize our playback. For example, consider an alarm clock that speaks text and the user can choose its settings. We would then like the text to be played on the stream type of *AudioManager*.STREAM_ALARM. We can use the *HashMap* parameter to change the stream type of our utterances:

```
HashMap<String, String> hashMap = new HashMap();
hashMap.put ( TextToSpeech.Engine.KEY_PARAM_STREAM,
            String.valueOf(AudioManager.STREAM_ALARM) );
tts.speak( text1, TextToSpeech.QUEUE_FLUSH, hashMap );
tts.speak( text2, TextToSpeech.QUEUE_ADD, hashMap );
```

The **put**() method of *HashMap* in the code associates the *String*

TextToSpeech.Engine.KEY_PARAM_STREAM,

which is the key, with the STREAM_ALARM *String*, which is the key value. We use this key pair to identify the utterance we need for some other purposes. For this to work, we also need to implement the *TextToSpeech.OnUtteranceCompletedListener* interface in our activity:

```
tts.setOnUtteranceCompletedListener (
                        (OnUtteranceCompletedListener) this);
hashMap.put(TextToSpeech.Engine.KEY_PARAM_STREAM,
                String.valueOf(AudioManager.STREAM_ALARM));
tts.speak( text1, TextToSpeech.QUEUE_FLUSH, hashMap );
// Add another optional parameter to hashMap
hashMap.put(TextToSpeech.Engine.KEY_PARAM_UTTERANCE_ID,
                                "Alarm message ID");
tts.speak( text2, TextToSpeech.QUEUE_ADD, hashMap );
```

This code notifies the activity of the application when it has finished synthesizing *text2*. The application can then do some desired task such as playing some music or displaying a message on the screen:

```
public void onUtteranceCompleted ( String utteranceId ) {
  if ( utteranceId.equals("Alarm message ID") )
    doSomething();
}
```

Note that the *OnUtteranceCompletedListener* can be assigned to the *TextToSpeech* object only after the TTS **onInit** has been called. However, this listener has been deprecated, and developers are recommended to use *UtteranceProgressListener*, which is added in API level 15. *UtteranceProgressListener* is a listener for events relating to the progress of an utterance through the synthesis queue. Each utterance is associated with a call to the method **speak**(String, int, HashMap) or **synthesizeToFile**(String, HashMap, String) with an associated utterance identifier, as per KEY_PARAM_UTTERANCE_ID. The **speak** method allows multiple threads to call its specified callbacks. *UtteranceProgressListener* is an abstract class, so we have to implement it, and we can do that using an inner class:

```
tts.setOnUtteranceProgressListener ( new
  UtteranceProgressListener()
  {
    @Override
    public void onDone(String utteranceId){
      if ( utteranceId == "Alarm message ID")
        onUtteranceCompleted ( utteranceId );
    }

    @Override
    public void onError(String utteranceId){
    }

    @Override
    public void onStart(String utteranceId){
    }
  });
```

We should replace the statement *tts.setOnUtteranceCompletedListener(this);* by the above code.

9.4.2 Saving Speech

We have discussed how to convert text to speech using the **speak**() method of the class *TextToSpeech*. There can be situations in which we would like the synthesized speech to be recorded in an audio file so that next time when we want to play the speech, we do not have to go through the synthesis process again. The class *TexttToSpeech* provides the method **synthesizeToFile**() to record the synthesized data in an audio format. The following code shows how this is done:

```
HashMap<String, String> hashMap = new HashMap();
String keyText = "A string for key";
String outFile = "sample1.wav";
hashMap.put(TextToSpeech.Engine.KEY_PARAM_UTTERANCE_ID, keyText);
tts.synthesizeToFile(keyText, hashMap, outFile);
tts.speak( text1, TextToSpeech.QUEUE_FLUSH, hashMap );
tts.speak( text2, TextToSpeech.QUEUE_ADD, hashMap );
```

The code saves the synthesized audio data in *sample1.wav* in the *.wav* format after the synthesis process has finished. (The completion of the synthesis can be notified by an optional utterance identifier as discussed above.) The *.wav* file can be played just like any other audio resource with *android.media.MediaPlayer*.

The **put**() method of *HashMap* in the example associates the String *keyText* with *TextToSpeech*.Engine.KEY_PARAM_UTTERANCE_ID, which is of type *String* and is a parameter key to identify an utterance in *TextToSpeech.OnUtteranceCompletedListener* or *UtteranceProgressListener* after the text has been spoken, or a file has been played back or a silence duration has elapsed.

There are other ways to associate audio resources with speech. Continuing the above example, suppose we have a *.wav* file that contains the synthesized data associated with *keyText*. We can also associate *keyText* with an audio resource, which can be accessed with one of the two **addSpeech**() methods:

tts.addSpeech(keyText, outFile);

This way any call to **speak**() using the key string "A string for key" will result in the playback of *outFile*. If the file is missing, then **speak**() will ignore the file and simply synthesize the given string to produce speech. We can take advantage of this feature to provide an option to the user to customize how "A string for key" sounds: she can record her own version or use the synthesized sound by removing the sound file. Regardless of the option, we can use the same code to add the text to the speech queue:

tts.speak(keyText, TextToSpeech.QUEUE_ADD, hashAlarm);

9.5   Speak From a Text File with Pause/Resume

9.5.1   Synchronization by Condition Variable

We have discussed how to convert a short text to speech using the class *TextToSpeech*. We may apply the same technique to speak the text from a file. This works fine if the file is small as we can simply read the whole file into a *String* object and speak the text of the *String* as we did in the above sections. However, if the file is large, this won't work because a *String* object cannot be infinitely large to hold any size of text. Neither can we keep adding text to the utterance queue, because this may make the queue overflow as a queue's capacity is also finite.

A simple solution to this problem is to let the engine finish speaking a certain text segment and notify the activity when it is done, before reading in new text from the file. This can be accomplished by reading the file line by line and using a condition variable to force the reading activity to wait after the utterance queue has accumulated a certain number of lines of text. We can use an integer variable *count* to keep track of the lines in the queue. By making use of the third parameter of the **speak** method that we discussed in previous sections, we can notify the reading activity and decrement *count*:

```
final Lock mutex = new ReentrantLock();
final Condition textSpoken = mutex.newCondition();
int count = 0;

private void speak() throws InterruptedException {
   String str = null;
   InputStream is = null;
   HashMap<String, String> hashMap = new HashMap();
   String keyText = "Text Spoken ID";
   hashMap.put(TextToSpeech.Engine.KEY_PARAM_UTTERANCE_ID,keyText);
   MyUtteranceProgressListener listener = new
                      MyUtteranceProgressListener();
   tts.setOnUtteranceProgressListener ( listener );
   try {
```

```
        is = getResources().openRawResource(R.raw.myfile);
        BufferedReader reader = new
                    BufferedReader(new InputStreamReader(is));
        while ((str = reader.readLine()) != null) {
          mutex.lock();
          count++;
          while ( count > 50 )
            textSpoken.await();    // Condition wait
          mutex.unlock();
          tts.speak( str, TextToSpeech.QUEUE_ADD, hashMap );
        }
      }  catch(IOException e) {
              Log.e(LOG_APP_TAG, e.getMessage());
      }
    }

    public void onUtteranceCompleted ( String utteranceId ) {
      if ( utteranceId.equals("Text Spoken ID")) {
        mutex.lock();
        count--;
        mutex.unlock();
        textSpoken.signal();
      }
    }
```

In this code, *textSpoken* is the condition variable we mentioned. The reading activity waits (sleeps) when the counter *count* is larger than 50. When the engine has completed speaking one line of text, it calls **onUtteranceCompleted**(), passing to it the utterance ID, "Text Spoken ID"; the method decrements the *count*, and wakes up any activity that waits on the condition variable *textSpoken*.

9.5.2 Speak Using a Different Thread

We can also add a pause button to the application, so that the app stops synthesizing when the button is clicked and resumes the task when the resume button is clicked. We can call the **stop**() method of *TextToSpeech* to stop synthesizing. However, the method will also discard all utterances in the queue. So we need to buffer the lines we have read from the file and keeps track of the current line the engine is speaking. When we resume the synthesis, we can add the text lines saved in the buffer to the utterance queue again to the engine, which has discarded them in the queue when executing **stop**().

Since the UI has to interact with the user all the time, we have to start the speech engine with a different thread so that the main activity will not be mostly consumed by the speech task. Suppose we again use Eclipse IDE to develop such an application. We call the names of the project and the application, *FileToSpeech* and the name of the package, *tts.filetospeech*. We create another class file *Speech.java*, which contains the code of the thread that manages the engine and our main program, *MainActivity.java* mainly manages the UI and the initialization of the speech engine. Listing 9-3 below shows the complete code of the activity class *MainActivity*.

Program Listing 9-3   *MainActivity.java* of Project *FileToSpeech*

```
package tts.filetospeech;
```

```
import java.io.*;
import java.util.*;
import android.app.Activity;
import android.os.*;
import android.util.Log;
import android.view.View;
import android.widget.*;
import android.speech.tts.TextToSpeech;
import android.speech.tts.TextToSpeech.*;

public class MainActivity extends Activity
                                    implements   OnInitListener
{
  ImageButton ttsButton;
  Button pauseButton;
  Button resumeButton;
  TextView msg;
  TextToSpeech tts;
  InputStream is = null;
  BufferedReader reader;
  boolean firstTime = true;   //First time reading text to synthesize
  Speech speech = null;

  @Override
  protected void onCreate(Bundle savedInstanceState) {
    super.onCreate(savedInstanceState);
    setContentView(R.layout.activity_main);
    ttsButton = (ImageButton) findViewById(R.id.ttsButton);
    msg = (TextView) findViewById(R.id.msg);
    pauseButton = (Button) findViewById(R.id.pauseButton);
    resumeButton = (Button) findViewById(R.id.resumeButton);
    tts = new TextToSpeech(this, this);
  }

  // Start button clicked
  public void onStart(View view) {
    if ( firstTime ) {
      is = getResources().openRawResource(R.raw.myfile);
      speech = new Speech ( tts, is );
      Thread speechThread = new Thread ( speech );
      speechThread.start();   // start thread to speak
      firstTime = false;
    }
  }

  // Pause button clicked
  public void onPause ( View view ) {
    if ( speech != null )
      speech.speechPause();
  }

  // Resume button clicked
  public void onResume ( View view ){
    if ( speech != null )
      speech.speechResume();
```

```
    }

    @Override
    public void onInit(int state) {
        if (state == TextToSpeech.SUCCESS) {
            msg.setText("TTS initialized successfully!\n " +
                    "Click TTS to start speaking.");
            int result = tts.setLanguage(Locale.US);
            if (result == TextToSpeech.LANG_MISSING_DATA
                    || result == TextToSpeech.LANG_NOT_SUPPORTED) {
                msg.setText("TTS: Language not supported!");
            } else {
                ttsButton.setEnabled(true);
            }
        } else {
            msg.setText("TTS: Initilization Failed!");
        }
    }

    @Override
    public void onDestroy() {
        if (tts != null) {
            tts.stop();
            tts.shutdown();
        }
        super.onDestroy();
    }
}
```

This class mainly handles the UI and initializes the speech engine. The code that speaks the text from the file is listed below:

Program Listing 9-4   *Speech.java* of Project *FileToSpeech*

```
package tts.filetospeech;

import java.io.*;
import java.util.*;
import android.util.Log;
import java.util.concurrent.locks.*;
import android.speech.tts.*;
import android.speech.tts.TextToSpeech.OnInitListener;

public class Speech  implements Runnable
{
    TextToSpeech tts;
    boolean firstTime = true;
    HashMap<String, String> hashMap;
    InputStream is = null;
    BufferedReader reader = null;
    final Lock mutex = new ReentrantLock();
    final Condition textSpoken = mutex.newCondition();
    final Lock mutex1 = new ReentrantLock();
    final Condition pauseCond = mutex1.newCondition();
```

```
int count = 0;
int position = 0;
final int LEN = 20;
String buffer[] = new String[LEN];
boolean pausing = false;
boolean starting = true;
boolean resuming = false;
// Constructor
public Speech ( TextToSpeech tts0, InputStream is0 )
{
  tts = tts0;
  is = is0;
}

@Override
public void run() {
  try {
    speak();
  } catch (InterruptedException e) {
    e.printStackTrace();
  }
}

private void speak() throws InterruptedException {
  String str = null;
  if ( firstTime ){  // Initialization only once
    String keyText = "Text Spoken ID";
    hashMap = new HashMap();
    hashMap.put(TextToSpeech.Engine.KEY_PARAM_UTTERANCE_ID,keyText);
    MyUtteranceProgressListene listener =
                      new MyUtteranceProgressListene();
    tts.setOnUtteranceProgressListener ( listener );
    firstTime = false;
  }
  try {
    if ( reader == null  )
      reader = new BufferedReader(new InputStreamReader(is));
    while ((str = reader.readLine()) != null) {
      mutex1.lock();
      while ( pausing )
        pauseCond.await();  // Condition wait
      mutex1.unlock();
      mutex.lock();
      count++;
      if ( starting ){
        tts.speak( str, TextToSpeech.QUEUE_FLUSH, hashMap );
        starting = false;     // starts once only
      } else {
        if ( resuming ) {
          // copy buffer string back
          int j =  position - 1;
          if ( j < 0 ) j = j + LEN;
          for ( int i = 1; i < count; i++){
            if ( i == 1 )
              tts.speak( buffer[j],
```

```
                              TextToSpeech.QUEUE_FLUSH, hashMap );
                else
                  tts.speak( buffer[j], TextToSpeech.QUEUE_ADD,
                                                        hashMap );
                j = ( j + 1) % LEN;
              }
            }  // if ( resuming )
            tts.speak( str, TextToSpeech.QUEUE_ADD, hashMap );
          } // else
          while ( count > LEN )
            textSpoken.await();    // Condition wait
          mutex.unlock();
          buffer[position] = str;
          position++;
          if ( position == LEN )
            position = 0;          // Circular buffer
        }  // while reader
      }  catch(IOException e) {
        Log.e("speak", e.getMessage());
      }
    }

    public void onUtteranceCompleted ( String utteranceId ) {
      if ( utteranceId.equals("Text Spoken ID")) {
        mutex.lock();
        count--;
        textSpoken.signal();
        mutex.unlock();
      }
    }

    // Innner class for UtteranceProgressListener
    class MyUtteranceProgressListener extends UtteranceProgressListener
    {
      @Override
      public void onDone(String utteranceId)
      {
        onUtteranceCompleted ( utteranceId );
      }
      @Override
      public void onError(String utteranceId){
      }
      @Override
      public void onStart(String arg0) {
      }
    }

    public void speechPause()
    {
      if ( pausing ) return;  // engine already stopped
      mutex1.lock();
      pausing = true;
      mutex1.unlock();
      tts.stop();      // stop engine, clears utterance queue
    }
```

```
public void speechResume ()
{
  if ( !pausing ) return;   // engine already running
  mutex1.lock();
  pausing = false;
  resuming = true;
  pauseCond.signal();    // Wake up the waiting method
  mutex1.unlock();
}
}
```

In this class, **speak**() is the method that does the reading of file and synthesizing. It uses the two condition variables, *textSpoken*, and *pauseCond* to block the engine. It blocks (waits) on *pauseCond* when the user clicks the *Pause* button, setting the variable *pausing* to true. It is woken up by the signal of *pauseCond*, when someone clicks *Resume*, setting *pausing* to false and executing the statement *pauseCond.signal();*. and making *pauseCond* to signal.

In this program, each utterance is a line of text. When the *Pause* button is clicked, the rest of the line is discarded. When it resumes, it starts from the next line. You can modify this program to handle this situation differently. It can start from the current line rather than the next, or it can finish speaking the current line before it stops. Or you can make an utterance to be a word instead of a line.

The UI layout, including the button listeners, is defined in *res/layout/activity_main.xml*, which is listed below.

Program Listing 9-5   *activity_main.xml* of Project *FileToSpeech*

```
<LinearLayout xmlns:android="http://schemas.android.com/apk/res/android"
    android:layout_width="fill_parent"
    android:layout_height="fill_parent"
    android:orientation="vertical" >
    <RelativeLayout
        android:id="@+id/linearLayout1"
        android:layout_width="match_parent"
        android:layout_height="wrap_content"
        android:layout_marginLeft="6pt"
        android:layout_marginRight="6pt"
        android:layout_marginTop="4pt" >
        <Button
        android:id="@+id/pauseButton"
        android:layout_width="wrap_content"
        android:layout_height="wrap_content"
        android:onClick="onPause"
        android:text="Pause" />
        <ImageButton
            android:id="@+id/ttsButton"
            android:layout_width="90dp"
            android:layout_height="90dp"
            android:layout_alignParentRight="true"
            android:layout_alignParentTop="true"
            android:layout_marginRight="60dp"
            android:adjustViewBounds="true"
            android:background="@drawable/tts"
```

```
            android:scaleType="centerCrop"
            android:onClick="onStart"
            android:src="@drawable/tts" />
    </RelativeLayout>
    <RelativeLayout
        android:id="@+id/linearLayout2"
        android:layout_width="match_parent"
        android:layout_height="wrap_content"
        android:layout_marginLeft="6pt"
        android:layout_marginRight="6pt"
        android:layout_marginTop="4pt" >
        <Button
          android:id="@+id/resumeButton"
          android:layout_width="wrap_content"
          android:layout_height="wrap_content"
          android:onClick="onResume"
          android:text="Resume" />
    </RelativeLayout>
    <TextView
        android:id="@+id/msg"
        android:layout_width="match_parent"
        android:layout_height="wrap_content"
        android:layout_marginLeft="4pt"
        android:layout_marginRight="4pt"
        android:layout_marginTop="2pt"
        android:gravity="center_horizontal"
        android:textSize="10pt" >
    </TextView>
</LinearLayout>
```

When we run the program, we will see a UI like the one shown in Figure 9-3 below.

Figure 9-3 UI of *FileToSpeech* Project

9.6   Playing Audio Clips

9.6.1   Playing Sound

Android provides resources for managing audio and video media. The Android multimedia framework includes support for playing a variety of common media types.

Android supports various audio streams for different purposes. For example, a phone volume button can be configured to control the sound volume of a specific audio stream, increasing or decreasing the volume according to the need. We can also configure a button to control the sound media stream type in our application.

There are two main API's for audio playback, the *SoundPool* class for playing small audio clips, and the more commonly used *MediaPlayer* class for playing any kind of audio clips. We can use *SoundPool*, which loads files asynchronously, to play several sounds at the same time and repeat the play. However, The sound files to be played must not exceed 1 MB. The *OnLoadCompleteListener* can be used to check whether the loading of a file is complete.

We can use the *MediaPlayer* class, which also loads files asynchronously, to control playback of audio/video files and streams. The player is is managed as a state machine. Using this class, we can easily integrate audio, video and images into our applications. We can play video and/or audio from media files stored in our application's resources (raw resources), from standalone files in the filesystem, or from a data stream of a remote server through a network connection. Often we also need the *MediaController* class to control playback, and use a *Service* instance to play audio when the user is not interacting with the app directly. The *ContentResolver* class is often used to retrieve tracks on the device.

The *MediaPlayer* class may be the most important component of the Android media framework. The class is particularly easy to use for simple applications. A *MediaPlayer* object can fetch, decode, and play both audio and video with minimal setup. It supports several different media sources including

1. Local resources
2. Internal URIs, such as one that can be obtained from a *ContentResolver*
3. External URLs (streaming)

The details of this class and its usage can be found at the web sites,
   http://developer.android.com/reference/android/media/MediaPlayer.html
and
   http://developer.android.com/guide/topics/media/mediaplayer.html

9.6.2   Simple Examples of Using *MediaPlayer*

As a simple example, we show how to play a local audio file from the main activity (which is not desirable as we normally play an audio in the background). The following code is the complete program of *MainActivity.java* that plays an audio file located in the local raw resource directory *res/raw*:

```
package tts.audiodemo;

import android.os.*;
import android.app.Activity;
import android.media.MediaPlayer;

public class MainActivity extends Activity
{
```

```
  @Override
  protected void onCreate(Bundle savedInstanceState) {
    super.onCreate(savedInstanceState);
    setContentView(R.layout.activity_main);
    MediaPlayer mp = MediaPlayer.create(this, R.raw.sound1_wav);
    // no need to call prepare(); create() has done that already
    mp.start();
  }
}
```

The audio file name in this example is *sound1_wav*. The system does not try to parse a raw file in any particular way. Also, a raw filename cannot contain any upper case letter or a dot '.'. Thus a filename cannot have the two conventional parts, a primary part followed by an extension after a dot. However, the content of this resource should not be raw audio. It should be a properly formatted and encoded media file in one of the formats that Android supports. For clarity, we use the underscore '_' to replace the role of the dot. Thus the file *sound1_wav* actually means *sound1.wav*, which is encoded in the WAV format. When you run the program, you should hear the sound generated from the encoded data of the file.

The code of the above example is simple enough. We modify it to play a file on the Internet and show that *MediaPlayer* loads file asynchronously. In our next simple example, we show that the **start**() method of *MediaPlayer* returns immediately, not waiting for the playback to finish. In this example, the app flashes a message on the screen after it has started and another message after it has finished using the *Toast* class. The example will play a source file residing on a Web site. So we need to add the Internet access permission statement in the file *AndroidManifest.xml*:

```
<?xml version="1.0" encoding="utf-8"?>
 <manifest xmlns:android="http://schemas.android.com/apk/res/android"
 .....
 <uses-permission android:name="android.permission.INTERNET"/>
 <application>
 .....
 </application>
</manifest>
```

Since we need to toast a message at the end, we need to know when the play completes. To accomplish this, we can add to the code a completion listener, which will call a method to perform the task when the player finishes playing. The following is the complete program (*MainActivity.java*) of this example:

```
package tts.audiodemo1;

import android.os.*;
import java.io.IOException;
import android.widget.Toast;
import android.app.Activity;
import android.media.MediaPlayer;
import android.media.AudioManager;
import android.media.MediaPlayer.OnCompletionListener;

public class MainActivity extends Activity
{
  MediaPlayer mp = null;

  @Override
  protected void onCreate(Bundle savedInstanceState) {
    super.onCreate(savedInstanceState);
```

```
  setContentView(R.layout.activity_main);
  mp = new MediaPlayer();
  String url = "http://www.forejune.com/android/files/sound1.wav";
  mp.setAudioStreamType(AudioManager.STREAM_MUSIC);
  try {
    mp.setDataSource(url);
    mp.prepare();     // might take long! (for buffering, etc)
  } catch (IllegalArgumentException | SecurityException
     | IllegalStateException | IOException e) {
    e.printStackTrace();
  }
  mp.start();
  mp.setOnCompletionListener(new
          OnCompletionListener() {
      @Override
      public void onCompletion(MediaPlayer mp) {
        onDone();
      }
    });
  if ( mp.isPlaying() )
    Toast.makeText(this, "Sound playback has started!",
                                    Toast.LENGTH_LONG).show();
}

protected void onDone()
{
   Toast.makeText(this, "Sound playback has finished!",
                                    Toast.LENGTH_LONG).show();
   mp.release();
   mp = null;
  }
}
```

In the code, the complete listener is implemented as an anonymous inner class. The **setOn-CompletionListener**() method register a callback to be invoked when the end of a media source has been reached during playback. In our example, when it finds the play is complete, it calls **onDone**(), which shows a *Toast* message, and calls **release**() to release the resources and then nullifies the *MediaPlayer*. It is important to always release the resources and not to hang to a *MediaPlayer* object that is no longer needed. This is because a *MediaPlayer* object can consume valuable system resources.

When we run the program, we should see a *Toast* message at the beginning of playing the sound (Figure 9-4 (a)), and another message at the end of the play (Figure 9-4 (b)).

(a)   (b)

Figure 9-4   Toast Messages at Beginning and End of Play in Example

9.6.3   Asynchronous Playback of *MediaPlayer*

In most applications, we do not want to start a *MediaPlayer* in the main activity because most
often we want the sound to be played in the background and leave the main activity to handle the
UI for user interactions. Also, the call to *prepare()* may take a long time to execute as it might
involve fetching and decoding media data. This may cause the UI to hang until the method returns,
which may frustrate any user and may cause an ANR (Application Not Responding) error. We may
manage and start a *MediaPlayer* object at the background with a new service as suggested by the
official Android developers site. Here, we present an example that uses an alternative approach.
We start the player using a worker thread running in the background, which is a traditional way
of handling background tasks. Mutual exclusion locks and condition variables are used to achieve
synchronization, sending the worker to sleep while the *MediaPlayer* is playing the sound and
waking it up when the play has finished. The worker thread then calls the main thread, which
handles the UI, informing it that the play is complete. The main thread displays a Toast message
on the screen to notify the user.

   We call this example project and application *AudioDemo2*, where the main activity class, *Main-
Activity*, handles only the UI, and the media player is managed by a class named *MyPlayer*. The
UI in *MainActivity* defines four buttons, *Start*, *Pause*, *Stop* and *Resume*, to start, pause, stop and
resume the media player respectively (see Figure 9-5). As we usually do, we define the UI layout
in the file *res/layout/activity_main.xml*. The following is the complete listing of the code of *Main-
Activity*:

   Program Listing 9-6   *MainActivity.java of AudioDemo2*

```
package tts.audiodemo2;

import android.os.*;
import android.widget.*;
import android.util.Log;
import android.view.View;
import android.app.Activity;

public class MainActivity extends Activity
{
  public  TextView textView;

  MyPlayer player = null;
  boolean started = false;    //player not started at beginning

  @Override
  protected void onCreate(Bundle savedInstanceState) {
    super.onCreate(savedInstanceState);
    setContentView(R.layout.activity_main);
    textView = (TextView) findViewById(R.id.status);
  }

  public  void playComplete ( View view )
  {
    showToast( "Play complete!");
    player = null;
    started = false;
  }
```

```
public void onStart(View view) throws InterruptedException {
  if ( !started ){
    player = new MyPlayer ( this, view );
    Thread playerThread = new Thread ( player );
    playerThread.start();   // start player thread
    Toast.makeText(this,"Play started!",Toast.LENGTH_LONG).show();
    textView.setText("Play started!");
    started = true;
  }
}

public void pausePlay ( View view )
{
  if ( player != null ) {
    if ( player.pausePlayer() )
      textView.setText("Player paused!");
  }
}

public void resumePlay ( View view )
{
  if ( player != null ) {
    if ( player.resumePlayer() )
      textView.setText("Player resumed!");
  }
}

// stop player
public void onStop ( View view )
{
  if ( player != null ) {
    if ( player.stopPlayer() )
      textView.setText("Player stopped!");
  }
}

// display a Toast message on UI thread
public void showToast(final String toast)
{
  runOnUiThread(new Runnable() {
    public void run()
    {
        Toast.makeText(MainActivity.this, toast, i
                              Toast.LENGTH_SHORT).show();
    }
  });
}
}
```

In the code, the method **playComplete**() will be called by the other class *MyPlayer*, when the media player detects that the playback is complete. It nullifies the current player (the zombie object will be handled by the Java garbage collector). To play the sound again, the user has to click the *Start* button again, which will create a new player object.

The method *Toast*.**makeText**() must be called from within the UI thread as do most methods that deal with the UI. If we call it from a worker thread, an exception error saying *Can't create handler inside thread that has not called Looper.prepare()* will occur. The function **showToast**() at the end of the code is to ensure that **makeText**() will be called from the UI thread. In this function, the method **runOnUiThread**(*Runnable action*) is a method of the class *Activity*. It runs the specified *action* on the UI thread.

The following listing shows the complete code of the other class, *MyPlayer*:

Program Listing 9-7   *MyPlayer.java* of *AudioDemo2*

```
package tts.audiodemo2;

import java.io.*;
import java.util.concurrent.locks.*;
import android.util.Log;
import android.view.View;
import android.content.Intent;
import android.media.MediaPlayer;
import android.media.AudioManager;
import android.media.MediaPlayer.OnCompletionListener;

public class MyPlayer  implements Runnable
{
  MediaPlayer mp = null;
  MyListener listener = null;
  final Lock mutex = new ReentrantLock();
  final Condition done = mutex.newCondition();
  Intent intent = null;   // not used in this demo
  boolean complete = false;
  MainActivity main;
  View view;              // not really needed

  public MyPlayer (){
     //super ("MyPlayer");
  }

  public MyPlayer ( MainActivity main0, View view0 ){
     main = main0;
     view = view0;
     listener = new MyListener();
  }

  public MyPlayer ( Intent i ) {
    //super ("MyPlayer");
    listener = new MyListener();
    intent = i;
  }

  @Override
  public void run() {
    onHandleIntent ( intent );
    main.playComplete( view );
  }
```

```
//@Override ( need Override if started as an IntentSerive )
protected void onHandleIntent(Intent intent) {
  mp = new MediaPlayer();
  String url = "http://www.forejune.com/android/files/sound1.wav";
  mp.setAudioStreamType(AudioManager.STREAM_MUSIC);
  try {
    mp.setDataSource(url);
    mp.prepare();      // might take long! (for buffering, etc)
  } catch (IllegalArgumentException | SecurityException
        | IllegalStateException | IOException e) {
    e.printStackTrace();
  }

  mp.start();
  mp.setOnCompletionListener ( listener );
  try {
    mutex.lock();
    while ( !complete )
      done.await();              //Condition wait
    mutex.unlock();
  } catch (InterruptedException e) {
    e.printStackTrace();
  }
}

// To detect when is the play complete
class MyListener implements OnCompletionListener
{
  @Override
  public void onCompletion ( MediaPlayer mp ) {
    complete = true;
    mutex.lock();
    done.signal();       //wake up sleeping thread
    mutex.unlock();
    mp.release();        //release resources
    mp = null;
  }
}

// stop the media player
public boolean stopPlayer()
{
  if( mp !=null && mp.isPlaying() ){
      mp.stop();
      return true;
  } else
    return false;
}

// pause the media player, which can be resumed by calling start()
public boolean pausePlayer()
{
  if( mp !=null && mp.isPlaying() ){
        mp.pause();
        return true;
```

```
      } else
        return false;
  }

  // resume the paused media player
  public boolean resumePlayer()
  {
    if( mp !=null && !mp.isPlaying() ){
          mp.start();
          return true;
    } else
      return false;
  }
}
```

After the worker thread has started to run, the method **onHandleIntent** is called. This method creates and prepares a *MediaPlayer*, which starts playing the sound from the hard-coded Web address in the example. It also sets the listener *OnCompletionListener*, which is implemented inside the class. It then waits on the condition variable *done* and goes to sleep. When the playback of the sound is complete, the method **onCompletion** of the listener is called; this method nullifies the *MediaPlayer* and releases its resources. It also wakes up the sleeping thread, which will return from **onHandleIntent** to **run**, which then calls **playComplete**() of *MainActivity* that will present messages about the completion to the user.

With minor modifications, the thread can also be started as an *IntentService* and the method, **onHandleIntent**() will be an *Override* and called asynchronously.

The variable *intent* is not used here. It is left in the code for the convenience of any reader who wants to make modifications to the code.

The xml code listed below is of the file *res/layout/activity_main.xml*, which defines the layout of the UI.

Program Listing 9-8   *activity_main.xml of AudioDemo2*

```xml
<?xml version="1.0" encoding="utf-8"?>
<LinearLayout xmlns:android="http://schemas.android.com/apk/res/android"
    android:layout_width="match_parent"
    android:layout_height="match_parent"
    android:orientation="horizontal" >

    <Button
        android:id="@+id/onstart"
        android:layout_width="wrap_content"
        android:layout_height="wrap_content"
        android:layout_margin="5dip"
        android:layout_weight="1"
        android:onClick="onStart"
        android:text="Start" />
    <Button
        android:id="@+id/pauseplay"
        android:layout_width="wrap_content"
        android:layout_height="wrap_content"
        android:layout_margin="5dip"
        android:layout_weight="1"
```

```
        android:onClick="pausePlay"
        android:text="Pause" />
    <LinearLayout
        android:layout_width="wrap_content"
        android:layout_height="wrap_content"
        android:orientation="vertical" >
    <Button
        android:id="@+id/stop"
        android:layout_width="wrap_content"
        android:layout_height="wrap_content"
        android:layout_margin="5dip"
        android:layout_weight="1"
        android:onClick="onStop"
        android:text="Stop" />

    <Button
        android:id="@+id/resume"
        android:layout_width="wrap_content"
        android:layout_height="wrap_content"
        android:layout_margin="5dip"
        android:onClick="resumePlay"
        android:text="Resume" />
    </LinearLayout>
    <LinearLayout
        android:layout_width="wrap_content"
        android:layout_height="wrap_content"
        android:orientation="vertical" >

    <TextView
        android:layout_width="wrap_content"
        android:layout_height="wrap_content"
        android:text="Status: " />
    <TextView
        android:id="@+id/status"
        android:layout_width="wrap_content"
        android:layout_height="wrap_content"
        android:text="Not started" />
    </LinearLayout>
</LinearLayout>
```

Since the source file is on the Internet. We have to set the permission in the *AndroidMani-fest.xml*:

<uses-permission android:name="android.permission.INTERNET"/>

Figure 9-5 shows the UI of this application when we run it. Figure 9-5(a) shows the buttons and the text layout at the beginning. The *Status* message shows *"Play started!"* implying that the button *Start* has been clicked and the audio is played in the background. Figure 9-5(b) shows the Toast message when the playback is complete.

Figure 9-5 UI of *Audiodemo2*

Chapter 10   Speech Recognition

10.1   Introduction

Speech recognition (SR) by machine, which translates spoken words into text has been a goal of research for more than six decades. It is also known as *automatic speech recognition* (ASR), *computer speech recognition*, or simply *speech to text* (STT). The research in speech recognition by machine involves a lot of disciplines, including signal processing, acoustics, pattern recognition, communication and information theory, linguistics, physiology, computer science and psychology. Figure 10-1 below shows a general block diagram of a task-oriented speech recognition system:

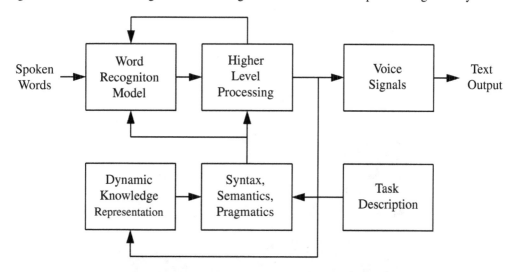

Figure 10-1 A Typical Speech Recognition System

The figure shows a general model for speech recognition, which starts with a speaker generating a speech to accomplish certain tasks. The speech is parsed into a sequence of words that makes sensible meaning according to the syntax, semantics and pragmatics of the recognition task. A higher level processor makes analysis of the spoken words and uses a dynamic knowledge representation to modify the syntax, semantics and pragmatics dynamically. The higher level processor feedback reduces the complexity of analysis and search.

Speech recognition research has been performed for about six decades. Only in recent years did it get widespread applications in the consumer products. The research in the field of speech recognition by machine started in the 1950s in large laboratories such as Bell Laboratories and RCA Laboratories, when researchers exploit the fundamental principles of how human perceives acoustic-phonetics. The speech recognition systems relied on spectral measurements. Later, researchers incorporate statistical techniques to improve upon earlier methods. In the 1960s several fundamental ideas in speech recognition emerged in the US and Japan. Significant milestones were achieved in 1970s by different groups of researchers in the world. In the 1980s, speech research shifted from template-based approaches to statistical modeling methods, especially the hidden Markov model approach. After the 1990s, the research in the field has become mature. Linguists, computer scientists, and engineers worked together to take advantage of large databases and the improvement in computing speed to create applications that had commercial usage. In recent years, mobile phones and desktop computing are inundated with speech recognition applications.

Nowadays, speech recognition (SR) mobile products are ubiquitous. There are many third party SR apps that support Android. The well known Google *Now project* allows a user to give a voice command to an Android device, which will then fetch the result for the user. It recognizes the voice and converts it into text or takes appropriate actions. Android's *Translate* app goes one step further. It lets a user dictate e-mails and text messages. It not only converts English into another spoken language such as French, but also has a *conversation mode* that will translate the French receiver's response back into English.

Some SR apps provide service to another user app through the use of *Intent*. For example, *Google Voice Search* is a Google product that allows users to use Google Search by speaking on a mobile device or a PC, rather than entering data via a keyboard. It is one of the popular recognizers available for Android and supports a wide variety of languages. The app has a very simple *Activity* to notify users for speaking, and the dialog closes promptly as soon as the user stops talking. (Google Now mentioned above is not exactly the same as Google Voice Search. Google Now is a feature of the Google Search app for Android. It shows information about what is currently happening now or will happen in the near future, such as reservations, calender events, weather, and travel information.) Figure 10-2 below shows a UI of a Google Voice Search app.

Figure 10-2 A UI of a Google Voice Search App

These applications are built upon the Android voice recognition APIs, which are fairly easy to use. The class *SpeechRecognizer* provides access to the speech recognition service, which allows access to the speech recognizer. The Android documentation recommends that we should not instantiate this class directly, but call **createSpeechRecognizer** (*Context*), and the class's methods must be invoked only from the main application thread. For most SR applications, audio data are sent to remote servers, where speech recognition is performed. Consequently. as most tasks are done remotely, the API should not be used for continuous recognition, which would consume a significant amount of battery and bandwidth. For the API to work properly, a voice recognizer must have been installed in the Android device where the app runs. Normally, the app must be run in a real device. The emulator cannot perform the recognition tasks properly.

Our examples discussed below use a recognizer based on Google Voice Recognition (GVR), which uses neural network algorithms to convert human audio speech to text. GVR works for a number of major languages but we have only considered English in our applications. A neural network consists of many processors working in parallel, mimicking a virtual brain. The usage of parallel processors allows for more computing power and better operation in real-time, but what truly makes a neural network distinct is its ability to adapt and learn based on previous data. A neural network does not use one specific algorithm to achieve its task. It learns by the example of other data. In our examples, GVR uses the Internet to access its large database for voice recognition attempted by previous users. It also looks at previous Google search queries so that the voice recognition engine can guess which phrases are more commonly used than others. This way, even if the user does not speak a certain word clearly, GVR can use the context of the rest of the spoken phrase or sentence to extrapolate what the user is most likely trying to say. In general, a neural network can learn from two major categories of learning methods : supervised or self-organized. In supervised training, an external teacher provides labeled data and the desired output. Meanwhile, self-organization network takes unlabeled data and finds groups and patterns in the data by itself. GVR learns from its own database through the self-organization method.

10.2   A Simple Example

We present here a very simple example of writing an app that converts spoken words to text by making use of the speech recognition API. In this example (*SttDemo0*), a button is presented to the user. When the user clicks on the button, a Google Speech dialog appears and the user can speak. As soon as the user stops speaking, the dialog vanishes and the text of the speech is shown (Figure 10-4). The complete Java code of this app is listed below:

Program Listing 10-1   *MainActivity.java* of Project *SttDemo0*

```java
package stt.sttdemo0;

import java.util.*;
import android.widget.*;
import android.os.Bundle;
import android.view.View;
import android.content.pm.*;
import android.app.Activity;
import android.content.Intent;
import android.speech.RecognizerIntent;

/**
 * A very simple SR application that starts speech recognition
 * activity through the use of RecognizerIntent.
 * Spoken words are saved as a list of words of String.
 */
public class MainActivity extends Activity
{
    private static final int REQUEST_CODE = 1989;
    private ListView words;

    @Override
    public void onCreate(Bundle savedInstanceState)
    {
        super.onCreate(savedInstanceState);
        setContentView(R.layout.activity_main);

        Button speechButton=(Button) findViewById(R.id.speechbutton);
        words = (ListView) findViewById(R.id.listview);

        PackageManager pm = getPackageManager();
```

```
      List<ResolveInfo> activities = pm.queryIntentActivities(
          new Intent(RecognizerIntent.ACTION_RECOGNIZE_SPEECH), 0);

      // Disable button in the absence of recognition service
      if ( activities.size() == 0 ) {
        speechButton.setEnabled ( false );
        speechButton.setText ( "Recognizer not present" );
      }
    }

  public void onClick( View view )
  {
    startSpeechRecognition();
  }

  // Start the speech recognition activity through an intent.
  private void startSpeechRecognition()
  {
    Intent intent = new Intent (
                    RecognizerIntent.ACTION_RECOGNIZE_SPEECH);
    intent.putExtra(RecognizerIntent.EXTRA_LANGUAGE_MODEL,
                    RecognizerIntent.LANGUAGE_MODEL_FREE_FORM);
    startActivityForResult(intent, REQUEST_CODE);
  }

  // Handle the results from the speech recognition activity.
  @Override
  protected void onActivityResult(int requestCode,
                                   int result, Intent intent)
  {
    if (requestCode == REQUEST_CODE && result == RESULT_OK)
    {
      // Populate the list by words recognized by engine
      ArrayList<String> matches=intent.getStringArrayListExtra(
                RecognizerIntent.EXTRA_RESULTS);
      words.setAdapter(new ArrayAdapter<String>(this,
                        android.R.layout.simple_list_item_1,
                matches));
    }
    super.onActivityResult(requestCode, result, intent);
  }
}
```

This class, *MainActivity*, defines a *ListView* variable named *words* for displaying strings. When a user speaks, the recognition engine guesses what the speaker says and puts all the guessed sentences in *words*.

Inside the **onCreate** method, the class *RecognizerIntent* consists of constants for supporting speech recognition through starting an *Intent*. The *String* constant ACTION_RECOGNIZE_SPEECH tells to start an activity that will prompt the user for speech and send it through a speech recognizer. If an appropriate recognizer is present, the *Activity* will be a started successfully and added to the List *activities*; if no recognizer is present then no activity will be added to the List. Therefore if *activities*.**size**() is 0, we disable the speech button with the statement

speechButton.setEnabled (false);

and display a message saying *Recognizer not present* (Figure 10-3(a)). If a speech recognizer exists in the system, the speech button is displayed (Figure 10-3(b)).

When we click on the speech button, the method **startSpeechRecognition**() is called. This method will call **startActivityForResult** (*Intent*, *int*), which is a method of the class *Activity*. We use *startActivityForResult* rather than *startActivity* because it allows us to get a result back from an activity when it ends. The second integer parameter of the method is a request code that identifies the call and the result will come back through our **onActivityResult** (int, int, Intent) method. In our example, the request code is REQUEST_CODE, which is set to 1989. The method puts all the strings that the recognition engine has recognized in the *ArrayList matches*. The *String RecognizerIntent*.EXTRA_RESULTS signifies an ArrayList<String> of the recognition results when performing ACTION_RECOGNIZE_SPEECH of *RecognizerIntent*. It will be present only when RESULT_OK is returned in an activity result. In a *PendingIntent*, the lack of this extra indicates failure.

To handle the returned results, we have used an *ArrayAdaptor*, which is one of the available adaptors in Android. An *Adaptor* is a collection handler that returns an item of the collection as a view. The *ArrayAdapter* class can handle a list or an array of Java objects as input, and every Java object is mapped to one row. We have used the *android.R.layout* class of the Android OS to display the strings; the class contains all of the publicly available layouts. In particular, we have used the layout *simple_list_item_1* for the display.

In the code, **setAdapter**(*ListAdapter*) is a public method of the class *ListView*. In the example, it sets the data behind the *ListView* object *words*; its input parameter is a *ListAdapter* object responsible for maintaining the data of the list and for producing a view to represent an item of the data set.

The xml layout code, *activity_main.xml* of this project is very simple. It is presented in Listing 10-2 below:

Program Listing 10-2   *activity_main.xml* of Project *SttDemo0*

```xml
<?xml version="1.0" encoding="utf-8"?>
<LinearLayout xmlns:android="http://schemas.android.com/apk/res/android"
    android:layout_width="fill_parent"
    android:layout_height="fill_parent"
    android:orientation="vertical">

    <TextView
        android:layout_width="fill_parent"
        android:layout_height="wrap_content"
        android:paddingBottom="4dip"
        android:text="Click Speech Button, then start speaking" />

    <Button android:id="@+id/speechbutton"
        android:layout_width="fill_parent"
        android:onClick="onClick"
        android:layout_height="wrap_content"
        android:text="Speech Button" />

    <ListView android:id="@+id/listview"
        android:layout_width="fill_parent"
        android:layout_height="0dip"
        android:layout_weight="1" />
</LinearLayout>
```

When we run the application, it presents one of the two displays shown in Figure 10-3. Figure 10-3(a) shows the UI when the app cannot find a valid recognition engine in the system. The button is disabled and will not respond to any clicks. Figure 10-3(b) shows the case when a valid recognizer is detected. The user activates the recognition engine by clicking on the button.

When the user clicks on the speech button, the app presents a dialog as shown in Figure 10-4(a). The user speaks to the phone and the engine guesses what the user says, converting all the possible guesses into text; the app saves the strings of text in a list. As soon as the user stops speaking, the dialog closes and the app presents the list of the guessed words. Figure 10-4(b) shows a sample output of the app. The user had spoken the sentence: *Hello, everyone*. The figure shows all the possible sentences that the engine thought it might have heard.

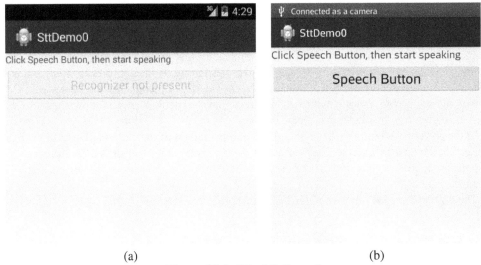

(a)   (b)

Figure 10-3   UI of *SttDemo0*

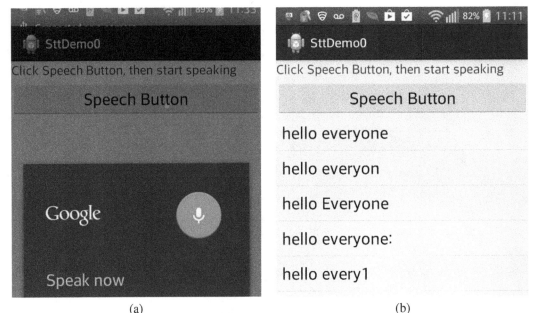

(a)   (b)

Figure 10-4   Input and Output of *SttDemo0*

Chapter 11 Playing Video

11.1 Introduction

We have discussed how to play audio in Chapter 9 using the class *MediaPlayer*. This class can also play video clips. In fact, the Android multimedia framework supports a wide variety of common media types to allow users to play audio or video from various sources, such as media files or data arriving from a network, and one can easily integrate audio, video and images into an application.

The class *MediaPlayer* is the main API for playing audio and video, while the class *AudioManager* manages audio sources and outputs on a device. However, unlike audio, which can be played in the background, we need to create a surface to play a video..

Like playing audio, to play video over a network, we need to request network access by adding the **uses-permission** statement in the manifest file *AndroidManifest.xml*:

```
<uses-permission android:name="android.permission.INTERNET"/>
```

While playing a video, if we do not want to keep the screen from dimming or the application process from sleeping, we also need to add the wake-lock statement in the manifest file:

```
<uses-permission android:name="android.permission.WAKE_LOCK" />
```

11.2 A Simple Example

We present here a simple example of playing video in Android. We call the project and application *VideoDemo1*, and the package *video.videodemo1*. We shall write two Java files, *MainActivity.java* and *VideoViewActivity.java* to play a video, and two layout files, *activity_main.xml* and *video-main_main.xml* to define the screen layout. We also create the directory *res/raw* and put the video file to be played in the directory.

The following is the code of *MainActivity*. Its main task is to set up a button, which listens to any clicking event. When the button is clicked, a new *Intent* of the class *VideoViewActivity* is created, and a new activity of this *Intent* is started:

Program Listing 11-1   *MainActivity.java* of Project *VideoDemo1*

```
package video.videodemo1;

import android.view.View.OnClickListener;
import android.content.Intent;
import android.widget.Button;
import android.app.Activity;
import android.os.Bundle;
import android.view.View;

public class MainActivity extends Activity
{
  Button button;

  @Override
  protected void onCreate(Bundle savedInstanceState) {
```

```
    super.onCreate(savedInstanceState);
    // Get the layout from activity_main.xml
    setContentView(R.layout.activity_main);

    // Locate the button in activity_main.xml
    button = (Button) findViewById(R.id.streamButton);

    // Listen to button clicks
    button.setOnClickListener(new OnClickListener() {
     public void onClick(View arg0) {
       // Start New Activity.class
       Intent intent=new Intent(MainActivity.this,VideoViewActivity.class);
       startActivity ( intent );
     }
    });
  }
}
```

When the activity *VideoViewActivity* is started, the class creates a *ProgressDialog* object, which is a dialog that shows a progress indicator with an optional text message or view, and progress range 0..10000. It then creates a *MediaController* with layout defined in *res/layout/videoview_main.xml* to play the specified video source:

Program Listing 11-2   *VideoViewActivity.java* of Project *VideoDemo1*

```
// VideoViewActivity.java
package video.videodemo1;

import android.media.MediaPlayer.OnPreparedListener;
import android.media.MediaPlayer;
import video.videodemo1.R;
import android.widget.*;
import android.app.*;
import android.net.Uri;
import android.util.Log;
import android.os.Bundle;

public class VideoViewActivity extends Activity
{
 ProgressDialog progressDialog;
 VideoView videoView;

 @Override
 protected void onCreate(Bundle savedInstanceState) {
   super.onCreate(savedInstanceState);
   // Get the layout from video_main.xml
   setContentView(R.layout.videoview_main);
   // Find your VideoView in video_main.xml layout
   videoView = (VideoView) findViewById(R.id.videoView);
   // Create a progressbar
   progressDialog = new ProgressDialog(VideoViewActivity.this);
   // Set progressbar title
   progressDialog.setTitle("Video Streaming");
```

```
   // Set progressbar message
   progressDialog.setMessage("Loading...");
   progressDialog.setIndeterminate ( false );
   progressDialog.setCancelable ( false );
   // Show progressbar
   progressDialog.show();

   try {
   // Create MediaController
   MediaController mediaController = new
                       MediaController(VideoViewActivity.this);
   mediaController.setAnchorView(videoView);
   //Note: omit extension here though the real filename has it
   Uri video=Uri.parse("android.resource://video.videodemo1/raw/android");
   videoView.setMediaController ( mediaController );
   videoView.setVideoURI(video);
   } catch (Exception e) {
   Log.e("Error", e.getMessage());
   e.printStackTrace();
   }
   videoView.requestFocus();
   videoView.setOnPreparedListener(new OnPreparedListener() {
   // Close the progress bar and play the video
   public void onPrepared(MediaPlayer mp) {
    progressDialog.dismiss();
    videoView.start();
   }
   });
  }
 }
```

In the example, we have hard-coded the video source, which is the 3gp video file *res/raw/android.3gp*. Note that we do not include the file extension ".3gp" in the specification. Even though the full file name is *android.3gp*, we just refer to it as *android*:

```
Uri video = Uri.parse ("android.resource://video.videodemo1/raw/android");
```

Here the video file is in a local directory. If we want to play a video from a web site, we have to specify the full file name full URL path like the following example:

```
String videoURL = "http://www.forejune.com/android/videos/android.3gp";
Uri video = Uri.parse ( videoURL );
```

The main layout file *activity_main.xml* has nothing special. It simply defines a clicking button, similar to some of our previous examples:

```
<LinearLayout xmlns:android="http://schemas.android.com/apk/res/android"
  xmlns:tools="http://schemas.android.com/tools"
  android:layout_width="match_parent"
  android:layout_height="match_parent"
  android:orientation="vertical" >

  <Button
    android:id="@+id/streamButton"
    android:layout_width="fill_parent"
    android:layout_height="wrap_content"
    android:text="@string/button" />
</LinearLayout>
```

The other layout file, *videoview_main.xml* is just as simple. It defines where on the screen the video should be presented:

```xml
<?xml version="1.0" encoding="utf-8"?>
<LinearLayout xmlns:android="http://schemas.android.com/apk/res/android"
  xmlns:tools="http://schemas.android.com/tools"
  android:layout_width="match_parent"
  android:layout_height="match_parent"
  android:orientation="vertical" >
  <VideoView
      android:id="@+id/videoView"
      android:layout_width="match_parent"
      android:layout_height="match_parent" />
</LinearLayout>
```

When we run this application, it will first present a UI consisting of a button for the user to click on as shown in Figure 11-1(a). When the user clicks on the button, the video is loaded and played. Figure 11-1(b) shows a frame of the video. When the video is finished, the screen is still of the *VideoView*. We can press the **ESC** key to exit the screen, returning to the parent activity, which shows the clicking button of Figure 11-1(a). Clicking on the button will play the video again.

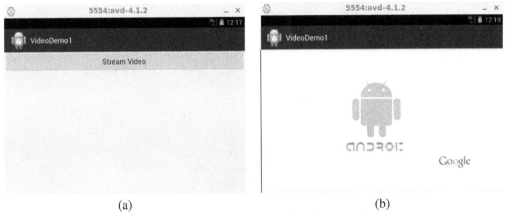

(a)   (b)

Figure 11-1   UI and Output of *VideoDemo1*

Chapter 12   OpenCV For Android

12.1   Introduction

OpenCV (Open Source Computer Vision Library) is a popular open source software library designed for computer vision application and machine learning. Its official web site is at:

http://opencv.org/

Since it is released under a BSD license, it is free for both academic and commercial use. It has a wide-range of interfaces, including C++, C, Python and Java, supporting Windows, Linux, Mac OS, iOS and Android platforms. OpenCV has been designed for computational efficiency with a strong focus on real-time applications and rich graphics features. The software has been adopted all around the world with more than forty-seven thousand people of user community and an estimated number of downloads exceeding 7 million.

OpenCV provides a common infrastructure for computer vision applications and helps accelerate the development of machine perception applications in commercial products. The library has more than 2500 optimized algorithms, including a comprehensive set of both classic and contemporary computer vision and machine learning algorithms, which can be used to detect and recognize faces, identify objects, classify human actions in videos, track camera movements and moving objects, extract 3D models of objects, and recognize scenery, etc. The library has been used extensively in companies, research groups and governmental bodies, such as Google, Yahoo, IBM, Sony and many startup companies.

12.2   OpenCV4Android SDK

12.2.1   Getting the SDK

OpenCV supports the Android platform by providing the OpenCV4Android SDK package. Detailed information about the package, including download links, installations, and tutorials for various systems, can be found at the OpenCV site at:

http://docs.opencv.org/doc/tutorials/introduction/android_binary_package/O4A_SDK.html

The download link for version 2.4.9 is at

http://sourceforge.net/projects/opencvlibrary/files/opencv-android/2.4.9/

Suppose we have downloaded the package. We can unzip it into a directory, say, */apps/android*, by the commands,

    $ cd /apps/android/
    $ unzip ~/Downloads/OpenCV-2.4.9-android-sdk.zip

Suppose we get into the OpenCV directory and list its files with the commands,

    $ cd OpenCV-2.4.9-android-sdk
    $ ls

We should the see the following files and directories listed:

    apk doc LICENSE README.android samples sdk

The package has the following file structure:

```
OpenCV-2.4.9-android-sdk
|_ apk
|    |_ OpenCV_2.4.9_binary_pack_armv7a.apk
|    |_ OpenCV_2.4.9_Manager_2.18_XXX.apk
|
|_ doc
|_ samples
|    |_ 15-puzzle
|    |_ camera-calibration
|    |_ color-blob-detection
|    .....
|    |_ example-15-puzzle.apk
|    .....
|_ sdk
|    |_ etc
|    |_ java
|    |_ native
|           |_ 3rdparty
|           |_ jni
|           |_ libs
|                 |_ armeabi
|                 |_ armeabi-v7a
|                 |_ x86
|
|_ LICENSE
|_ README.android
```

12.2.2 Import OpenCV Library and Samples

It is better to start working with OpenCV for Android from a new clean workspace. Suppose we choose our workspace to be */apps/android/opencv-work*. As usual, we use Eclipse IDE for development. We can **import** the OpenCV library into our workspace using Eclipse:

1. Click **File** > **Import..**
2. Select **Android** > **Existing Android Code Into Workspace** and click **Next**.
3. Enter */apps/android/OpenCV-2.4.9-android-sdk* for the **Root Directory**.
4. Check all the projects to import and check *Copy projects into workspace* as shown in Figure 12-1. Check **Finish** to import the projects.

5. You may or may not need to do the following, depending on how you have installed your Eclipse IDE.
   (a) If you do not have a copy of Android NDK, you need to download it from the site:
       https://developer.android.com/tools/sdk/ndk/index.html
       Unzip and unpack the package. Install it in Eclipse IDE:
       Click **Window** > **Preferences** > **Android** > **NDK**. Then enter the root directory of the NDK for **NDK Location** (e.g. */apps/android/android-ndk-r10*), and click **Apply** > **OK**. (You may need to restart Eclipse.)
   (b) You may need to install the OpenCV Manager manually. In our example, the command to install it is:
       $ adb install /apps/android/OpenCV-2.4.9-android-sdk/
          apk/OpenCV_2.4.9_Manager_2.18_armeabi.apk

Figure 12-1 Importing OpenCV Projects From SDK

12.2.3   Run OpenCV Samples

After the import and the setup, we should be able to run the Open CV samples. (You may need to do some configuration of the Eclipse IDE to run them, depedning on how your Eclipse environement has been setup.) For example, to run the *15 puzzle*, we do the following:

1. Click on the first project, *OpenCV Sample - 15 puzzle*, in the *Package Explorer*. You may need to first clean the project by clicking **Project** > **Clean..** ... If you still see red error indicators at the import statements of the source code, you can click on an error indicator and choose **Fix project setup ..**, and then click **Add project 'OpenCV Library - 2.4.9' to build path ...**
2. Add the OpenCV library in Eclipse: Click **File** > **Properties** > **Android** > **Library** > **Add**. Select **OpenCV Library - 2.4.9** and click **OK**.
3. Include 'Emulated Camera' in AVD: Click **Window** > **Android Virtual Device Manager**. Then click the tab **Android Virtual Devices** of the Android Virtual Device Manager dialog, select the AVD you are going to run the project, click **Edit**. The *Edit Android Virtual Device (AVD)* panel appears. Choose **Emulated** for both of the entries *Front Camera* and *Back Camera*. Click **OK** to go back to the *Android Virtual Device Manager*. Press the escape key *Esc* to return to the Eclipse editing screen.
4. Now we can run the application by clicking **Run** > **Run** > **Android Application**. We should see a moving pattern as shown in Figure 12-2.

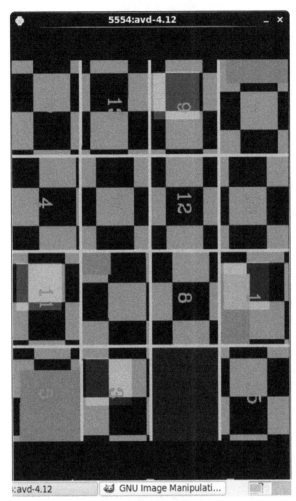

Figure 12-2 OpenCV Samples Outputs

If you "C/C++ Build" is not in the *Build Property* of your project (right-click project and select **Properties** to check) and you need it in the project, you can add it by:

1. Close all projects.
2. Open the library project and right-click on it. Select **Android Tools** > **Add Native Support..**
3. Enter a unique library name that does not contain any space and click **Finish**.
4. Right-click the project (at package explorer) and select **Properties**. The *C/C++ Build* should be there. Change the build command to ${*NDKROOT*}/*ndk-build*, assuming *NDKROOT* has been setup properly.
5. Build the project by clicking **Project** > **Build Project**.

Index

UDP, 199, 200
URL, 221
utterance, 239

vertex shader, 117
video, 269
virtual machine, 6

Wall Street Journal, 1
Webkit, 5
Weta Digital, 2
Wi Fi, 5
Win-32, 189

Yahoo, 273

Other books by the same author (Fore June):

1. *Windows Fan, Linux Fan*, CreateSapce, 2002

2. *An Introduction to Video Compression in C/C++*, CreateSpace, 2010

3. *An Introduction to Digital Video Data Compression in Java*, CreateSapce, 2011

4. *An Introduction to 3D Computer Graphics, Stereoscopic Image, and Animation in OpenGL and C/C++*, CreateSpace, 2011

Advertisement

A Fiction by Vani Venkatesan:

Badminton Kid 1, Vani Venkatesan, CreateSpace, 2013